HAMBURG
DRAMATURGY

By

G. E. LESSING

With a New Introduction by

VICTOR LANGE

Chairman, Department of Germanic Languages and Literatures
Princeton University

DOVER PUBLICATIONS, INC.
NEW YORK

This new Dover edition, first published in
1962, is an unabridged and unaltered republication of the "Dramatic Notes (Hamburg
Dramaturgy)" as translated by Helen Zimmern and included in *Selected Prose Works of
G. E. Lessing*, published circa 1890 as a volume
in Bohn's Standard Library.

This volume also contains a new Introduction especially written for this Dover edition
by Victor Lange.

Standard Book Number: 486-20032-9
Library of Congress Catalog Card Number: 62-4220

Manufactured in the United States of America
Dover Publications, Inc.
180 Varick Street
New York, N.Y. 10014

INTRODUCTION TO DOVER EDITION

Whoever reasons rightly, invents, and whoever desires to invent must be able to reason. Only those who are not fitted for either believe that they can separate the one from the other.

—Lessing

1.

THE eighteenth century was, even more perhaps than our own time, an age of criticism: the emergence since Leibnitz of a rational and secular philosophy, the interplay, in all areas of thought and action, of traditional and revolutionary values, and the steady increase in the self-confidence of the new middle class—these aspects of one of the most imaginative periods in modern history brought about an intellectual climate that was at times academic and ponderous, at others tense and militant, but always uncompromisingly critical of its own beliefs. In England and France the structure of social life had for long offered a suitable frame within which philosophical and aesthetic debates could appropriately take place. London and Paris provided a coherent metropolitan society that attracted, produced and consumed an unending supply of literary merchandise; writers, patrons and publishers, journals, theatres and academies sustained and enlivened the creative life in a fashion quite unknown in other parts of Europe. It was certainly different in Germany, which was divided by dynastic allegiances and religious predilections and where countless small and self-important principalities could but copy the fashionable life of their European cousins. The society of the German courts and of their educated bureaucracy lacked the energy and independence

v

that accrues, even to the life of the mind, from a widely
shared sense of political effectiveness. Well into the eighteenth century foreign models of behavior and taste were
readily accepted, and the German book market depended
in large measure upon English and French plays and
novels that conveyed, often in miserable translations, something of the cosmopolitan life beyond the Rhine.

It was in the community of learning, in such university
centers as Halle, Leipzig and Göttingen that historical,
theological and even philological controversies assumed an
importance that soon transcended the academic sphere and
began to attract the curiosity and interest of the literate
German middle class. Between these two worlds an in-
creasing number of knowledgeable and independent writers
attempted in three or four influential journals to mediate,
and to create a common sensibility not merely for the intellectual issues of the day but for the wider social relevance of literature and the arts. The most brilliant of
these, and the ablest German representative of the European enlightenment, was undoubtedly Gotthold Ephraim
Lessing. His career reflects more characteristically than
that of any other contemporary man of letters the aggressive but disjointed cultural life that was emerging in
Germany. After early studies in theology, Lessing turned
in 1748 to literary journalism and to writing for the stage,
which he soon recognized as the most promising instrument
for the kind of moral and intellectual persuasion he wished
to achieve. His plays are the work of remarkable imaginative originality coupled with a firm attachment to the traditions of the European stage and of dramatic criticism;
their effect, not only upon the literature of the day, but
upon the subsequent history of the German theatre from
Goethe and Schiller to our own time, is incalculable.
Although Lessing hoped at times for a position as scholar
or librarian where his extensive knowledge of history,
archaeology and literary criticism might be usefully and
quietly employed, the detached and sheltered life was not
really to his taste. He continued to the end as a ceaseless
and indomitable fighter for an awareness among his
countrymen of the great issues that stirred Europe in
every sphere of life during the thirty years before the
French Revolution. When he died in 1781 German litera-

ture, enlightened and encouraged by his convictions and his work, had begun to make its important contribution to the shaping of the modern mind.

2.

In his *Letters Concerning Contemporary Literature* Lessing devoted himself, between 1759 and 1765, to a survey of the impulses that dominated, for better or for worse, the centers of European writing. Ostensibly addressing himself to a friend in the army, he subjected the sentimental or pedantic German imitators of French and English literature to that brilliant and dialectical irony that made his criticism at once admired and immensely feared. But it was in the collection of essays entitled *Hamburg Dramaturgy* that Lessing's polemical talent became most productive, largely because it is there constrained by a clear and explicit moral purpose and made impressive by his critical maturity. This expansive series of reviews was originally commissioned by the enterprising director of what was to have been the first permanent German theatre devoted to the performance of serious European plays and supported by a group of Hamburg business men. Lessing was asked to continue the weekly articles begun by J. F. Löwen, who had succeeded, by persistent attacks on K. E. Ackermann's troupe, in being invited himself to take over the direction of that company. His assignment was ambiguous: he was to act as consultant to this new theatre and, at the same time, to supply regular critical commentaries on its performances. When he accepted this proposal —in December, 1766—he did not know that Löwen's irresponsible management and the scandalous relations between some of the financial backers and the chief actresses had already deprived the new venture of much of its public credit: the "Hamburg National Theatre" which opened on April 27, 1767, was forced to close less than eight months later, on December 4 of the same year. In the final essays of the *Hamburg Dramaturgy*, Lessing looks back upon the somewhat melancholy circumstances of his connection with this venture:

> When some time ago some people in this town conceived the idea of trying whether something more could not be done for the German theatre, than was

possible under the type of old-fashioned manager, I
do not know how it was that they thought of me and
dreamed that I could be useful to such an undertaking. I was just standing idly in the marketplace,
no one wanted to hire me—beyond doubt because no
one knew how to use me—except for these friends.
Until now all occupations of my life have been indifferent to me; I have never pushed myself into any or
offered myself, but neither have I ever refused even
the most insignificant to which I felt myself drawn by
any kind of predilection.

Whether I would join in the founding of the local
theatre? To this I could reply easily. My only reasons
for hesitation were that I did not know whether I
would be able to do the job, and how I could best
do so. . . .

At last they hit upon the plan to use even that in
me which makes me such a slow, or as my more
energetic friends deem, such a lazy workman: criticism. And thus arose the idea of these papers.

Lessing reviewed in a total of 104 essays most of the
plays that were offered by the company. His articles appeared at first twice a week, later less frequently; they
were widely read and, to his own financial loss, eagerly
pirated. In 1769 he published them himself in two volumes
under the title *Hamburgische Dramaturgie*. It was inevitable that the irregular manner of its appearance had its
effect upon the character of the work as a whole: what had
begun as appealing accounts of the current theatrical
repertoire gradually turned into more and more severe
exercises in dramatic criticism. Midway in his work, in the
fiftieth essay, Lessing presents with characteristic irony
his oblique apologies for making such strenuous demands
upon his readers:

I pity my readers who promised themselves in this
journal a theatrical newspaper as varied and manifold, as entertaining and comical, as a theatrical
newspaper should be. Instead of containing the story
of the plays performed, told in short, lively and
touching romances; instead of detailed biographies
of absurd, eccentric, foolish beings, such as those
must be who concern themselves with writing comedies; instead of amusing, even perhaps scandalous
anecdotes of actors and especially actresses; instead

of all these pretty things which they expected, they
got long, serious, and dull criticisms of old familiar
plays, and ponderous enquiries into what tragedy
should or should not be, at times even expositions of
Aristotle. And are they really to read all this? As I
say, I pity them; they have been grievously deceived.
But let me add in confidence: better that they should
be deceived than I. And I for one should be much
deceived if I made their expectations my law. Not
that their expectations would be very difficult to fulfil; no indeed, I should find them very easy, if only
they agreed better with my own intentions.

3.

To define the nature and function of tragedy and to
examine the contemporary dramatic repertoire through a
better understanding of Aristotelian assumptions was
Lessing's primary purpose. He focuses his attention upon
the view of tragedy represented by the French neo-classi-
cal drama, and contrasts it with what seemed to him the
far more moving—and more genuinely Aristotelian—conception of the tragic which he thought characteristic of
the English drama from Shakespeare to his own time. If
Shakespeare is Lessing's admired model, he chooses Corneille and Voltaire as his chief targets. Almost for the first
time he thus formulates a judgment that was subsequently
to become one of the axioms of German criticism. When
Lessing developed the antithesis, it was felt to carry
strong patriotic overtones, but its central impulse was
not so much a nationalistic bias as a growing dissatisfaction with the baroque view of the function of art. To the
writers of the mid-century this highly sophisticated and
rhetorical literary tradition had lost much of its earlier
splendor and appeared to be lacking in authenticity. It was,
above all, no longer compatible with the imaginative as-
pirations of the new middle class.

For Lessing the balance between authenticity and convention was one of the precarious indications of the civilized life which required the continuous scrutiny of the
critical intelligence. He was by training and dedication
deeply attached to the traditions of European criticism;
but to destroy the pretensions of empty conformity was
one of the tasks which he had set for himself. Indeed, all
his writings were undertaken in order to provide answers

to the question as to what is essentially, and not merely by
dubious convention, the nature and justification of certain
forms of human conduct, of human faith and of human
creativity. Whether Lessing speaks on theological issues
or deals with social foibles or with literary criticism, he
seeks to remove with skill and seriousness the crust of
prejudice or bigotry from the "natural" core of the spirit.

As a critic he insists therefore, above all, on the com-
pelling and continuing validity of that "golden chain" of
informed tradition that reaches from classical antiquity
to the present. This is the body of formulated judgment
to which Lessing remains attached and which he wishes,
as a true classicist, to protect and preserve. It is this purpose that gives to the *Hamburg Dramaturgy* its character
and specific critical gravity. To restore the Aristotelian
—and this was for Lessing tantamount to saying the
Greek—idea of tragedy with all its human and by no
means only academic implications and consequences, this
was what he hoped to achieve. And those to whom he
wished to address himself were not the unruly anti-Aris-
totelians among the younger German writers, but the false
and irresponsible interpreters of the classical ideals who
drew beliefs and precepts from the tradition of the French
drama and, in particular, from the example of Corneille.
"Corneille," he concludes in the eighty-first essay, "has
done the greatest harm and exercised the most pernicious
influence. . . . Racine seduced only by his example, Corneille by his example and doctrines together."

Lessing's attacks on the French theatre were undertaken
in a spirit at once philological and moral: the true meaning of Aristotle's notions of tragedy was to be recovered
from its French perverters, and a more profound and
dynamic understanding was thus to be gained of the efficacy of the drama, the highest form, as he was convinced,
of artistic creation and the most telling mirror of the
moral life.

His respect for Aristotle was considerable; he had himself translated parts of the *Poetics*, and planned a detailed
commentary of it. Throughout his earlier critical writings
he had deplored the obtuseness which the French dramatists seemed to him to have displayed in their use of
Aristotelian principles; they had, he reiterated in the

Hamburg Dramaturgy, made a mockery of Aristotle's thoughtful and essentially functional requirements of a unity of time, of place and of action; they had misunderstood his central doctrine of imitation and had, in disregard of Aristotle's philosophical insights, abused the portentous subject matter of history for baldly didactic ends.

We would, of course, do Lessing an injustice if we thought that he was insensitive to the immense competence and to the impressive intellectual style of the French theatre; his criticism was directed at the heart of their concept of tragedy and not at the quality of their craft. "Various French plays," he is ready to admit, "are most intelligent and instructive works which I think worthy of all praise—only, they are not tragedies! Their authors could not be otherwise than of high intellect; some of them take no mean rank among poets—only, they are not tragic poets. Their Corneille and Racine, their Crébillon and Voltaire have little or nothing of what makes Sophocles Sophocles, Euripides Euripides, Shakespeare Shakespeare. These latter are rarely in opposition to Aristotle's demands, the former are so constantly." Only Diderot among the French can be ranked in depth of philosophical perception and in aesthetic judgment next to Aristotle himself. In the *Dramaturgy* Lessing apostrophizes him as "the best of all French critics."

4.

Tragedy is for Lessing the effective dramatic form par excellence; through it the human being is made aware of his most profound emotional and intellectual resources; it represents at once a private and a collective experience; it has an historical and a contemporary dimension; and its power is derived from the acceptance of a religious sense which, however enlightened and "natural," yet enables us to transcend our individual preoccupations. Like Aristotle, Lessing defines the nature of tragedy not primarily in terms of subject matter but of the sort of impact which it makes upon the audience. In his earlier writings "tragic" had stood for a complex of experience that produced in the spectator beyond a high degree of intellectual or aesthetic involvement, a sense of pity; its effect was directly and pragmatically moral in that it produced that

humanitarian and philanthropic sensibility without which
the emotional climate of the age could not have become
effective. In the *Dramaturgy* Lessing returns to an acceptance of Aristotle's view of the tragic as having the double
impact of pity and fear. In connection with a review of
Shakespeare's *Richard III* he attempts in the seventy-
fourth essay to clarify the meaning of the term "fear"
(*phobos*). It cannot, he concludes, refer simply to the
melodramatic terror which the villain arouses in us;
Aristotle "speaks of pity and fear, not of pity and terror;
and his fear is by no means the fear excited in us by misfortune threatening another person. It is the fear which
arises for ourselves from the similarity of our position
with that of the sufferer; it is the fear that the calamities
impending over the sufferers might also befall ourselves;
it is the fear that we ourselves might thus become objects
of pity. In a word this fear is compassion referred back
to ourselves." Terror, Lessing means to say, is an instinc-
tive reaction, fear the reflection of a contemplative attitude which should enable the spectator to face in an
almost religious experience the "tremendum"—that which
is to be feared—without either indifference or cowardice.

It may be surprising that Lessing, the author of *Minna
von Barnhelm*, one of the most accomplished of German
comedies, should in the *Dramaturgy* pay so little attention
to that form. Comedy, he is inclined to think, produces in
the audience an effect far less profound than tragedy. It
is—and here Lessing betrays his classicist prejudices—too
much concerned with the defects and peculiarities, however
serious, of individuals; for unlike tragedy which, in keeping with Aristotelian principles, gathers its impact by the
all-important play of *action*, comedy must turn primarily
upon representative *characters*. "Similar situations produce similar tragedies, but not similar comedies; similar
characters, on the other hand, produce similar comedies
while between several tragedies this similarity is of no
importance." The purpose of comedy is not so much to
move our total spiritual resources by demonstrating the
ineluctable nature of our "moral" decisions, as to sharpen
our intellectual capacities. It aims essentially at our sense
of social effectiveness: "its true use consists in laughter
itself in the practice of our powers to discern the ridicu-

lous. . . . It is enough for comedy that, if it cannot cure an incurable disease, it can confirm the healthy in their health."

It was his conception of the tragic possibilities of great drama which led Lessing to attack what he believed to be an inadequate or a false view of tragedy in the French classicist writer. Corneille, he insists, aims at arousing not so much pity and fear in his audience as admiration; his premises are Stoic, not Greek, and his adherence to the classical theory of tragedy is merely mechanical. It is not difficult to detect in Lessing's dislike of Corneille a profound resentment of aristocratic attitudes, or at least of a courtly view of the function of theatre. It was Shakespeare and not Corneille whom Lessing regarded as the "modern" poet: his subject matter, his realistic devices and his immense grip on the emotions of an individualistic and non-aristocratic public are, Lessing argues, more congenial to the contemporary middle-class perception than the "artificial" conventions of the French drama.

We are today far more relativistic in our aesthetic judgments and recognize Lessing's position, no less than that of the Corneillean or Shakespearean theatre, as historically determined. But what makes Lessing's argument in praise of Shakespeare still plausible is his conviction that it is the "natural" resources of the great poet which alone give validity to his "form." Several years before the *Dramaturgy* Lessing had in the celebrated seventeenth of the *Letters Concerning Contemporary Literature* (1759) first praised Shakespeare as the incomparable "natural genius"—an attribute which remained for German critics well into the nineteenth century synonymous with the supreme achievement of poetry. The term "genius" echoes throughout the *Dramaturgy*; for Lessing it carried a connotation that had little or nothing in common with the torrential and undisciplined effusiveness of the German "Storm and Stress" sensibility. Indeed, the wave of "enthusiasm" among the young writers for a dithyrambic sort of poetry had given to the word "genius" a meaning that was most distasteful to Lessing. In the *Dramaturgy* he takes special pains to define his own understanding of "genius" in phrases not unlike those first used by J. Warton in his *Essay on the Genius and Writings of Pope*

(1760). Genius is a more creative disposition than that of wit or *esprit* which merely impose a precarious intellectual unity upon a haphazard variety of facts and attitudes. "Genius is concerned only with events that are rooted in one another, that form a chain of cause and effect. To reduce the latter to the former, to weigh the latter against the former, everywhere to exclude chance, to cause everything that occurs to occur so that it could not have happened otherwise, this is the part of genius when it deals with matters of history and converts the useless treasures of memory into nourishment for the soul."

Genius was for Lessing not an intuitive display of talent but in its highest form the result of knowledge and craftsmanship as well as imaginative energy. It is the very distinction of the genius that he should organize the natural order so as to produce in the play or poem a maximum of palpable truth. "The world the genius creates endeavours to copy in miniature the Highest Genius; it transposes, exchanges, reduces or increases the various particles of the given world in order to form a whole therefrom that corresponds to his own artistic aims and ends."

5.

If Lessing thought it was in the genius that the full force of a vision of truth became apparent, this corresponded to his altogether pragmatic convictions. For him truth appeared, whether in life or in art, only in those deeds and works that had the unmistakable stamp of authenticity about them; to establish the intense relationship between the "natural" truth of the "Highest Genius" and the correspondence of a work of art to this natural order is Lessing's everpresent intention. His central requirement of criticism is therefore that it should demonstrate, and in the audience awaken, an awareness of the double nature of truth: truth as an immanent structure, and truth as an object, however elusive, of the human desire for order and form. Few among the critics of his day seemed to Lessing capable of correlating in their judgments the demands of genius and of critical detachment. He reflects ironically in the ninety-sixth essay:

Heaven be praised, we have now a generation of critics whose highest critical activity consists in making all criticism suspicious. They shout: "Genius! Genius! Genius may disregard all rules! What genius produces is rules!" Thus they flatter genius; I fancy in order that they too may be held geniuses. But they betray at the same time that they do not feel a spark of it in themselves, when they add in one and the same breath: "Rules oppress genius," as if genius could be oppressed by anything in the world! Moreover, oppressed by something that, as they themselves admit, is deduced from it. Not every critic is a genius; but every genius is a born critic. He has the proof of all rules within himself. He comprehends, remembers and follows only those rules that express his own feelings in words. And these feelings expressed in words should be capable of limiting his activity? Reason with him about this as much as you will, he only understands you in so far as he recognizes your general axioms in a particular instance; he remembers only this particular instance, and as he works this memory affects his energies neither more nor less than the remembrance of a felicitous example or of a happy experience. To maintain that rules and criticism can oppress genius, means to maintain in other words, that example and practice can do this; it means not only restricting genius to itself but even to its very first attempts.

To insist on an awareness of what is ultimately formal discipline—this is the meaning of Lessing's defense of a continuing relevance of the classical "rules" properly understood—cannot possibly diminish the power of genius. On the contrary, not merely talent but the measure of critical perception and a mastery of the devices of poetry determine the poet's rank:

To act with a purpose is what raises man above the brutes, to invent with a purpose, to imitate with a purpose, is what distinguishes genius from the petty artists who only invent in order to invent, imitate in order to imitate. They are content with the small enjoyment that comes from their use of these means; they make these means their whole purpose and demand that we, too, should be satisfied with this lesser enjoyment, that springs from the contemplation of their ingenious but aimless use of their means.

In Corneille, the most widely admired writer of tragedies, Lessing missed the true understanding of poetic re-
sponsibility: his plays appear to him mere inventions of a
fertile imagination. "Why all these fictions? Do they render anything more probable in the history wherewith he
overloads them? . . . He should have known that not the
mere fact of invention but invention adequate to its purpose, marks a creative mind."

Again and again, in these hundred and four essays
Lessing searches in the large conception of a play as well
as in the subtlest suggestions of a performance for the
creative force that gives shape to an intention. He urges
us to examine the evidence of genius in the most elusive
detail. "Shakespeare must be studied, not plundered. If
we have genius, Shakespeare must be today what the
camera obscura is to the landscape-painter. He must look
into it diligently to learn how nature reflects herself upon
a flat surface, but he must not borrow from it." There are
not many who understand the profound exigencies of art:
"Few will be able to recognize the wool from which the
threads have been spun. Those few who comprehend art,
will not betray the master, for they know that a grain of
gold may be wrought so skillfully that the value of the
form far surpasses the value of the material."

6.

It is, at any rate, one of the most attractive features of
Lessing's own criticism that it is always the specific critical reflection, elicited by the play or the performance, that
engages our interest. This concrete criticism, sustained
as it is by an impressive knowledge of historical and contemporary assumptions and by an uncompromising insist-
ence upon wisdom as well as craftsmanship, is what makes
Lessing's work extraordinarily alive today.

It is of course true that the large number of names of
little-known dramatists and of barely remembered titles
to which Lessing refers requires on the part of the modern
reader a good deal of patience. But if we read him intelli-
gently we shall soon realize that the author of a play, or
the actress, or any generalities of taste are to Lessing in
themselves of very little concern; he is unwilling to satisfy

"the childish curiosity of the public or the vain complaisance of the poet." "What do people think a poet looks like? Not like other mortals? And how weak must be the impression made by his work if in the end one desires nothing more ardently than to see the face of its maker. The true masterpiece, so it seems to me, fills us so entirely with itself that we forget its author over his work." Lessing is, in any case, skeptical of a view which regards the work of art as the accretion of personal experience; he is as yet attached to the classical notion that the artist must above all satisfy the demands of a canon of aesthetic considerations rather than indulge in the kind of confession or self-expression which the romantic poets were soon to advocate.

To formulate this critical attitude in a series of reflections rather than in an academic treatise corresponded to Lessing's temperament as a writer; he knew that he was neither a scholar nor a creative mind but essentially a critic:

> I do not feel within myself the living spring that rises from its native strength and breaks forth from its own strength into such rich, fresh, clear streams. I must draw everything out of myself by pressure and pipes. I should be poor and cold and shortsighted if I had not learnt in a measure to borrow from the treasures of others, to warm myself at the fires of others, and to strengthen my eyes by the glasses of art. I am always ashamed or annoyed when I hear or read anything in disparagement of criticism. It is said to suppress genius, and I flattered myself that I had gained from it something very nearly approaching to genius. I am a lame man who cannot possibly be edified by an abusive pamphlet against his crutch.

7.

There is no pretense in the *Dramaturgy* at systematic coherence; on the contrary, Lessing reminds his readers "that these sheets are to contain anything rather than a dramatic system. I am therefore not bound to resolve all the difficulties I raise. My thoughts may seem less and less connected, may even seem to contradict themselves, what matter if only they are thoughts amid which may be found matter for individual thinking! I only want here to scatter *Fermenta cognitionis*."

Still, these scattered observations are yet held together by a resolute purpose. Assuming the dramatic form to be the most stirring vehicle of the life of the mind, it seemed essential to Lessing to provide for it an audience that not only comprehended something of the possible scope of art but that could, in the long-discredited community of the theatre, be brought to experience a sense of common conviction. No theatre of serious pretensions existed in Germany before the end of the century; occasional efforts at establishing repertory troupes devoted to anything but the most popular entertainment had met with little success. The picture of an irresponsible and aimless theatrical life which Goethe draws in *Wilhelm Meister* is in Germany eminently true for most of the eighteenth century. At the same time a decided preoccupation with the drama as one of the three traditional forms of literature continued among the more academic critics. But theatre and drama existed in large measure as separate concerns. To bring the two realms into a productive relationship was for Lessing a most urgent task; the poet, the performer and the audience, he hoped, were to pool their resources once again, as they had often done in Greece, towards making articulate the moral and intellectual strength which the emerging age of reason demanded. Criticism of the drama as a literary form occupies much of the *Dramaturgy*; the space devoted to matters of acting and stagecraft is no less extensive. It is well to remember that before Lessing there was almost no work in which the principles of theatrical presentation had been coherently set forth. Garrick's acting was everywhere in Europe widely discussed and imitated; his Shakespearean performances became exemplary for the German "Storm and Stress" and offered Lessing the more naturalistic style with which he wished to replace the declamatory rhetoric of the French stage. In France Rémond de Saint Albine had in his *Comédies* (1747) outlined a system of acting to which Lessing occasionally refers with favor. But never before Lessing had a critic so convincingly insisted on the absolute interdependence of the word of the poet and the speech, expression and gestures of the actor. "A beautiful figure, a fascinating mien, a telling eye, a charming gait, a sweet intonation, a melodious voice, all these are things that cannot be expressed in words. Still they are neither the only nor the greatest assets of the actor. These valuable gifts of nature are, of course, necessary to his calling, but they by no means suffice for it. He must everywhere think with the poet; he must even think for him in places where the poet has shown himself human."

Lessing's analysis of stagecraft and acting is as specific as is his more general literary criticism. He is here as skeptical as he is in the case of the poet, of mere individual enthusiasm: "Feeling," he says in the third essay, "is altogether the most controverted among the talents of an actor. It may be present where we do not recognize it, and we can fancy we recognize it where it does not exist. For feeling is something internal of which we can only judge by its external signs." These "external signs" have seldom been analyzed with greater intelligence: we need only read the fourth essay of the *Dramaturgy* to recognize Lessing's eye for the gestures, whether "significant," "picturesque" or "pantomimic," that make a poetic or moral proposition effective.

> Among significant gestures there is one kind that the actor must note above all and with which alone he can impart life and light to the moral. These are the articulating gestures. A moral proposition is a general axiom extracted from the particular circumstances of an action; by means of its generality the proposition becomes, so to speak, alienated from the action, it becomes a digression whose connection with the actual present is not noticed or comprehended by the less observant or less astute spectators. If there is a way of making this connection evident, of relating the symbolical quality of the moral to the visible, and if this can be done through certain gestures, then the actor must on no account fail to do so.

For us today, these reflections on the art of the theatre are among the most stimulating in the *Dramaturgy;* but Lessing himself had little hope that what he had to say would be accepted by those to whom it was directed. He concludes in his final essay:

VICTOR LANGE

We have actors, but no mimetic art. If in the past
there was such an art, we have it no longer; it is
lost; it must be discovered anew. There is enough
superficial chatter on the subject in various languages, but precise rules, accepted by everyone,
formulated with distinctness and precision, according to which blame or praise can be bestowed upon
an actor in a particular case — of such I scarcely
know two or three. This is the reason why all our
thinking about this subject seems so vacillating and
ambiguous; small wonder if the actor who has nothing but a happy routine, feels offended. He will never
think himself sufficiently praised and will always
believe himself blamed too much; he will often not
even know whether he has been praised or blamed.
Indeed the observation was made long ago, that the
sensitiveness of artists with regard to criticism,
increases in just that ratio in which the number,
certainty, and precision of their artistic principles
decrease.

"There can be no doubt," Schiller wrote to Goethe on
June 4, 1799, "that Lessing, among all Germans of his
time, had the clearest judgment as to matters of art, that
he thought most precisely and at the same time most
liberally about it, and that he kept the essentials firmly
before himself." This is a judgment of Lessing's empirical
intelligence as a critic which we can only today, after a
century of metaphysical and speculative criticism, fully
appreciate and comprehend.

But however specific and objective Lessing's critical pro-
cedure may be, it never fails to transcend its primary
aesthetic impulse. By the incisive and often aggressive
manner of his writing he hoped to bridge the gap that
existed in his time between theory and practice, and to
engage the interest of an ever wider body of literate
readers. His dramatic, even forensic style was superbly
suited to this deliberate purpose of persuasion: "His manner of writing," said Herder, "is that of a poet, i.e. of an
author who offers us not a product but a process, who does
not claim to have thoughts, but thinks in our presence; we
see a work that comes into being much like Achilles' shield
in Homer. He seems to demonstrate to us the very operation of one of his reflections, to take it apart and to put it

together again: the spring begins to work, the wheel turns — one thought, one conclusion leads to another, the next step seems near — this is the gist of his thinking." If Lessing's attitude, particularly in the *Dramaturgy*, was polemical it was because he had no placid illusions about the expectations, by and large, of his audience. All his efforts were from beginning to end directed at this one goal: to create an informed and articulate public for a literature and a theatre that should be "the school of the moral world" and that would engage the most serious concerns of an emerging, enlightened society. As a writer he reflected the faith of his age in the efficacy of discourse to move his readers in the direction of truth; but as a critic he meant to remind them of Aristotle's tenet that the truth in poetry has its own irrefutable logic and its own forms of compulsion towards understanding and order.

*   *   *

The present translation, prepared by Helen Zimmern and published in Bohn's Standard Library, has certain disadvantages. It is somewhat archaic and the translator has omitted a few brief passages, though none of great importance. It is, nevertheless, accurate and may be used with reliance. The sad truth is that to date no one has attempted to prepare a new translation. It is to be hoped that the appearance of the *Hamburg Dramaturgy* at the present time will encourage translators to offer more satisfying English versions of Lessing's works.

Victor Lange
*Chairman, Department of Germanic Languages
and Literatures
Princeton University*

*Princeton, New Jersey
March, 1961*

Selected Bibliography

Garland, H.B. *Lessing*. Cambridge, 1937.

Gombrich, E.H. "Lessing," in *Proceedings of the British Academy, 1957*. London, 1958, 133–156.

Kommerell, M. *Lessing und Aristoteles*. Frankfurt, 1957.

Lessing, G.E. *Werke*, ed. Petersen-Olshausen. Berlin, 1925–1929. (Volume V contains the best German text of the *Hamburgische Dramaturgie*).
——. *Hamburgische Dramaturgie*, ed. O. Mann. Stuttgart, 1958.

Pascal, R. *Shakespeare in Germany*. Cambridge, 1937.

Robertson, G.J. *Lessing's Dramatic Theory*, ed. E. Purdie. Cambridge, 1939.

Sime, J. *Lessing: His Life and Writings*. 2 vols. London, 1877.

Vail, C.C.D. *Lessing's Relation to the English Language and Literature*. New York, 1936.

PREFACE.

It will be easily guessed that the new management of the local theatre is the occasion of the present publication. Its object is to respond to the good intentions that must be attributed to the gentlemen who propose to undertake the management. They have themselves amply explained their intentions, and the better portion of the public, both within and without our city, have given to their utterances the approval which every voluntary exertion for the general good may expect to meet with in our day.

It is true that people are always and everywhere to be found who, judging others by themselves, see nothing but hidden designs in every good undertaking. This form of self-consolation might gladly be permitted to them. Only when the assumed hidden designs provoke them against the object itself, when their malicious envy is busy undermining this object in order to frustrate these assumed designs, then they must be informed that they are the most contemptible members of human society.

Happy the spot where these wretches do not give the tone to society, where the greater mass of well-disposed citizens keep them in the bounds of respect, and do not suffer that the better portion of a whole community become the prey of their cabals, that patriotic objects become a reproach to their petty sneering wit!

May Hamburg be so happy in all that concerns its wealth and its freedom: for it deserves to be thus happy!

1

When Schlegel made suggestions for the improvement of the Danish theatre (a German poet for the Danish theatre !)—suggestions that may long form a subject of reproach to Germany, which gave him no opportunity of making them for the improvement of her own—this was his first and foremost saying : " The care of working for their own gain and loss must not be left to the actors themselves." But the best managers have degraded a free art to the level of a trade which permits its master to carry on the business as negligently and selfishly as he likes if only necessity or luxury bring him customers.

If therefore nothing further has been attained here than that an association of friends of the stage have laid their hands to the work and have combined to work according to a common plan for the public good, even then, and just through this, much would have been gained. For out of this first change, even with only meagre encouragement from the public, all other improvements needed by our theatre could quickly and easily spring.

In matters of expense and industry assuredly nothing will be economised; whether taste and judgment will be wanting only time can teach. And is it not in the hands of the public to improve and redress whatever it may here find defective? Only let it come, and see and hear, and examine and judge ! Its voice shall never be contemptuously ignored, its judgment shall always be respectfully heard.

Only every little criticaster must not deem himself the public, and he whose expectations have been disappointed must make clear to himself in some degree of what nature his expectations have been. For not every amateur is a connoisseur. Not every one who can feel the beauties of one drama, the correct play of one actor, can on that account estimate the value of all others. He has no taste who has only a one-sided taste; but he is often the more partisan. True taste is general; it spreads over beauties of every kind, and does not expect more enjoyment or delight from each than its nature can afford.

The steps are many that a growing stage must traverse before it attains the climax of perfection; but a corrupt stage is naturally still further removed from this height, and I greatly fear that the German stage is more the latter than the former.

Everything consequently cannot be done at once. But what we do not see growing we find after some time has grown. The slowest person, who does not lose sight of his goal, will always outstrip him who wanders aimlessly.

This "Dramaturgie" is to form a critical index of all the plays performed, and is to accompany every step made here either by the art of the poet or the actor. The choice of the plays is no trifle, for choice presupposes quantity, and if masterpieces should not always be performed it is easy to perceive where the fault lies. At the same time it is well that the mediocre should not pretend to be more than it is, so that the dissatisfied spectator may at least learn to judge from it. It is only needful to explain to a person of healthy mind the reasons why something has not pleased him if one desires to teach him good taste. Some mediocre plays must also be retained on account of their containing certain excellent parts in which this or that actor can display his whole strength. A musical composition is not immediately rejected because its libretto is miserable.

The great discrimination of a dramatic critic is shown if he knows how to distinguish infallibly, in every case of satisfaction or dissatisfaction, what and how much of this is to be placed to the account of the poet or the actor. To blame the actor for what is the fault of the poet is to injure both. The actor loses heart, and the poet is made self-confident.

Above all, it is the actor who may in this particular demand the greatest severity and impartiality. The justification of the poet may be attempted at any time; his work remains, and can be always brought again before our eyes. But the art of the actor is transitory in its expression. His good and bad pass by rapidly, and not seldom the passing mood of the spectator is more accountable than the actor for the more or less vivid impression produced upon him.

A beautiful figure, a fascinating mien, a speaking eye, a charming gait, a sweet intonation, a melodious voice, are things that cannot be expressed in words. Still they are neither the only nor the greatest perfections of the actor. Valuable gifts of nature are very necessary to his calling, but they by no means suffice for it. He must everywhere think with the poet; he must even think for him in places where the poet has shown himself human.

.   .   .   .   .
.   .   .   .   .
.   .   .   .   .

DRAMATIC NOTES.

—◆◆—

THE theatre was successfully opened on the 22nd of last month with the tragedy ' Olindo and Sophronia.' ' Olindo and Sophronia ' is the work of a young poet, and is a posthumous incomplete work. Its theme is the well-known episode in Tasso. It is not easy to convert a touching little story into a touching drama. True, it costs little trouble to invent new complications and to enlarge separate emotions into scenes. But to prevent these new complications from weakening the interest or interfering with probability; to transfer oneself from the point of view of a narrator into the real standpoint of each personage; to let passions arise before the eyes of the spectator in lieu of describing them, and to let them grow up without effort in such illusory continuity that he must sympathise, whether he will or no; this it is which is needful, and which genius does without knowing it, without tediously explaining it to itself, and which mere cleverness endeavours in vain to imitate.

In his ' Olindo and Sophronia ' Tasso appears to have had Virgil's ' Nisus and Euryalus ' before his eyes. As Virgil in the latter has depicted the strength of friendship, so Tasso in the former wished to depict the strength of love. There it was the heroic zeal of duty that gave rise to the test of friendship, here it is religion that gives to love the opportunity of evincing itself in all its power. But religion, which Tasso only uses as a means by which love

5

is shown efficient, has become the main end in Cronegk's
treatment. He wished to glorify the triumph of the one
in the triumph of the other. Beyond doubt a pious
amendment—only nothing more than pious! For it has
misled him into making that which is simple and natural,
true and human, in Tasso into all that is confused and
fabulous, wonderful and transcendental!

In Tasso it is a wizard, a fellow who is neither a
Christian nor a Mahommedan, but one who has spun together his own particular superstition out of both religions,
who gives Aladin the advice to bring the miraculous image
of the Virgin out of the temple into the mosque. Why did
Cronegk convert this wizard into a Mahommedan priest?
If this priest was not as ignorant of his religion as the
poet seems to be, he could not possibly have given this
advice. It tolerated no images in its mosques. Cronegk
betrays in several things what an erroneous idea he enter-
tains of the Mahommedan faith. In Tasso the image of
Mary disappears from the mosque without our knowing
precisely whether human hands have removed it or
whether a higher power has been in play. Cronegk
makes Olindo the perpetrator. True he converts the
image of Mary into "an image of our Lord on the Cross,"
but an image is an image, and this wretched superstition
makes Olindo very contemptible. It is impossible to be
reconciled to him after he could venture for so paltry a
deed to bring his nation to the verge of destruction. If he
does afterwards openly confess his deed it is nothing but
his duty and no magnanimity. In Tasso it is only love
that impels him to this step; he will save Sophronia or
perish with her, die, only to die with her. If one couch
cannot unite them, let it be one scaffold; at her side, bound
to the same stake, destined to be consumed by the same
fire, he is only sensible of the happiness of such sweet
vicinity, he thinks of nothing he has to hope for beyond
the grave or wishes for nothing but that this union may
be yet closer and more intimate, that he may press heart
to heart and that he may give forth his soul upon her
lips.

This admirable contrast between a lovable, calm,
entirely transcendental dreamer and a hot passionate youth

is utterly lost in Cronegk's version. They are both of the chilliest uniformity, both have their heads full only of martyrdom. And not enough that he and she wish to die for religion, Evander wishes to do the same and even Serene is not ill inclined.

Here I wish to make a double remark which, borne in mind, will save young tragic poets from committing some great faults. If heroic sentiments are to arouse admiration, the poet must not be too lavish of them, for what we see often, what we see in many persons, no longer excites astonishment. Every Christian in ' Olindo and Sophronia ' holds being martyred and dying as easy as drinking a glass of water. We hear these pious bravadoes so often and out of so many mouths, that they lose all their force.

The second remark concerns Christian tragedies in particular. Their heroes are generally martyrs. Now we live in an age when the voice of healthy reason resounds too loudly to allow every fanatic who rushes into death wantonly, without need, without regard for all his citizen duties, to assume to himself the title of a martyr. We know too well to-day how to distinguish the false martyr from the true, but despise the former as much as we reverence the latter, and at most they extort from us a melancholy tear for the blindness and folly of which we see humanity is capable. But this tear is none of those pleasing ones that tragedy should evoke. If therefore the poet chooses a martyr for his hero let him be careful to give to his actions the purest and most incontrovertible motives, let him place him in an unalterable necessity of taking the step that exposes him to danger, let him not suffer him to seek death carelessly or insolently challenge it. Else his pious hero becomes an object of our distaste, and even the religion that he seeks to honour may suffer thereby. I have already said that it could only be a superstition that led Olindo to steal the image from the mosque as contemptible as that which we despise in the wizard Ismenor. It does not excuse the poet that there were ages when such superstition was general and could subsist side by side with many excellent qualities, that there still are countries where it would be nothing strange for pious ignorance. For he wrote his tragedy as little for those ages as he intended that it should be performed in Bohemia or Spain. The good author, be he of whatever species he will, if he does not write merely to show his wit and learning, has ever the best and most intelligent of his time and country before his eyes and he only condescends to write what pleases and can touch these. Even the dramatic author, if he lowers himself to the mob, lowers himself only in order that he may enlighten and improve the mass and not to confirm them in their prejudices or in their ignoble mode of thought.

No. 2.

Yet another remark, also bearing on Christian tragedies might be made about the conversion of Clorinda. Convinced though we may be of the immediate operations of grace, yet they can please us little on the stage, where everything that has to do with the character of the personages must arise from natural causes. We can only tolerate miracles in the physical world; in the moral everything must retain its natural course, because the theatre is to be the school of the moral world. The motives for every resolve, for every change of opinion or even thoughts, must be carefully balanced against each other so as to be in accordance with the hypothetical character, and must never produce more than they could produce in accordance with strict probability. The poet, by beauty of details, may possess the art of deluding us to overlook misproportions of this kind, but he only deceives us once, and as soon as we are cool again we take back the applause he has lured from us. Applying these remarks to the fourth scene of the third act, it will be seen that Sophronia's speeches and acts could have roused pity in Clorinda, but were much too impotent to work conversion on a person who had no natural disposition to enthusiasm. Tasso also makes Clorinda embrace Christianity, but only in her last hour, only after she has recently heard that her parents were also inclined to this faith, subtle weighty reasons by whose means the operations of a higher power are, as it were, entwined with the course of natural events.

No one has better understood how far this point may be carried on the stage than Voltaire. After the sensitive noble soul of Zamor has been shaken to its depths by example and entreaties, by generosity and exhortation, he allows him to divine rather than believe in the truths of a religion whose adherents evince such greatness. And perchance Voltaire would have suppressed even this surmise if it had not been needful to do something for the pacification of the spectator.

Even Corneille's 'Polyeucte' is to be condemned in view of the above remarks, and since the plays made in imitation of it are yet more faulty, the first tragedy that deserves the name of Christian has beyond doubt still to appear. I mean a play in which the Christian interests us solely as a Christian. But is such a piece even possible? Is not the character of a true Christian something quite untheatrical? Does not the gentle pensiveness, the unchangeable meekness that are his essential features, war with the whole business of tragedy that strives to purify passions by passions? Does not his expectation of rewarding happiness after this life contradict the disinterestedness with which we wish to see all great and good actions undertaken and carried out on the stage?

Until a work of genius arises that incontestably decides these objections,— for we know by experience what difficulties genius can surmount,—my advice is this, to leave all existent Christian tragedies unperformed. This advice, deduced from the necessities of art, and which deprives us of nothing more than very mediocre plays, is not the worse because it comes to the aid of weak spirits who feel I know not what shrinking, when they hear sentiments spoken from the stage that they had only expected to hear in a holier place. The theatre should give offence to no one, be he who he may, and I wish it would and could obviate all preconceived offence.

Cronegk only brought his play to the end of the fourth act. The rest has been added by a pen in Vienna: a pen—for the work of a head is not very visible. The "continuator" has, to all appearance, ended the story quite otherwise than Cronegk intended to end it. Death best dissolves all perplexities, therefore he despatches both

Olindo and Sophronia. Tasso lets them both escape, for
Clorinda interests herself for them with noble generosity.
But Cronegk had made Clorinda enamoured, and that
being the case, it was certainly difficult to guess how he
could have decided between two rivals, without calling
death to his aid. In another still worse tragedy where one
of the principal characters died quite casually, a spectator
asked his neighbour, "But what did she die of?"—"Of
what? Of the fifth act," was the reply. In very truth
the fifth act is an ugly evil disease that carries off many
a one to whom the first four acts promised a longer life.

But I will not proceed more deeply with the criticism
of the play. Mediocre as it is, it was excellently performed. I keep silence concerning the external splendour,
for this improvement of our stage requires nothing but
money. The art whose help is needful to this end is
as perfect in our country as in any other, only artists
wish to be paid as well as in any other.

We must rest satisfied with the performance of a play if
among four or five persons some have played excellently
and the others well. Whoever is so offended by a beginner
or a makeshift in the subordinate parts, that he turns up
his nose at the whole, let him travel to Utopia and there
visit the perfect theatre where even the candle-snuffer is
a Garrick.

. . . .

Interspersed moral maxims are Cronegk's strong point.
. . . Unfortunately he often tries to persuade us that
coloured bits of glass are gems, and witty antitheses common sense. Two such lines in the first act, had a peculiar
effect upon me.
The one:

"Heaven can pardon, but a priest never."
The other:

"Who thinks ill of others is himself a scoundrel."

I was taken aback to see a general movement in the
parterre and to hear that murmur with which approval is
expressed when close attention does not permit it to break
out. I thought on the one hand : Most excellent! they love

morality here, this parterre finds pleasure in maxims, on this stage Euripides could have earned fame, and Socrates would gladly have visited it. But on the other I noticed as well how false, how perverted, how offensive were these presumed maxims, and I greatly wished that disapproval had had its share in this murmur. For there has only been one Athens and there will ever remain but one Athens, where even the mob has moral feelings so fine and delicate that actors and authors run the risk of being driven from the stage on account of impure morality. I know full well that the sentiments in a drama must be in accordance with the assumed character of the person who utters them. They can therefore not bear the stamp of absolute truth, it is enough if they are poetically true, if we must admit that this character under these circumstances, with these passions could not have judged otherwise. But on the other hand this poetical truth must also approach to the absolute and the poet must never think so unphilosophically as to assume that a man could desire evil for evil's sake, that a man could act on vicious principles, knowing them to be vicious and boast of them to himself and to others. Such a man is a monster as fearful as he is uninstructive and nothing save the paltry resource of a shallow-head that can deem glittering tirades the highest beauties of a tragedy. If Ismenor is a cruel priest, does it follow that all priests are Ismenors? It is useless to reply that the allusion refers to priests of a false religion. No religion in the world was ever so false that its teachers must necessarily be monsters. Priests have worked mischief in false religion as well as in true, but not because they were priests but because they were villains who would have abused the privileges of any other class in the service of their evil propensities.

If the stage enunciates such thoughtless judgments on priests, what wonder if among these are found some foolish enough to decry it as the straight road to hell?

But I am falling back into the criticism of the play and I wanted to speak of the actors.

No. 3.

Why is it that we like to hear the commonest maxim
spoken by this actor (Herr Eckhof)? What is it that
another must learn from him if we are to find him equally
entertaining in the same case? All maxims must come
from the abundance of the heart with which the mouth
overflows. We must appear to have thought of them as
little as we intend to boast of them. It therefore follows
as a matter of course that all the moral parts must be
very well learnt by heart. They must be spoken without
hesitation, without the faintest stammer, in an unbroken
easy flow of words, so that they may not appear a trouble-
some unburdening of memory but spontaneous promptings
of the actual condition. It must also follow that no false
accentuation lead us to suspect that the actor is chattering
what he does not understand. He must convince us by a
firm assured tone of voice that he is penetrated by the
full meaning of his words.

But true accentuation can, if needful, be imparted to a
parrot. Yet how far is the actor, who only understands
a passage, removed from him who also feels it! Words
whose sense we have once grasped, that are once impressed
upon our memories, can be very correctly repeated even
when the soul is occupied with quite other matters; but
then no feeling is possible. The soul must be quite present,
must bestow its attention solely and only on its words,
and then only——

And yet even then the actor may really feel very much
and still appear to have no feeling. Feeling is altogether
the most controverted among the talents of an actor. It
may be present where we do not recognise it, and we can
fancy we recognise it where it does not exist. For feeling
is something internal of which we can only judge by its
external signs. Now it is possible that certain outer
things in the build of a body do not permit of these
tokens or else weaken them and make them dubious. An
actor may have a certain cast of features, certain gestures,
a certain intonation, with which we are accustomed to
associate quite different sentiments from those which he is
to represent and express at that moment. If this is the

case, he may feel ever so much, we do not believe him for he is at variance with himself. On the other hand another may be so happily formed, may possess such decisive features, all his muscles may be so easily and quickly at his command, he may have power over such delicate and varied inflexions of voice; in short he may be blessed in such a high degree with all the gifts requisite for dramatic gesture, that he may appear animated with the most intense feeling when he is playing parts that he does not represent originally but after some good model, and where everything that he says and does is nothing but mechanical imitation.

Beyond question, this man for all his indifference and coldness is more useful to the theatre than the other. When he has for a long spell done nothing but copy others, he will at last have accumulated a number of little rules according to which he begins to act and through the observance of which (in consequence of the law that the modifications of the soul that induce certain changes of the body, in return are induced by these bodily changes) he arrives at a species of feeling that has not, it is true, the duration or the fire of that which arises in the soul, but is yet powerful enough in the moments of representation to bring about some of the involuntary changes of body whose existence forms almost the only certain clue we have as to the presence of inner feeling. Such an actor is to represent for instance, the extremest fury of anger. I will suppose that he does not even properly understand his part, that he neither comprehends fully the reasons for this anger nor can imagine them vividly enough in order to arouse anger in his soul. And yet I say that if he has only learnt the very commonest expressions of anger from an actor of original feeling and knows how to copy him faithfully—the hasty stride, the stamp of the foot, the voice now harsh, now smothered, the play of the eyebrows, the trembling lip, the gnashing teeth, &c.—I say that if he only imitates well these things that can be imitated, his acting will thus infallibly cast on his mind a dim feeling of anger that will react on his body and will there produce such changes as do not depend solely upon his will. His face will glow, his eyes will sparkle, his

muscles will dilate; in short he will seem to be truly
furious without being so, without comprehending in the
least why he should be so.

From these principles of feeling in general I have endeavoured to ascertain what external tokens accompany
those feelings with which moral axioms should be spoken,
and which of these tokens are within our command, so
that every actor, whether he have the feeling himself or
not, may represent them. I think they are the following.

Every moral maxim is a general axiom, which as such
demands a degree of calm reflexion and mental composure. It must therefore be spoken with tranquillity and
a certain coldness.

But again, this general axiom is also the result of impressions made by individual circumstances on the acting
personages. It is no mere symbolical conclusion, it is a
generalised sensation and as such it requires to be uttered
with a certain fire and enthusiasm.

Consequently with enthusiasm and composure; with
coldness and fire?

Not otherwise; with a compound of both, in which
however, according to the conditions of the situation, now
one and now the other, predominates.

If the situation is a placid one, the soul must desire to
gain a sort of elevation by the moral maxim; it must
seem to make general observations on its happiness or its
duties, in such a manner that by help of this very general-
ising it may enjoy the former the more keenly and observe
the latter the more willingly and bravely.

If on the other hand the situation is turbulent, the soul
must appear to recall itself by means of the moral axiom
(under which definition I comprehend every general
observation); it must seem to give to its passions the
appearance of reason and to stormy outbursts the look of
premeditated resolves.

The former requires an elevated and inspired tone; the
latter a tempered and solemn one. For in the one reason
must fire emotion, while in the other emotion must be
cooled by reason.

Most actors exactly reverse this. In their agitated
scenes they bluster out the general observations as excit-

edly as the other speeches, and in the quiet scenes repeat·
them just as calmly as the rest.   It therefore follows that
moral maxims are not distinguished either in the one or
the other, and this is the cause why we find them either
unnatural or stupid and chilly.   These actors have never
reflected that embroidery must contrast with its ground,
and that to embroider gold on gold is wretched taste.

Finally they spoil everything by their gestures.   They
neither know whether they should make any nor of what
kind.   They usually make too many and too insignificant
ones.   When in an agitated scene the soul suddenly seems
to collect itself to cast a reflective glance upon itself or
that which surrounds it, it is natural that it should command all the movements of the body that depend upon its
will.   Not only the voice grows more composed, the limbs
also fall into a condition of rest, to express the inner rest
without which the eye of reason cannot well look about
it.   The unquiet foot treads more firmly, the arms sink,
the whole body draws itself up into a horizontal position;
a pause—and then the reflexion.   The man stands there
in solemn silence as if he would not disturb himself from
hearing himself.   The reflexion is ended—again a pause—
and then, according to whether the reflexion was intended
to subdue his passions or to inflame them, he suddenly
bursts forth again or gradually resumes the play of his
limbs.   Only the face during the reflexion still retains
the traces of agitation; mien and eye are still on fire
and moved, for mien and eye are not so quickly within
our control as foot and hand.   In this therefore, in these
expressive looks, in this fiery eye, and in the composure
of the rest of the body, consists the mixture of fire and
calm with which I believe that moral reflexions should be
spoken in passionate situations.

And with this same mixture they should be spoken in
quiet situations; only with the difference that the part of
the action which is fiery in the former, is here calm; and
that which is calm here must be fiery there.   For instance,
when the soul has nothing but gentle sensations, and endeavours to give to these gentle sensations a higher degree
of vivacity, the limbs that are under control will be
brought into play, the hands will be in full movement,

only the expression of the face cannot follow so quickly
and in mien and eye the quiet will yet reign out of which
the rest of the body is trying to work itself.

No. 4.

But of what kind are the movements of the hand, with
which in quiet situations, maxims should be spoken?

We know very little concerning the Chironomia of the
ancients, that is to say, the nature of the rules prescribed
by the ancients in the use of the hands. We know this,
that they carried gestures to a perfection of which we can
scarcely form an idea from what our orators can compass
in this respect. Of this whole language we seem to have
retained nothing but an inarticulate cry, nothing but the
power to make movements without knowing how to give
these movements an accurately determined meaning and
how to connect them together so that they may be capable
of conveying not only one idea, but one connected
meaning.

I am quite aware that among the ancients the pantomimist must not be confounded with the actor. The
hands of the actor were by no means as talkative as those
of the pantomimist. In the one case they supplied the
place of speech, while in the other they were only to lend
emphasis, and as natural signs of things to lend life and
truth to the preconcerted signs of the voice. In panto-
mimes the movements of the hands were not merely
natural signs, many of them had a conventional meaning
and from these the actor had to refrain completely. He
therefore used his hands less than the pantomimist, but
as little in vain as he. He did not move his hand if he
could not mean something thereby or emphasise something. He knew nothing of those indifferent movements
through whose constant monotonous use a large portion
of actors, especially women, give to themselves the appearance of mere marionettes. Now the right hand, now the
left, now a swing from the body, now agitating the air
with both hands is what they call action, and whoever
can practise it with a certain ballet-master's grace deems
that he can fascinate us.

I know well that even Hogarth advises actors to learn how to move their hands in beautiful undulatory lines, but in all directions with all the possible variations of which these lines are capable in consideration of their sweep, size and duration. And finally he only advises it as an exercise to make them supple in movement, to make the movements of grace familiar to the arms, but not in the belief that acting itself consists in nothing more than in always describing such beautiful lines in the same direction.

Away therefore with these insignificant *portebras*; especially away with them in reflective scenes. Grace in the wrong place is affectation and grimace, and the very same grace too often repeated, becomes at last cold and then repulsive. I seem to see a schoolboy say his task when the actor tenders to me moral reflexions with the same movements with which a hand is given in the minuet, or as if he spun them down from a spindle.

Every movement made by the hand in such passages should be significant. It is possible often to be picturesque if only the pantomimic be avoided. Perhaps another time I may find an occasion to explain by examples these various gradations from significant to picturesque and from picturesque to pantomimic gestures. Just now it would lead me too far and I will only remark that among significant gestures there is one kind that the actor must note above all and with which alone he can impart to the moral life and light. These are in one word the individual gestures. The moral is a general axiom extracted from the particular circumstances of the acting personages; by means of its generality it becomes foreign to the action, it becomes a digression whose connexion with the actual present is not comprehended or noticed by the less observant or less acute spectators. If consequently a means exists to make this connexion evident, to bring back the symbolical of the moral to the visible, and if this means lies in certain gestures, the actor must on no account omit making them.

No. 5.

.   .   .   .   .

.   .   .   .   .

If Shakespeare was not as great an actor as he was a dramatist, at least he knew as well what was needed for the art of the one as the other. Yes, perhaps he even pondered more about the former because he had the less genius for it. Certainly every word that he puts into Hamlet's mouth when addressing the players should be a golden rule for all actors who care for sensible approbation. "I pray you," he says among other things, "speak the speech as I pronounced it to you, trippingly on the tongue: but if you mouth it, as many of your players do, I had as lief the town crier had spoke my lines. Nor do not saw the air too much with your hand, thus: but use all gently; for in the very torrent, tempest, and (as I may say) the whirlwind of passion, you must acquire and beget a temperance that may give it smoothness."

The fire of the actor is often mentioned, discussions are common as to whether the actor can show too much animation. If those who maintain this cite as an instance that an actor may be passionate or at least more passionate than circumstances require; then those who deny it have a right to say that in such cases the actor has not shown too much animation, but too little intelligence. Altogether it depends greatly what we understand under the word fire. If screams and contortions are fire then it is incontestable that the actor can carry these too far. But if fire consists in the rapidity and vivacity with which all those parts that make the actor, bring their properties to bear, to give to his acting the semblance of truth, then we should not desire to see this semblance of truth carried to the extremest illusion, if we deemed it possible that the actor could apply too much fire in this sense. It can therefore not be this fire the moderation of which Shakespeare requires even in the torrent, tempest, and whirlwind of passion. He can only mean that violence of voice and movement; and it is easy to discover why, where the poet has not observed the least moderation, the actor must yet moderate himself in both points. There are few voices that do not become displeasing at their utmost pitch, and movements that are too rapid, too agitated will rarely be dignified. Now our eyes and our ears are not to be offended, and only when everything is avoided in the expression of violent passion that can be unpleasant to these, can acting possess that smoothness and polish which Hamlet demands from it even under these circumstances, if it is to make the deepest impression and to rouse the conscience of stiffnecked sinners out of its sleep.

The art of the actor here stands midway between the plastic arts and poetry. As visible painting beauty must be its highest law, but as transitory painting it need not always give to its postures the calm dignity that makes ancient sculpture so imposing. It may, it must at times permit to itself the wildness of a Tempesta, the insolence of a Bernini; and they have in this art all that which is expressive and peculiar without the offensive element that arises in the plastic arts through their permanent posture. Only it must not remain in them too long, it must prepare for them gradually by previous movements, and must resolve them again into the general tone of the conventional. Neither must it ever give to them all the strength which the poet may use in his treatment. For though the art is silent poetry, yet it desires to make itself comprehended immediately to our eyes, and every sense must be gratified if it is to convey unfalsified the proper impressions to the soul.

It might easily come about that the moderation demanded by art, even in the extremes of passion, does not consort well with applause. But what applause? It is true the gallery greatly loves the noisy and boisterous, and it will rarely omit to repay a good lung with loud hand-clappings. The German parterre also shares this taste in part; and there are actors cunning enough to derive advantage from this taste. The most sleepy actor will rouse himself towards the end of the scene, when he is to make his exit, raise his voice and overload the action, without reflecting whether the sense of his speech requires this extra exertion. Not seldom it even contradicts the mood in which he should depart; but what matters that to him? Enough that he has thus reminded the parterre to

look at him, and, if it will be so good, to applaud after him.
They should hiss after him! But, alas! the spectators
are partly not connoisseurs, and in part too good-natured,
and they take the desire to please them for the deed.

.   .   .   .   .

[No. 6 consists mainly of a Prologue and Epilogue
spoken on the first night. They were not written
by Lessing.]

No. 7.

The Prologue shows us the drama in its highest
dignity, inasmuch as it regards it as supplementary to
the laws. There are matters in the moral conduct of men
which, in regard to their immediate influence upon the
well-being of society, are too insignificant and in themselves too changeable to be worth while placing under the
protection of the law. There are others again, against
which the whole force of legislation falls powerless.
They are too incomprehensible in their mainsprings, too
abnormal in themselves, and too unfathomable in their
consequences, so that they either escape totally from the
penalty of the law, or cannot possibly be punished according to their due. I do not attempt to restrict comedy to
the former as a species of the ludicrous; or tragedy to
the latter, as extraordinary manifestations in the domain
of morals that astonish our reason and rouse tumult in
our breast. Genius laughs away all the boundary lines
of criticism. Only so much is indisputable, that drama
chooses its themes this side or beyond the frontiers of
law, and only touches its objects in so far as they either
lose themselves in the absurd, or extend to the horrible.

The Epilogue dwells upon one of the chief lessons that
a great part of the fable and character of the tragedy was
to teach. True it was rather rash of Herr von Cronegk to
preach toleration in a play whose subject was taken from
the unhappy time of the Crusades, and to endeavour to
show the enormity of a spirit of persecution as practised
by the adherents of Mahommedanism. For these Crusades
themselves, at the outset a political subterfuge of the popes,
proved one of the most inhuman of persecutions of which

Christian superstition has been guilty. True religion possessed the greatest number of bloodthirsty Ismenors. The punishment of an individual who had robbed a mosque, could that be placed in opposition to the unholy madness that depopulated orthodox Europe to lay waste heterodox Asia? But what the tragedian has brought into his work clumsily, the author of the Epilogue may very well take up. Humanity and charity deserve to be commended on every occasion, and no inducement thereto can be so far-fetched but that our heart finds it most natural and imperative. . . . . .

A passage in the Epilogue was open to a misconstruction from which it deserves to be rescued. The poet says :—

" Bedenkt dass unter uns die Kunst nur kaum beginnt,
    In welcher tausend Quins für einen Garrick sind."[1]

To this I have heard it replied that Quin was no bad actor. No, that he certainly was not. He was Thomson's especial friend, and the friendship that united a poet like Thomson with an actor must awaken in posterity a prejudice in favour of his powers. Besides, Quin has more claims than this mere prejudice. It is known that he acted with great dignity in tragedy, that he was especially distinguished for the manner in which he did justice to Milton's sublime language, and that in comedy he brought the *rôle* of Falstaff to the greatest perfection. Still all this does not make him a Garrick, and the misconstruction of the passage consists in the assumption that the poet meant to oppose to this universal and extraordinary actor one who was bad, and was universally recognised as bad. Quin was meant to represent one of the usual type as they are to be found every day, a man who does his work so well that we are content with him, a man who may even play this or that part excellently when it happens that his figure, his voice, and his character come to his aid therein. Such a man is very useful, and may truthfully be called a good actor. But how much he still lacks before he can be the Proteus of his art which unanimous

[1] " Consider that our art is only in its infancy, and that we have a thousand Quins for one Garrick."

rumour has long voted Garrick to be! No doubt such a
Quin played the King in 'Hamlet' when Tom Jones and
Partridge went to the playhouse together, and such
Partridges exist in shoals who do not hesitate for a
moment to prefer him far beyond a Garrick. "What!"
they cry; "Garrick, the best player who was ever on the
stage! Why, he did not seem frightened at the ghost,
but he really was frightened. What kind of an art is
that to be frightened by a ghost? Why I could act as
well myself. Most surely if I had seen a ghost I should
have looked in the very same manner, and done just as he
did. Now the actor, the king, looked as if he was
touched, but like a good actor he took all pains to hide
it. Then he spoke all his words distinctly, half as loud
again as the other little man about whom you make such
to do."

In England every new play has its prologue and
epilogue composed either by the author himself or by a
friend. They do not, however, employ it for the purpose
for which the ancients used the prologue, namely, to
inform the spectators of various matters that would help
them to a more rapid comprehension of the main points of
the play. But it nevertheless is not without its use. The
English know how to say many things in it that serve to
dispose the spectators in favour of the poet or of his subject, and that obviate unfavourable criticisms both of him
and of the actors. Still less do they employ the epilogue
as Plautus sometimes employed it, to tell the complete
solution of the play for which the fifth act had not space.
They use it as a kind of moral application, full of good
maxims and pretty remarks on the morals portrayed and
on the art wherewith they have been rendered, and all
this is written in a droll, humorous tone. Nor do they
alter this tone willingly even in the case of tragedies, so
that it is nothing unusual that satire causes loud laughter
to resound after the most piteous or murderous drama,
and that wit becomes so wanton that it would seem to be
express design that every good impression should be
turned into an object of ridicule. It is notorious how
Thomson inveighed against this fool's rattle that was
thus jingled after Melpomene. If, therefore, I wish that

our new original plays should not be brought before the
public without introduction or recommendation, it follows
of course that in the case of tragedies I should wish the
tone of the epilogue to be more suited to our German
gravity. After a comedy it may be as burlesque as it
likes. In England it is Dryden who has written masterpieces of this kind, and they are still read with the greatest
pleasure, although many of the plays for which they were
written have long been wholly forgotten. . . .

No. 8.

. . . On the third evening 'Melanide' was performed. This play by Nivelle de la Chaussée is well
known. It is of the pathetic genus to which the name
larmoyant has been given in ridicule. . . .

The translation was not bad; it was indeed far better
than an Italian one contained in the second volume of the
Theatrical Library of Diodati. I must admit for the
comfort of the great mass of our translators that their
Italian colleagues are usually more pitiable than they
are. Still to transcribe good verses into good prose needs
something more than exactitude, or, I would rather say,
something else. A too faithful rendering makes a translation stiff, because it is impossible that all which is
natural in one language should be so also in the other.
But a translation from verse becomes at once watery and
crooked. For where is the happy versifier whom a
syllabic measure, a rhyme has not forced into saying here
and there something a little stronger or weaker than he
would have said if free from this restraint? Now when
the translator does not know how to distinguish this, if he
has not good taste and courage enough to omit a digressio n,
to substitute the real meaning for a metaphor, or supply or
conclude an ellipsis, he will give us all the careless fault
of the original, while depriving it of the excuses that
existed for the original in the difficulties of symmetry or
in the euphony demanded by its language.

The part of Melanide was played by an excellent actress
. . . . . Her declamation was accentuated correctly but
not obtrusively. The total want of marked accentuation

gives rise to monotony; but without being able to accuse
her of this, she knows how to come to the aid of its rare
employment by another subtle trait of which, alas! most
actors know little or nothing. I will explain myself.
People know what is meant by movement in music; not
the time but the degrees of slowness or quickness in which
the time is played. This movement is uniform throughout the whole piece. The same degree of quickness in
which the first bars are played must be sustained to the
last. This uniformity is needful in music, because one
piece can only express the same kind of thing, and without this uniformity there can be no combination of different
instruments and voices. In declamation, on the other
hand, it is very different. Regarding a period of many
phrases as one musical piece, and regarding the phrases as
the bars, yet these phrases, even if they were of the same
length and consisted of the same number of syllables of
the same time quantity, they ought never to be spoken
with the same degree of rapidity. For as they cannot be
of equal value and importance either in reference to clear-
ness and expression, or in reference to the main idea of
the period, it follows that the voice should enunciate the
least important quickly, and skim them lightly and carelessly, and should rest on the more important ones in
marked detail, giving to every word and every letter its
full value. The degrees of these differences are infinite,
and although they cannot be marked out and measured by
artificial divisions of time, yet they are distinguished by
the most uncultivated ear and are observed by the most
uncultivated tongue when speech comes from a full heart
and not merely from a ready memory. The effect produced by this constant change is incredible, and if besides
this all changes of voice are taken into account, not only
with regard to pitch and strength but also with regard to
its various tones of sweetness, roughness, harshness, mel-
lowness, used in their proper places, then that natural
music arises to which every heart is sure to respond
because we feel that it issues from the heart, and that art
has only part in it in so far as art is nature. And I say
that in this music the actress of whom I speak is excellent,
and no one can be compared to her but Herr Eckhof, who

by superadding a more marked accent to certain words,
which she regards less, is able to give to his declamation
a higher degree of perfection. . . .

On the fourth evening a new German original play was
performed, called ' Julia, or the Conflict between Love
and Duty.' Herr Heufeld of Vienna is the author. He
tells us that two plays of his have already met with the
approval of the Viennese audience. I do not know them,
but to judge by this one, they cannot be wholly bad.

The main points of the fable and a greater part of the
situations are borrowed from Rousseau's 'Nouvelle Héloïse.'
I wish that Herr Heufeld, before setting to work, had
read and studied the criticism of this novel in the ' Letters
concerning Contemporary Literature.' [1] He would have
worked with a more just comprehension of the beauties of
the original, and would perhaps have been more felicitous
in various points.

From the point of view of invention, the worth of the
' Nouvelle Héloïse' is very slight, and the best parts in it are
by no means adapted to dramatic purposes. The situations
are commonplace or unnatural, and the few good ones so
far apart, that they cannot be constrained into the
narrow limits of a drama of three acts without violence.
It was impossible that the story should end on the stage
as it does not end, but rather loses itself in the novel.
The lover of Julia had to be happy here, and Herr Heufeld lets him be happy. He gets his pupil. But has Herr
Heufeld considered that his Julia is now no more the
Julia of Rousseau? But Julia of Rousseau or no, who
cares, if only she be a person who interests? But just
that she is not, she is nothing but a little enamoured fool,
who at times chatters prettily enough whenever Herr
Heufeld remembers a fine passage in Rousseau. "Julia,"
say the critics whom I have before named, "plays a twofold *rôle* in the story. At first she is a weak and even a
seductive maiden, then at last she becomes a woman who
surpasses all ever dreamt of as a model of virtue." This

---

[1] A periodical publication written in great part by Lessing, but the
letters to which he here refers are from the pen of his friend, the
philosopher Moses Mendelssohn. (TR.)

last she becomes through her obedience, through the sacrifice of her love, through the mastery she gains over her heart. But if nothing is seen or heard of all this in the play, what remains of her but as I said a weak seductive maiden who has wisdom and virtue on her tongue and foolishness in her heart?

Herr Heufeld has changed the name St. Preux into Siegmund. The name Siegmund savours of the footman. I wish that our dramatic poets would be a little more choice even in such details, and more attentive to the tone of good society. St. Preux is an insipid personage already in Rousseau. "They all call him the philosopher," says the above-named critic. The philosopher! And what, I should like to know, has this young man done or said in the whole story that earns him this name? In my eyes he is the most absurd creature in the world, who exalts wisdom and reason in all manner of general declamations and does not possess the faintest spark of either. His love is romantic, bombastic, wanton, and the rest of his doings reveal no trace of reflexion. He has the proudest confidence in his reason, and is yet not resolute enough to venture the smallest step without being led either by his pupil or his friend. But how far below St. Preux is this German Siegmund!

No. 9.

In the novel St. Preux has occasion now and then to show his enlightened mind, and to play the active part of a worthy man. But the Siegmund of our comedy is nothing more than a little conceited pedant, who makes a virtue of his weakness, and is much offended that his tender little heart does not everywhere meet with justice. His whole activity is concentrated in a few follies. The boy wants to fight and to stab himself.

The author himself felt that his Siegmund did not act sufficiently, but he thought to meet this objection when he bids us consider "that a man of this kind is not like a king to whom in the space of four-and-twenty hours opportunity is afforded every moment of doing great actions. We must assume beforehand that Siegmund is a worthy man as he is described, and be satisfied since Julia, her mother, Clarissa, and Edward, all worthy people, so regard him."

It is right and well if in every-day life we start with no undue mistrust of the character of others, if we give all credence to the testimony of honest folk. But may the dramatic poet put us off with such rules of justice? Certainly not, although he could much ease his business thereby. On the stage we want to see who the people are, and we can only see it from their actions. The goodness with which we are to credit them, merely upon the word of another, cannot possibly interest us in them. It leaves us quite indifferent, and if we never have the smallest personal experience of their goodness it even has a bad reflex effect upon those on whose faith we solely and only accepted the opinion. Far therefore from being willing to believe Siegmund to be a most perfect and excellent young man, because Julia, her mother, Clarissa and Edward declare him to be such, we rather begin to suspect the judgment of these persons, if we never see for ourselves anything to justify their favourable opinion. It is true, a private person cannot achieve many great actions in the space of four-and-twenty hours. But who demands great actions? Even in the smallest, character can be revealed, and those that throw the most light upon character, are the greatest according to poetical valuation. Moreover how came it that four-and-twenty hours was time enough to give Siegmund opportunity to compass two of the most foolish actions that could occur to a man in his position? The occasion was suitable, the author might reply, but he scarcely will reply that. They might have arisen as naturally as possible, be treated as delicately as possible; for all that the foolish actions, that we see him commit, would leave a bad impression on our minds concerning this young impetuous philosophist. That he acts badly we see; that he can act well we hear, not even by examples but in the vaguest of general terms.

Rousseau scarcely touches upon the severity with which Julia's father treats her when she is to take another husband than him whom her heart has chosen.

Herr Heufeld had the courage to show us the whole scene.
I like it when a young poet ventures something. He lets
the father throw his daughter to the ground. . . . Herr
Heufeld demands that when Julia is raised by her mother,
there should be blood on her face. He may be glad that
this was omitted. Minute effects must never be carried
to the extremity of repulsiveness. It is well if our
heated phantasy can see blood in such cases, but the eye
must not really see it.

.   .   .   .

In conclusion the 'Treasure'[1] was performed; an
imitation of the 'Trinummus' of Plautus, in which the
author has tried to concentrate into one act all the comic
scenes of the original. It was excellently played. The
actors all knew their parts with that perfection that
is absolutely requisite to low comedy.

If questionable fancies, indiscretions, and puns are
brought out slowly and haltingly, if the actors have to
try and recollect petty jokes that were intended to do no
more than raise a smile; the ruin is inevitable. Farces
must be spoken sharply and quickly, so that the spectator
has not a moment's time to examine whether they are witty
or stupid. There are no women in this play. The only
one that could have been introduced would have been a
chilly charmer, and it is certainly better to have none,
than such. But I would not counsel any one to cultivate
this peculiarity. We are too much accustomed to the
mixture of both sexes, so that the total absence of the
fairer leaves a sense of emptiness in our minds. . . . . .

No. 10.

The play of the fifth evening was 'The Unexpected
Hindrance; or, A Hindrance without Hindrance,' of
Destouches.

If we refer to the annals of the French stage, we shall
find that just the very merriest plays of this author met
with the very least success. Neither the present play, nor
the 'Buried Treasure,' nor 'The Ghost with the Drum,'

---

[1] This play was by Lessing. (TR.)

nor 'The Poetical Yeoman' have maintained themselves
upon the stage, and they were acted only a few times even
when they were novelties. Much depends upon the keynote a poet strikes at his first appearance, or in which he
composes his best works. It is silently assumed that he
thus makes a contract never to depart from this given
tone, and if he does so the world holds itself justified in
being startled. The author is sought in the author, and
they think they have found something worse as soon as
they do not find the same.

In his ' Married Philosopher,' his ' Boaster,' his
' Spendthrift' Destouches had produced models of more
refined and elevated comedy even than Molière in his most
serious plays. At once the critics, who love to classify,
pronounced that to be his peculiar sphere. What was
perchance nothing but accidental choice on the poet's
part, they declared as marked bias and ruling power;
what he once or twice had not tried to do, they thought
he could not; and when he did try, what do the critics
do? They rather refuse to do him justice than abate
their hasty judgment. I do not want to say by this that
the low comedy of Destouches is of the same goodness as
that of Molière. It is much more formal; the witty-head
is more prominent than the faithful portrait-painter; his
fools are rarely of those comfortable fools such as they
issue from the hands of nature, but rather of the wooden
sort such as art carves them, overladen with affectation,
pedantry, and absence of *savoir vivre;* his school-wit, his
Mazures are therefore more chilly than ridiculous. But
notwithstanding this—and this is all I wanted to say—
his merry plays are not so deficient in the truly comic
element as an over-delicate taste thinks them. There are
scenes in them that make us laugh most heartily, that
alone should secure to him no mean rank among the comic
writers.

.   .   .   .   .

On the sixth evening was performed 'Semiramis,' by
M. de Voltaire.

This tragedy was first brought out on the French stage
in 1748, was greatly applauded, and in a measure formed

an epoch in the history of this stage. After M. de Voltaire
had produced his 'Zaire and Alzire,' his 'Brutus and
Cæsar,' he was confirmed in his opinion that the tragic
poets of his nation had in many points outstripped the
Greeks. "From us French," he said, "the Greeks might
have learnt a more graceful exposition and the great art
how to combine the scenes one with another in such a mode
that the stage never remains empty and no personage
enters or leaves without a reason. From us," he said,
"they might have learnt how rivals speak to each other
in witty antitheses, and how the poet can dazzle and
astonish by a wealth of sparkling elevated thoughts."
From us they could have learnt—oh yes, what cannot be
learnt from the French! Here and there, it is true, a
foreigner who has also read the classics a little would
like humbly to beg permission to differ from them. He
would perhaps object that all these prerogatives of the
French have no great influence on the essential element of
tragedy; that they are beauties which the unaffected
grandeur of the ancients despised. But what does it
avail to raise objections against M. de Voltaire? He
speaks and the world believes. There was only one thing
he missed in the French theatre: that its masterpieces
should be brought upon the stage with all the splendour
that the Greeks accorded to the trifling attempts of their
young art. He was very properly offended at the theatre
of Paris, an old ball-room, decorated in the worst taste,
where the people pushed and jostled in a dirty pit.
Especially was he offended at the barbarous custom of
tolerating spectators on the stage, leaving the actors
barely room enough for their most necessary movements.
He was convinced that this bad practice alone had deprived France of much that would have been attempted
under freer conditions and in a theatre better adapted to
comfort and action. To prove by example he wrote his
'Semiramis.' A queen who assembles her parliament
to announce to them her marriage; a ghost who rises
from his grave to hinder incest and to revenge himself
on his murderer; the grave into which a fool steps to
issue as a criminal; all this was indeed something quite
new for the French. It created as much noise on the stage,

it demanded as much pomp and transformation as had been
known only in opera. The poet believed he had given the
model for a special genus, and though he had made it for
the French stage not such as it was, but such as he wished
to see it, nevertheless it was played there for the present
as well as circumstances would permit. At the first representation the spectators still sat on the stage; and I
should like much to have seen a ghost of old appear in
this gallant circle. Only after the first performances was
this blemish in artistic fitness removed. The actors
cleared the stage and what was then an exception for the
benefit of an extraordinary play became in time the constant practice But only for the Parisian stage, for which
as we have said, 'Semiramis' formed an epoch. The
provincials love to retain old fashions and would rather be
deprived of all illusions than renounce their privilege of
treading on the long trains of Zaires and Meropes.

No. 11.

The appearance of a ghost was so bold a novelty on
the French stage, and the poet who ventured upon it
justified it by such curious reasons, that it really repays
the trouble of investigating them a little.

"They cry and write on all sides," says M. de Voltaire, "that we no longer believe in ghosts and that the
apparition of a ghost is held childish in the eyes of
an enlightened nation. But how," he replies to this;
"should all antiquity have believed in such miracles
and should we not be permitted to adapt ourselves to
antiquity? How? Our own religion has hallowed the
belief in such extraordinary dispensations of Providence
and it should be held ridiculous to revive them!"

These exclamations appear to me to be more rhetorical
than philosophical. Above all things I should wish
religion to be left out of the question. In matters of
taste and criticism, reasons extorted from religion are all
very well to silence an opponent, but not well suited to
convince him. Religion as religion has nothing to decide
here, and regarded as a form of ancient tradition her
testimony has neither more nor less value than all other

testimonies of antiquity. Consequently in this instance we have only to deal with antiquity.

Very good then; all antiquity believed in ghosts. Therefore the poets of antiquity were quite right to avail themselves of this belief. If we encounter ghosts among them, it would be unreasonable to object to them according to our better knowledge. But does this accord the same permission to our modern poets who share our better knowledge? Certainly not. But suppose he transfer his story into these more credulous times? Not even then. For the dramatic poet is no historian, he does not relate to us what was once believed to have happened, but he really produces it again before our eyes, and produces it again not on account of mere historical truth but for a totally different and a nobler aim. Historical accuracy is not his aim, but only the means by which he hopes to attain his aim; he wishes to delude us and touch our hearts through this delusion. If it be true therefore that we no longer believe in ghosts; and if this unbelief must of necessity prevent this delusion, if without this delusion we cannot possibly sympathise, then our modern dramatist injures himself when he nevertheless dresses up such incredible fables, and all the art he has lavished upon them is vain.

Consequently?—It is consequently never to be allowed to bring ghosts and apparitions on the stage? Consequently this source of terrible or pathetic emotions is exhausted for us? No, this would be too great a loss to poetry. Besides does she not own examples enough where genius confutes all our philosophy, rendering things that seem ludicrous to our cooler reason most terrible to our imagination? The consequence must therefore be different and the hypotheses whence we started false. We no longer believe in ghosts? Who says so? Or rather, what does that mean? Does it mean: we are at last so far advanced in comprehension that we can prove their impossibility; that certain incontestable truths that contradict a belief in ghosts are now so universally known, are so constantly present even to the minds of the most vulgar, that everything that is not in accordance with these truths, seems to them ridiculous and absurd! It cannot mean this. We no longer believe in ghosts can therefore only mean this : in this matter concerning which so much may be argued for or against, that is not decided and never can be decided, the prevailing tendency of the age is to incline towards the preponderance of reasons brought to bear against this belief. Some few hold this opinion from conviction, and many others wish to appear to hold it, and it is these who raise the outcry and set the fashion. Meanwhile the mass is silent, and remains indifferent, and thinks now with one side, now with the other, delights in hearing jokes about ghosts recounted in broad daylight and shivers with horror at night when they are talked of.

Now a disbelief in ghosts in this sense cannot and should not hinder the dramatic poet from making use of them. The seeds of possible belief in them are sown in all of us and most frequently in those persons for whom he chiefly writes. It depends solely on the degree of his art whether he can force these seeds to germinate, whether he possesses certain dexterous means to summon up rapidly and forcibly arguments in favour of the existence of such ghosts. If he has them in his power, no matter what we may believe in ordinary life, in the theatre we must believe as the poet wills.

Such a poet is Shakespeare and Shakespeare only and alone. His ghost in ' Hamlet ' makes our hairs stand on end, whether they cover a believing or an unbelieving brain. M. de Voltaire did not do well when he referred to this ghost, he only made himself and his ghost of ' Ninus ' ridiculous by so doing.

Shakespeare's ghost appears really to come from another world. For it comes at the solemn hour, in the dread stillness of night, accompanied by all the gloomy, mysterious accessories wherewith we have been told by our nurses that ghosts appear. Now Voltaire's ghost is not even fit for a bugbear wherewith to frighten children. It is only a disguised actor, who has nothing, says nothing, does nothing that makes it probable that he is that which he pretends to be. All the circumstances moreover, under which he appears, disturb the illusion and betray the creation of a cold poet who would like to deceive and

terrify us without knowing how to set about it. Let us
only consider this one thing. Voltaire's ghost steps out
of his grave in broad daylight, in the midst of an assembly
of the royal parliament, preceded by a thunder-clap.
Now where did M. de Voltaire learn that ghosts are thus
bold? What old woman could not have told him that
ghosts avoid sunshine and do not willingly visit large
assemblies? No doubt Voltaire knew this also; but he
was too timid, too delicate to make use of these vulgar
conditions, he wanted to show us a ghost but it should
be of a higher type, and just this original type marred
everything. A ghost that takes liberties which are
contrary to all tradition, to all spectral good manners,
does not seem to me a right sort of ghost, and everything
that does not in such cases strengthen the illusion seems
to weaken it.

If Voltaire had paid some attention to mimetic action
he would for other reasons have felt the impropriety of
allowing a ghost to appear before a large assembly. All
present are forced at once to exhibit signs of fear and
horror, and they must all exhibit it in various ways
if the spectacle is not to resemble the chilly symmetry of
a ballet. Now suppose a troupe of stupid walking
gentlemen and ladies have been duly trained to this end,
and even assuming that they have been successfully
trained, consider how all the various expressions of the
same emotion must divide the attention of the spectator
and withdraw it from the principal characters. For
if these are to make their due impression on us, it is not
only needful we should see them but it is well we should
see nothing but them. Shakespeare let only Hamlet see
the ghost, and in the scene where his mother is present,
she neither sees nor hears it. All our attention is therefore fixed on him, and the more evidences of terror and
horror we discover in this fear-stricken soul, the more
ready are we to hold the apparition that has awakened
such agitation as that for which he holds it. The spectre
operates on us, but through him rather than by itself.
The impression it makes on him passes on to us, and the
effect is too vivid and apparent for us to doubt its supernatural cause. How little has Voltaire understood this

artistic touch! At his ghost many are frightened, but not much. Semiramis exclaims once: "Heaven! I die," while the rest make no more ado about him than we might make about a friend whom we deemed far away and who suddenly walks into the room.

No. 12.

I must note another difference that exists between the ghosts of the English and French poets. Voltaire's ghost is nothing else but a poetical machine that is only employed to help the unravelling of the plot; it does not interest us in the very least on its own account. Shakespeare's ghost, on the contrary, is a real active personage, in whose fate we take an interest, who excites not only our fear but our pity.

This difference arose beyond question out of the different points of view from which the two poets regarded ghosts. Voltaire looked upon the reappearance of a dead man as a miracle; Shakespeare as quite a natural occurrence. Which of the two thought the more philosophically cannot be questioned, but Shakespeare thought the more poetically. Voltaire's ghost presents no claims to be regarded as a being who even beyond the grave is capable of pleasant and unpleasant sensations. He only wishes to instruct us how divine power would occasionally make an exception to its eternal laws in order to discover and punish secret crimes.

I will not say that it is a fault when the dramatic poet arranges his fable in such a manner that it serves for the exposition or confirmation of some great moral truth. But I may say that this arrangement of the fable is anything but needful; that there are very instructive and perfect plays that do not aim at such a single maxim, and that we err when we regard the moral sentences that are found at the close of many ancient tragedies, as the keynote for the existence of the entire play.

If therefore the 'Semiramis' of M. de Voltaire had no further merit but this on which he so greatly prides himself, namely that we can therefrom learn to reverence almighty justice that selects extraordinary means to punish

extraordinary crimes, then I say 'Semiramis' would seem to
me a very indifferent play, especially as its moral is by no
means the most edifying. For it is incontestably more
becoming to assume that Providence does not need to
employ such extraordinary means, and to suppose that
the punishment of the bad and the reward of the good
follow in the ordinary chain of events.

.   .   .   .

The play of the eighth evening was the ' Coffee-house,
or the Scotchwoman' of M. de Voltaire.

A long story might be made out of this comedy. Its
author sent it into the world as a translation from the
English of Hume ; not the historian and philosopher but
another of that name, who made himself known by his
tragedy, ' Douglas.' In some points it has resemblances
with Goldoni's ' Caffè'; especially the Don Marzio of
Goldoni seems to have been the prototype of Frelon. But
what was only a malicious fellow is here also a miserable
scribbler, whom Voltaire named Frelon, that the critics
might the more easily discover his sworn enemy, the
journalist Freron. He wanted to annihilate him by this
play, and doubtless he gave him no mean blow therewith.
We foreigners, who take no interest in the jealous
bickerings of these French *literati*, overlook the personalities contained in the play, and find in Frelon merely
the faithful portrait of a certain set of people who are not
strange to us either. We have our Frelons as well as the
French and the English, only that they raise less
comment among us because we are more indifferent to
our literature. But even if the meaning of this character
were lost for Germany, the play has interest enough
without, and honest Freeport alone could insure it our
favour. We love his rough nobility and even the English
were flattered by him.

For only for his sake have they lately transplanted the
whole trunk to the soil where it purported to have grown.
Colman, unquestionably their best living comic writer,
has translated the piece under the title of ' The English
Merchant,' and has given to it the national colouring
that was still wanting in the original. Well as M. de
Voltaire claims to know English customs, yet he has often

blundered, for instance, when he makes his Lindane live at
a coffee-house; Colman lodges her instead with a worthy
female who lets furnished rooms, and this woman is far
more suited to be the friend and benefactress of the
young deserted beauty than Fabrice. Colman has also
tried to define the characters more strongly for the
English taste. Lady Alton is not only a jealous fury
she desires to be a lady of genius, taste, and learning
a patroness of literature. He thus thought to make her
connexion with the wretched Frelon (whom he calls
Spatter) more natural. Freeport also obtains a larger
sphere of usefulness, he protects Lindane's father as
warmly as Lindane, and that which Lord Falbridge does
in the French version towards the father's pardon, is here
done by Freeport; it is he alone who brings all to a
happy conclusion.

The English critics have commended Colman's adapta-
tion as excellent in feeling, delicate and vivacious in
dialogue, and well defined as to the characters. But yet
they far prefer Colman's other plays. . . . ' The English
Merchant' has not action enough for them; curiosity is
not sufficiently fostered, the whole complication is visible
in the first act. . . . Much in this criticism is not un-
founded. However we Germans are well content that
the action is not richer and more complex. The English
taste on this point distracts and fatigues us, we love
a simple plot that can be grasped at once. The English
are forced to insert episodes into French plays if they are
to please on their stage. In like manner we have to weed
episodes out of the English plays, if we want to introduce
them on to our stage. The best comedies of a Congreve
and Wycherley would seem intolerable to us without this
excision. We manage better with their tragedies. In
part these are not so complex and many of them have
succeeded well amongst us without the least alteration,
which is more than I could say for any of their
comedies.

The Italians also have a version of the 'Scotchwoman.'
It is in the first portion of Diodati's Theatrical Library.
Like the German, it follows the original closely, only the
Italian has added a scene at the end. Voltaire said that

Frelon was punished in the English original, but merited as was this punishment, it seemed to him to hurt the chief interest of the play and he had therefore omitted it. The Italian did not deem this excuse sufficient, he completed the punishment of Frelon out of his own head, for the Italians are great lovers of poetical justice.

No. 13.

.   .   .   .   .

.   .   .   .   .

On the eleventh evening 'Miss Sara Sampson'[1] was performed.

It is not possible to demand more from art than what Mdlle. Henseln achieved in the *rôle* of Sara, and indeed the play altogether was well performed. It is a little too long and it is therefore generally shortened at most theatres. Whether the author would be well satisfied with all these excisions, I almost incline to doubt. We know what authors are, if we want to take from them a mere bit of padding they cry out : You touch my life! It is true that by leaving out parts the excessive length of a play is clumsily remedied, and I do not understand how it is possible to shorten a scene without changing the whole sequence of a dialogue. But if the author does not like these foreign abbreviations, why does he not curtail it himself, if he thinks it is worth the trouble and is not one of those persons who put children into the world and then withdraw their hands from them for ever.   .   .   .   .

.   .   .   .

No. 14.

Domestic tragedies found a very thorough defender in the person of the French art critic who first made 'Sara' known to his nation. As a rule the French rarely approve anything of which they have not a model among themselves.

The names of princes and heroes can lend pomp and majesty to a play, but they contribute nothing to our emotion. The misfortunes of those whose circumstances most resemble our own, must naturally penetrate most

[1] By Lessing himself.

deeply into our hearts, and if we pity kings, we pity them
as human beings, not as kings.   Though their position
often renders their misfortunes more important, it does
not make them more interesting.   Whole nations may be
involved in them, but our sympathy requires an individual
object and a state is far too much an abstract conception
to touch our feelings.

" We wrong the human heart," says Marmontel, " we
misread nature, if we believe that it requires titles to rouse
and touch us.   The sacred names of friend, father, lover,
husband, son, mother, of mankind in general, these are far
more pathetic than aught else and retain their claims for
ever.   What matters the rank, the surname, the genealogy
of the unfortunate man whose easy good nature towards
unworthy friends has involved him in gambling and who
loses over this his wealth and honour and now sighs in
prison distracted by shame and remorse ?   If asked, who is
he ? I reply : He was an honest man and to add to his
grief he is a husband and a father ; his wife whom he loves
and who loves him is suffering extreme need and can only
give tears to the children who clamour for bread.   Show
me in the history of heroes a more touching, a more moral,
indeed a more tragic situation !   And when at last this
miserable man takes poison and then learns that Heaven
had willed his release, what is absent, in this painful
terrible moment, when to the horrors of death are added
the tortures of imagination, telling him how happily he
could have lived, what I say is absent to render the situation worthy of a tragedy ?   The wonderful, will be replied.
What ! is there not matter wonderful enough in this sudden
change from honour to shame, from innocence to guilt,
from sweet peace to despair ; in brief, in the extreme
misfortune into which mere weakness has plunged him !"

But no matter how much their Diderots and Marmontels
preach this to the French, it does not seem as though
domestic tragedies were coming into vogue among them.
The nation is too vain, too much enamoured of titles and
other external favours ; even the humblest man desires to
consort with aristocrats and considers the society of his
equals as bad society.   True, a happy genius can exert great
influence over his nation.   Nature has nowhere resigned

her rights and she is perhaps only waiting there for the
poet who is to exhibit her in all her truth and strength.

.   .   .   .   .

The objections raised by the above critic against the
German 'Sara' are in part not without foundation.   Yet
I fancy the author would rather retain all its faults than
take the trouble of entirely rewriting the play.   He recalls
what Voltaire said on a similar occasion : " We cannot do
all that our friends advise.   There are such things as
necessary faults.   To cure a humpbacked man of his hump
we should have to take his life.   My child is humpbacked,
but otherwise it is quite well."   .   .

.   .   .   .   .

No. 15.

The sixteenth evening 'Zaire' by Voltaire was performed.   "To those who care for literary history," says
M. de Voltaire, " it will not be displeasing to know how
this play originated.   Various ladies had reproached the
author because his tragedies did not contain enough about
love.   He replied, that in his opinion, tragedy was not the
most fitting place for love; still if they would insist on
having enamoured heroes he also could create them.   The
play was written in eighteen days and received with
applause.   In Paris it is named a Christian tragedy and
has often been played in place of ' Polyeucte.' "
To the ladies therefore we are indebted for this tragedy
and it will long remain the favourite play of the ladies.   A
young ardent monarch, only subjugated by love ; a proud
conqueror only conquered by love ; a Sultan without poly-
gamy ; a seraglio converted into the free and accessible
abode of an absolute mistress ; a forsaken maiden raised to
the highest pinnacle of fortune, thanks solely to her lovely
eyes ; a heart for which religion and tenderness contest,
that is divided between its god and its idol, that would like
to be pious if only it need not cease loving ; a jealous man
who recognises his error and avenges it on himself: if
these flattering ideas do not bribe the suffrages of the fair
sex, then what indeed could bribe them ?
Love itself dictated 'Zaire' to Voltaire ! said a polite art
critic.   He would have been nearer the truth had he said

gallantry; I know but one tragedy at which love itself has laboured and that is 'Romeo and Juliet' by Shakespeare. It is incontestable, that Voltaire makes his enamoured Zaire express her feelings with much nicety and decorum. But what is this expression compared with that living picture of all the smallest, most secret, artifices whereby love steals into our souls, all the imperceptible advantages it gains thereby, all the subterfuges with which it manages to supersede every other passion until it succeeds in holding the post of sole tyrant of our desires and aversions? Voltaire perfectly understands the—so to speak—official language of love; that is to say the language and the tone love employs when it desires to express itself with caution and dignity, when it would say nothing but what the prudish female sophist and the cold critic can justify. Still even the most efficient government clerk does not always know the most about the secrets of his government; or else if Voltaire had the same deep insight as Shakespeare into the essence of love, he would not exhibit it here, and therefore the poem has remained beneath the capacities of the poet.

Almost the same might be said of jealousy. His jealous Orosman plays a sorry figure beside the jealous Othello of Shakespeare. And yet Othello has unquestionably furnished the prototype of Orosman. Cibber says [1] Voltaire avails himself of the brand that lighted the tragic pile of Shakespeare. I should have said: a brand from out of this flaming pile and moreover one that smoked more than it glowed or warmed. In Orosman we hear a jealous man speak and we see him commit a rash deed of jealousy, but of jealousy itself we learn neither more nor less than what we knew before. Othello on the contrary is a complete manual of this deplorable madness; there we can learn all that refers to it and awakens it and how we may avoid it.

But is it always Shakespeare, always and eternally Shakespeare who understood everything better than the

---

[1] " From English plays, Zara's French author fir'd
Confessed his Muse, beyond herself inspir'd,
From rack'd Othello's rage, he raised his style
And snatched the brand that lights this tragic pile."

French, I hear my readers ask? That annoys us, because
we cannot read him. I seizè this opportunity to remind
the public of what it seems purposely to have forgotten.
We have a translation of Shakespeare. It is scarcely
finished and yet seems already forgotten. Critics have
spoken ill of it. I have a mind to speak very well of it.
Not in order to contradict these learned men, nor to defend the faults they have discovered, but because I believe
there is no need to make so much ado about these faults.
The undertaking was a difficult one, and any other person
than Herr Wieland would have made other slips in their
haste, or have passed over more passages from ignorance
or laziness and what parts he has done well few will do
better. Any way his rendering of Shakespeare is a book
that cannot be enough commended among us. We have
much to learn yet from the beauties he has given to us,
before the blemishes wherewith he has marred them offend
us so greatly that we require a new translation.

To return to ' Zaire.' It was brought out on the Parisian
stage in 1733 by the author ; and three years after it was
translated into English and played in London at Drury
Lane. The translator was Aaron Hill, himself no mean
dramatic poet. This greatly flattered Voltaire, and what
he said of it in his dedication to the Englishman Falkener
deserves to be read, for it is in his peculiar strain of proud
humility. Only we must not think everything is as true
as he asserts.

Woe to him who does not always read Voltaire's
writings in the sceptical spirit wherein he has written a
portion of them.

For instance, he says to his English friend " Your poets
had a custom to which even Addison himself submitted ;
for custom is as mighty as reason or law. This unreasonable custom was that every act must be concluded by
verses in a style quite different from that of the rest of
the play, and also these verses must of necessity contain a
comparison. Phædra before her exit, compares herself
poetically to a stag, Cato to a rock, and Cleopatra to children who weep themselves to sleep. The translator of
' Zaire ' is the first who has ventured to maintain the
laws of nature against such an abnormal taste. He has

abolished this custom, for he felt that passion must speak
its own language and that the poet must everywhere
conceal himself in order that we may recognise the hero."

There are only three untruths in this passage; that is
not much for M. de Voltaire. It is true that the English
since Shakespeare or perhaps even before him, had the
habit of ending their blank verse acts with a few rhyming
lines. But that these rhyming lines consisted only of
comparisons, that they necessarily contained such comparisons, is entirely false; and I cannot imagine how
M. de Voltaire could say such things to the face of an
Englishman who might also be presumed to have read the
tragic poets of his nation. Secondly it is not true that
Hill departed from this custom in his translation of
'Zaire.' It is indeed almost incredible that M. de Voltaire should not have looked more closely at a translation
of his own play than I or some one else. And yet so it
must be. For as certainly as it is in blank verse, so certainly does every act close with two or four rhymed lines.
Comparisons, it is true, they do not contain, but as I said,
among all the rhymed lines with which Shakespeare and
Jonson and Dryden and Lee and Otway and Rowe and
all the rest conclude their acts, there are certainly a hundred against five that likewise do not contain them.
Therefore where is Hill's speciality? But even had he
had the speciality that Voltaire confers on him, it is not
true, in the third place, that his example has had the influence that Voltaire accords it. Of the tragedies that even
now appear in England, half, if not more, have their acts
ending with rhymes, rather than without them. Hill
himself has never entirely abandoned the old custom even
in those plays he has written since the translation of
'Zaire.' And what does it matter whether we hear
rhymes at the end or no? If they are there, they may
perhaps be useful to the orchestra to warn them to take
up their instruments; a sign which in this way would be
more prettily given out of the play itself than by means
of a whistle or other signal.

No. 16.

In Hill's day English actors were somewhat unnatural, and especially their acting of tragedy was wild and exaggerated, when they wished to express violent emotions they screamed and behaved like maniacs, and the rest they drawled off with a stilted pompous solemnity that betrayed the comedian in every syllable. When therefore Hill intended to have his translation of 'Zaire' performed, he confided the *rôle* of Zaire to a young woman who had never yet acted in tragedies. He concluded thus : this young person has feeling, voice, figure, and decorum, she has not yet acquired the spurious taste of the stage, she does not need to unlearn faults, and if she can be persuaded to be for a few hours what she represents, then she may speak as she likes and all will go well. And it did go well, and the theatrical pedants who had maintained against Hill that only a very practised and experienced person could do justice to this part, were silenced. This young actress was the wife of the comedian Colley Cibber and her first attempt in her eighteenth year was a *chef-d'œuvre*. It is curious that the French actress who played Zaire first was also a *débutante*.

The young fascinating Mdlle. Gossin became suddenly famous through Zaire, and even Voltaire himself was so enchanted that he lamented his age very piteously.

The *rôle* of Orosman was played by a connexion of Hill's, no actor by profession but a man of position. He acted from mere love of the art, and had no hesitation in appearing in public and exhibiting a talent that is as estimable as any other. In England examples are not rare of such distinguished persons who act merely for their pleasure. "All that appears strange to us in this," says M. de Voltaire, "is that it appears strange. We should reflect that all things in the world depend on custom and opinion. The French court formerly danced on the stage with opera singers, and nothing further is thought about it except that this mode of entertainment is gone out of fashion. What is the difference between the two arts but that the one is far above the other? as talents that require mind are above mere bodily agility. . . .

It is curious how far the German taste is removed from

the Italian. The Italians find Voltaire too short, we find
him too long. Scarcely has Orosman spoken his last
words and given himself the death-thrust than down goes
our curtain. But is it really true that German taste demands this? We curtail many plays thus, but why do
we so curtail them? Do we seriously require that a tragedy should end like an epigram? always with the point
of the dagger or with the last sigh of the hero? Whence
do we grave slow Germans take this impetuous impatience
that will not suffer us to listen to anything more as soon
as the execution is over, even if it were the fewest of words
and quite necessary to the proper conclusion of the play?
But I search in vain for the cause of a thing that is not. Our
blood is calm enough to allow of our listening to the poet
until the end, if only the actor would let us. We would
gladly listen to the last will of the magnanimous Sultan
and admire and pity Nerestan, but we are not allowed.
Why are we not allowed? To this why I know no because. Are the Orosman actors to blame? It is obvious
why they might like to have the last word—stabbed and
applauded. Well, we must pardon little vanities to artists.

Among no nation has ' Zaire ' found a severer critic than
among the Dutch. Frederick Duim, perhaps a relation of
the famous Amsterdam actor of that name, found so much
to object to in it, that it was really less trouble to make
a better one. He really did make another![1]

In this Zaire's conversion plays the chief part, the Sultan
conquers his love and sends back christian Zaire into her
fatherland with all the pomp due to her contemplated
dignity, while old Lusignan dies of joy. Who wants to
know more about this? The only unpardonable fault of
a tragic poet is this, that he leaves us cold ; if he interests
us he may do as he likes with the little mechanical rules.
It is easy for the Duims to blame, but they must not try to
bend the bow of Ulysses. I say this because I do not wish
conclusions drawn from Duim's unsuccessful improvement
as to the untenability of his criticisms. Duim's objections
are well founded in part, and especially has he remarked
the indecorum of Voltaire's choice of scene and the

[1] Zaire, bekeerde Turkinne. Treurspiel, Amsterdam, 1745.

awkwardness of the exits and entrances without sufficient reason. Neither has he overlooked the absurdity of the sixth scene in the third act. "Orosman," he says, "comes to fetch Zaire from the mosque; Zaire refuses to go without giving the smallest reason for this refusal, she departs and Orosman is left standing like a fool ('als eenen lafhartigen'). Is that in accordance with his dignity? Does it rhyme with his character? Why does he not urge Zaire to explain herself? Why does he not follow her into the seraglio? Might he not follow her thither?" But my good Duim, if Zaire had explained herself clearly, whence should the other acts have come? Would not the whole tragedy have been destroyed? Quite so, the second scene of the third act is absurd. Orosman again comes to Zaire and Zaire again departs without the least explanation, and Orosman, good soul ("dien goeden hals") consoles himself again by a monologue. But as I said before, the uncertainty or complication had to continue until the fifth act; and if the whole catastrophe hangs on a hair, many more important things in this life hang on nothing stronger.

In other respects the last-named scene is the one in which the actor who plays Orosman can show his highest art in all the modest splendour which only delicate connoisseurs can appreciate. He must change from one emotion to another and must make this dumb transition so naturally that the spectator is not carried away by a leap, but by a series of rapid but still perceptible gradations.

     .   .   .   .   .

No. 17.

The seventeenth evening, 'Sydney' by Gresset was performed.

This play was first brought out in 1745. A comedy against suicide could find little favour in Paris. The French said : This is a play for London. I do not know about that. The English might perhaps find 'Sydney' a little un-English, he does not act quickly enough, he philosophizes too much before his act, and after he thinks he has committed it, too little ; his remorse might seem like contemptible pusillanimity. Indeed to be thus imposed on by a French man-servant would be deemed by many shame enough to justify hanging.

But such as the play is, it seems very good for us Germans. We like to cloak a folly with a little philosophy, and do not find it at variance with our honour if we are held back from a stupid step and are forced to confess that we have philosophized falsely.

. . . .

On the eighteenth evening the 'Ghost with the Drum' was played.

This piece really originates from the English of Addison. Addison wrote only one tragedy and one comedy. Dramatic poetry was not his speciality; but a good head always knows how to set about a matter and therefore his two plays are very estimable works, even though they do not contain the highest beauties of their genus. In both he tried to approach to the French unities and rules, but given twenty Addisons and these rules will never be to the taste of the English. Let those be satisfied therewith who know no higher beauties.   .   .

. . . . .
. . . . .

No. 18.

On the twenty-first evening Marivaux's comedy, 'The False Intimacies' was performed.

Marivaux worked nearly half a century for the Parisian theatres, his first play dates from 1712, he died in 1763 aged seventy-two. The number of his comedies amounts to some thirty, of which more than two-thirds possess a harlequin, because he composed them for the Italian stage. To these · The False Intimacies' belongs, which was played in 1763 without much success, and was then brought out again two years after and met with great applause.

His plays, rich as they are in manifold characters and complications, still resemble one another closely. In all there is the same dazzling and often too far-fetched wit; the same metaphysical analysis of passions; the same flowery neological language. His plots are of a limited range, but like a true Kallipides of his art, he knows how to traverse this range in a variety of tiny and yet plainly emphasised steps, so that in the end we fancy that we have compassed a large tract under his guidance.

Since Frau Neuber, *sub auspiciis* of His Magnificence, Professor Gottsched, openly banished harlequin from her theatre, all German stages, that lay claim to correct taste, seem to have indorsed this banishment. I say seem advisedly, for at bottom they have only abolished the coloured jacket and the name, and retained the fool. Frau Neuber herself acted a number of plays in which harlequin was the chief personage. Only she called harlequin Jacky, and he was dressed in white instead of in many colours. Truly this is a great triumph achieved by good taste!

'The False Intimacies' has its harlequin, who has become Peter in the German translation. Frau Neuber is dead, Gottsched is dead, I think we might put his jacket on him again. Seriously, if he can be tolerated under a strange name, why then not under his own? "He is a foreign creation" they say. What matters that? I would all fools among us were foreigners! "He dresses as no one dresses amongst us." This relieves us from the necessity of saying who he is. "It is absurd to see the same individual appear every day in a different way." We must not look upon him as an individual but as a species. It is not harlequin who appears to-day in 'Timon,' to-morrow in 'The Falcon,' the day after in 'The False Intimacies' like a ubiquitous *gamin*, but there are harlequins and harlequins, and the species admits of a thousand varieties. He in 'Timon' is not the one in 'The Falcon'; the latter lived in Greece, the other in France. It is only because their characters have the same essential traits that they have retained the same name. Why should we be more captious, more choice in our pleasures, and give way more to jejune hypercriticisms than—I will not say the French and Italians—but than even the Greeks and Romans? Was their parasite aught but our harlequin? Had he not his especial peculiar dress in which he appeared in one play after another? Had the Greeks not an especial drama into which Satyrs had at all times to be introduced, whether or no they fitted into the story of the play?

.   .   .   .

On the twenty-second evening M. du Belloy's 'Zelmire' was played.

The name Du Belloy cannot be unfamiliar to any one who is not quite a stranger to modern French literature.

The author of 'The Siege of Calais'! If this play does not merit all the noise the French made about it, yet the noise itself reflects honour on the French. It showed them as a nation that is jealous of its fame; that has not forgotten the great deeds of its ancestors and that, convinced of the worth of a poet, and the influence of the theatre upon morality and manners, does not reckon the one among its useless members, or the other as an object concerning only busy idlers. How far in this respect are we Germans behind the French! To say it right out, compared with them we are true barbarians! Barbarians more barbaric than our oldest ancestors who deemed a minstrel a man of worth, and who, for all their indifference to art and science, would have held the question whether a bard or one who deals with bearskins and amber was the more useful citizen, to be the question of a fool. I may look about me in Germany where I will, the town has yet to be built which might be expected to have a thousandth part of the esteem and gratitude for a German poet, that Calais has had for Du Belloy. It may be called French vanity; how far we must still advance before we could even be capable of such vanity. And what marvel? Our scholars themselves are petty enough to encourage the nation in its contempt for everything that does not fill the purse. If we speak of a work of genius, whichever you will, if we speak of encouragement to artists, if we express the wish that a rich flourishing city should help by mere sympathy towards furnishing a decent place of recreation for men whose work obliges them to bear the heat and burden of the day, or a useful amusement for those who have no business (at least the theatre may lay claim to this), what do we hear and see? It is not only the usurer, Albinus, who exclaims: Heaven be praised that our citizens have more important things to do.

" Eu!
Rem poteris servare tuam!——"

More important? More lucrative; that I admit. For certainly nothing is lucrative amongst us that has the least connexion with the fine arts. But—

" ——hæc animos ærugo et cura peculi
Cum semel imbuerit——"

But I forget myself. How does all this belong to 'Zelmire'?

Du Belloy was a young man who wanted or was to study law. "Was to" will probably be nearer the truth. For the love of the stage retained the upper hand, he put aside the Bartolus and became a comedian. For some time he played at Brunswick in the French troupe, and wrote several plays; he then returned to his fatherland and soon became as happy and famous, thanks to a few tragedies, as law could ever have made him, even if he had become a Beaumont. Woe to the young German genius that should tread this path! Contempt and beggary would be his certain lot!

Du Belloy's first tragedy was called 'Titus,' 'Zelmire' was his second. 'Titus' found no favour and was only played once. But 'Zelmire' found the more favour; it was played fourteen consecutive times and the Parisians are not sated yet. The subject is of the author's own invention.

A French critic [1] took this occasion to declare himself against tragedies of this species. "We should have preferred," he said, "a subject drawn from history. The annals of the world are so rich in notorious crimes, and the especial purpose of tragedy is to present to our admiration and imitation the great deeds of real heroes. In thus paying the tribute posterity owes to their ashes, we also fire the hearts of contemporaries with the noble desire to resemble them. It will be objected that 'Zaire,' 'Alzire,' 'Mahomet,' are the creations of fancy. The two former names are creations, but the foundations of the stories are historical. There really were crusades in which Christians and Turks hated and murdered one another for the honour of God, their common father. At the conquest of Mexico the great and happy contrasts between European and American manners, between false sentiment and true religion had necessarily to evince themselves. And as for

---

[1] Journal Encyclopédique, Juillet 1762.

'Mahomet,' it is the epitome, the quintessence so to speak, of the life of this impostor : fanaticism shown in action ; the most beautiful and philosophical picture that has ever been drawn of this dangerous monster."

No. 19.

It is permitted to everybody to have his own taste, and it is laudable to be able to give the reasons why we hold such taste. But to give to the reasons by which we justify it a character of generality, and thus make it out to be the only true taste if these be correct, means exceeding the limits permitted to the investigating amateur and instituting oneself an independent lawgiver. The French critic above quoted begins with a modest "we should have preferred," and then passes on to pronounce such universally binding dicta, that we could almost believe this "we" was the utterance of personified criticism. A true art critic deduces no rules from his individual taste, but has formed his taste from rules necessitated by the nature of the subject.

Now Aristotle has long ago decided how far the tragic poet need regard historical accuracy : not farther than it resembles a well-constructed fable wherewith he can combine his intentions. He does not make use of an event because it really happened, but because it happened in such a manner as he will scarcely be able to invent more fitly for his present purpose. If he finds this fitness in a true case, then the true case is welcome ; but to search through history books does not reward his labour. And how many know what has happened ? If we only admit the possibility that something can happen from the fact that it has happened, what prevents us from deeming an entirely fictitious fable a really authentic occurrence, of which we have never heard before ? What is the first thing that makes a history probable ? Is it not its internal probability ? And is it not a matter of indifference whether this probability be confirmed by no witnesses or traditions, or by such as have never come within our knowledge ? It is assumed quite without reason, that it is one of the objects of the stage, to keep alive the memory of great men. For that we have history and not the stage. From the stage we are not to learn what such and such an individual man has done, but what every man of a certain character would do under certain given circumstances. The object of tragedy is more philosophical than the object of history, and it is degrading her from her true dignity to employ her as a mere panegyric of famous men or to misuse her to feed national pride.

.   .   .   .

The translation of 'Zelmire' is in prose. But would we not rather hear nervous melodious prose than vapid and forced verses? Among all our rhymed translations there will be scarcely half a dozen that are tolerable. And I must not even be taken at my word and asked to name them! . . .

But does it repay our labour to expend industry on French verses until we have produced some in our language as watery and correct, as grammatical and cold? If on the contrary we transfer the whole poetical dress of the French into our prose, our prose will not through this become very poetical. It will be still far removed from the hybrid tone that has resulted out of the prose translations of English poets, in which the use of the boldest metaphors and images, together with a measured cadenced construction, recalls drunkards who dance without music. The expressions will, at most, not be raised above everyday speech, more than theatrical declamation should be raised above the common tone of social conversation. And therefore I wish our prosaic translators right many imitators, although I am not at all of the opinion of Houdar de la Motte, that metre is of itself a childish constraint to which the dramatic poet least of all should submit. For here the only question is to choose the lesser of two evils; either to sacrifice sense and emphasis to versification, or to sacrifice the latter to the former. Houdar de la Motte can be pardoned for his opinion, he was thinking of a language in which the rhythm of poetry is mere tickling of the ears, and cannot contribute to the strength of expressions. In our language on the other hand it is something more, we

approach far more closely to the Greeks who were able to
indicate by the mere rhythm of their verses what passions
were expressed.   The French verses have only the value
of surmounted difficulties, and certainly this is a miserable
value.

Herr Borchers played the part of Antenor uncommonly
well . . . Herr Borchers has very much talent and this
alone should insure our favourable opinion of him, that he
is as ready to act old parts as young ones.   This shows his
love for his art, and a connoisseur thus distinguishes him
at once from many other young actors who want for ever to
shine on the stage, and whose petty vanity to be seen and
admired in nothing but gallant amiable parts often constitutes their foremost and only vocation for the stage.

.   .   .   .   .   .
.   .   .   .   .   .
.   .   .   .   .   .
.   .   .   .   .   .

No. 21.

On the twenty-seventh evening 'Nanine,' by M. de
Voltaire, was performed.

'Nanine'? asked so-called critics when this piece first
appeared in 1749.   What sort of a title is that?   What
idea does that give us?   Nothing more and nothing
less than a title should.   A title must be no bill of fare.
The less it betrays of the contents, the better it is.   It is
better for both poet and spectator.   The ancients rarely
gave to their comedies any other than insignificant titles.
I barely know three or four that indicate the chief personage or reveal anything of the plot.   To these belong
Plautus's *Miles Gloriosus*.   But how is it that no one
has noticed that only half this title belongs to Plautus?
Plautus called his play *Gloriosus*, as he named another
Truculentus.   Miles must be the addition of some grammarian.   It is true that the boaster whom Plautus portrays
is a soldier, but his boasts do not only concern his position
and his military deeds.   He is quite as boastful on the subject of love; he vaunts himself to be not only the bravest,
but also the most amiable and beautiful of men.   Both can

be included in the word *gloriosus*, but as soon as we add
Miles, gloriosus is restricted.   Perhaps the grammarian who
made this addition was misled by a passage of Cicero,[1] but
in this case he should have esteemed Plautus himself more
than Cicero.   Plautus himself says:—

> " ALAZON Græce huic nomen est Comœdiæ,
> Id nos latine GLORIOSUM dicimus——"

And in the passage of Cicero it is by no means established
that just this play of Plautus is intended.   The character
of a boasting soldier appeared in many plays.   Cicero
may just as well have aimed at the ' Thraso ' of Terence.
But this is by the way.   I remember that I have already
spoken my opinion on the titles of comedies in general.
It may be that the subject is not so insignificant.   Many
a bungler has made a bad comedy to a good title and
merely on account of the good title.   I should prefer a
good comedy with a bad title.   If we investigate what
characters have already been treated, scarcely one can be
thought of from which the French at least have not
already named a play.   This has been there long ago, is
the exclamation.   And so has this.   This is borrowed
from Molière, that from Destouches.   Borrowed?   That
comes from these beautiful titles.   What right of possession in a certain character does a poet gain by the fact
that he takes his title therefrom?   If he had used it
quietly I could also use it quietly again, and no one would
on that account deem me an imitator.   But let a man
venture to write, for instance, a new Misanthrope.   If he
does not even take a trait from Molière, yet his misanthrope will be always called only a copy.   Enough.
Molière has used the name first.   The other is in the
wrong that he lives fifty years later and that language
has not endless varieties of designation for the endless
varieties of the human mind.
     But if the title ' Nanine ' says nothing, the second title
says the more: ' Nanine, or Prejudice Conquered.'   And
why should a play not have two titles?   Have we not
two or three names?   Names are given to distinguish,
and with two names confusion is more difficult than with

---

[1] De Officiis, lib. I. cap. 38.

one. Concerning the second title M. de Voltaire does not
seem to have been quite decided. In the same edition of
his works it is called on one page, 'Conquered Prejudice'
and on another, 'The Man without Prejudices.' But
the two do not really differ much. The prejudice in
question is, that to the formation of a reasonable marriage
equality of birth and station are requisite. In short, the
history of Nanine is the history of Pamela. Doubtless
M. de Voltaire did not wish to use the name Pamela,
because several plays had already appeared some years ago
under that name, which had not met with great success.
Boissy and De la Chaussée's 'Pamela' are tolerably vapid
plays, and Voltaire did not need to be Voltaire to make
something better.

'Nanine' belongs to pathetic comedy. It has also
many laughable scenes, and only in so far as these laughable scenes alternate with the pathetic, Voltaire would
admit of them in comedy. An entirely serious comedy,
wherein we never laugh, not even smile, wherein we
should rather always weep, is to him a monstrosity. On
the other hand he finds the transition from the pathetic
to the comic, and from the comic to the pathetic, very
natural. Human life is nothing but a constant chain of
such transitions, and comedy should be a mirror of human
life. "What is more common," he says, "than to find
in one house an angry father who storms; an enamoured
daughter who sighs, a son who mocks at both, while
each relative feels something different in the same scene?
Very often we sneer in one room at that which is agitating
the feelings of those in the next room, and not rarely
the self-same person laughs and cries over the self-same
subject in the self-same quarter of an hour. A very
venerable matron sat by the bed of one of her daughters
who was dangerously ill. She was surrounded by the
whole family. She was weeping bitterly, and wringing
her hands, cried: 'O God! leave me, leave me this child,
only this one, you may take all the others instead.' At
this moment a man who had married one of the other
daughters, approached the matron, pulled at her sleeve
and asked: 'Madame, the sons-in-law as well?' The
cold-bloodedness and the comic tone in which he spoke

these words, made such an impression on the afflicted
lady, that she had to quit the room shaken by laughter,
all followed her laughing; the invalid herself, when she
heard it, nearly choked with laughing."

"Homer," he says in another place "even allowed his
gods to laugh while they were deciding the fate of the
world, over the ludicrous scruples of Vulcan. Hector
laughs at the fears of his little son while Andromache
is shedding hot tears. It will even happen that in the
middle of the horrors of battle, of a fire, or some such
event, an idea, a casual joke, evokes uncontrollable
laughter, notwithstanding all our anxiety, all our pity.
At the battle of Speyer a regiment was commanded to
give no quarter. A German officer begged for it, and the
Frenchman, whom he petitioned, replied: 'Ask for what
you like, sir, only not for life, I cannot accommodate you
with that!' This *naïveté* ran from mouth to mouth; the
soldiers laughed and murdered. How much sooner then
will laughter follow pathetic emotions in a comedy?
Does not Alcmena touch us? Does not Sosia make us
laugh? What miserable and futile labour then, to contest this experience!"

Very good. But does not M. de Voltaire also contend
against experience when he declares a wholly serious
comedy to be a species as tedious as it is faulty? Perhaps
his contention, when he wrote, was not yet against experience. But at that time there was no 'Cenie,' no 'Père
de famille'; and there is much that genius must really
create first, before we can recognise it as possible.

No. 22.

On the thirtieth evening Thomas Corneille's play of
'The Earl of Essex' was performed.

This tragedy is almost the only one of the considerable number of plays written by the younger Corneille
that has maintained its character as an acting play on
the French stage. And I believe it is still more frequently performed on the German stage than on the
French. It dates from 1678, forty years after Calprenede
had treated the same theme.

"It is certain," writes Corneille, "that the Earl of Essex stood in especial favour with Queen Elizabeth. By nature he was proud. The services he had rendered to England inflated his pride still more. His enemies accused him of a secret understanding with the Earl of Tyrone, whom the Irish rebels had chosen as their leader. The suspicion that rested on him because of this matter, deprived him of the commandership-in-chief. He was embittered, returned to London, incited the mob to rebel, was arrested, and condemned, and finally beheaded on Feb. 25, 1601, because he would not entreat pardon. Thus much has history lent me. If I should be accused of having violated history in an important point, because I have not used the incident of the ring, given to the Earl by the Queen as a guarantee of her unconditional pardon should he ever prove guilty of high treason; I must own it would surprise me. I am assured that this ring-story is an invention of Calprenede's; at least I have found nothing about it in any historian."

Unquestionably Corneille was at liberty to use or leave alone this incident of the ring; but he went too far when he declared it as a poetical invention. Its historical truth has recently been placed almost beyond doubt; and such careful sceptical historians as Hume and Robertson have admitted it into their works.

Robertson, when speaking in his 'History of Scotland,' of the deep melancholy that overcame Elizabeth shortly before her death, says: "The common opinion at that time and perhaps the most probable was, that it flowed from grief for the Earl of Essex. She retained an extraordinary regard for the memory of that unfortunate nobleman; and though she often complained of his obstinacy, seldom mentioned his name without tears. An accident happened soon after her retiring from Richmond which revived her affection with new tenderness and embittered her sorrows. The Countess of Nottingham, being on her death-bed, desired to see the Queen, in order to reveal something to her, without discovering which she could not die in peace. When the Queen came into her chamber she told her that while Essex lay under sentence of death, he was desirous of imploring pardon in the manner in which the Queen had herself prescribed, by returning a ring, which during the height of his favour she had given him, with a promise that if, in any future distress, he sent that back to her as a token, it should entitle him to her protection, that Lady Scrope was the person he intended to employ in order to present it; that, by a mistake, it was put into her hands instead of Lady Scrope's, and that she, having communicated the matter to her husband, one of Essex's most implacable enemies, he had forbid her to carry it to the Queen, or return it to the Earl. The Countess having thus disclosed her secret, begged the Queen's forgiveness, but Elizabeth, who now saw both the malice of the Earl's enemies, and how unjustly she had suspected him of inflexible obstinacy, replied: 'God may forgive you, but I never can!' and left the room in great emotion. From that moment her spirit sank entirely, she could scarce taste food, she refused all the medicines prescribed by her physicians; declaring that she wished to die and would live no longer. No entreaty could prevail on her to go to bed; she sat on cushions during ten days and nights, pensive and silent, holding her finger almost continually in her mouth, with her eyes open and fixed on the ground. . . . Wasted at last, as well by anguish of mind as by long abstinence, she expired without a struggle."

No. 23.

M. de Voltaire has criticised this 'Essex' in a very curious manner. I should not like to maintain in opposition to him that 'Essex' is an excellent play, but it is easy to prove that many of the faults he blames, in part are not there at all, or are such petty matters that they show on his part a want of proper and dignified perception of the nature of tragedy.

It is one of the weaknesses of M. de Voltaire to be a very profound historian. When therefore he criticised 'Essex' he mounted this battle-steed and proudly galloped round about the arena. What a pity therefore, that all the heroic deeds he performed thus mounted, were not worth the dust that he raised!

According to him Thomas Corneille knew little of

English history, and happily for the poet, the public of
his day was yet more ignorant. Now, says M. de Voltaire,
we know Queen Elizabeth and the Earl of Essex better;
now such gross blunders against historical accuracy
would be more sharply censured in a poet.

And what are these blunders? Voltaire has reckoned
out that the queen was sixty-eight years old at the time
when she caused Essex to be condemned. It would be
ludicrous therefore, he says, to suppose that love had the
faintest share in this transaction. Why so? Do no
ludicrous things happen in this world? Or is it so
ludicrous to fancy a ludicrous thing has happened?
Hume tells of the state of agitation and painful uncertainty in which the queen found herself after the
verdict had been pronounced on Essex. Revenge and
inclination, pride and pity, concern for her own safety
and sorrow for the life of her favourite were at war
within her; she was perhaps even more to be pitied
in this state of self-torture than Essex himself. She
signed and countermanded the warrant for his execution
time after time; now she was resolved to deliver him
over to death; a moment after and her tenderness for
him arose afresh and he was to live. Essex's enemies did
not lose sight of her, they told her that he himself desired
to die and that he had asserted that she could never be in
safety while he lived. It is likely that this proof of
penitence and concern for the safety of the queen
produced an effect quite contrary to that intended by
these enemies. It fanned the flame of the old passion
she had so long indulged towards the unhappy prisoner.
But what chiefly hardened her heart against him was
his supposed obstinacy in never suing for pardon. She
hourly expected such an application for mercy and it was
only from anger that it did not come, that she at last
allowed justice to take its course.

Why should Elizabeth not have loved in her sixty-
eighth year, she who so loved to be loved? she who was
so flattered when her beauty was praised? she who was
so gratified if any seemed to bear her chains? In every
respect the world can rarely have seen a vainer woman.
Her courtiers therefore all simulated love for her and
employed terms of absurdest gallantry with all appearance

of sincerity when addressing Her Majesty. When Raleigh fell into disgrace, he wrote a letter to his friend Cecil, that was intended beyond doubt to be shown to the queen, in which he named her a Venus, a Diana and 1 know not what else. And yet this goddess already numbered sixty years. Five years later Henry Unton, her ambassador in France, held the same language to her. In short Corneille was amply justified in giving her character all the amorous weaknesses whereby he could produce the interesting conflict between the tender woman and the haughty queen.

Neither has Corneille falsified or distorted the character of Essex. Essex, says Voltaire, was not the hero that Corneille makes him, he never did anything remarkable. But if he was not this, he believed that he was. The destruction of the Armada, the conquest of Cadiz, in which Voltaire allows him little or no share, he held to be so much his achievement, that he would not tolerate any one else to claim the least honour in the matter. He offered to prove it, sword in hand against the Earl of Nottingham under whom he had held his command; against his son; against each of his relations.

Corneille lets the Earl speak contemptuously of his enemies, especially of Raleigh, Cecil and Cobham. Neither will Voltaire suffer this. It is not permissible, he says, thus to distort modern history and to treat men of such noble birth and such great merit thus unworthily. But it is not the question here what these men were, but what Essex deemed them, and Essex was proud enough of his own merits to be convinced they could have none.

When Corneille lets Essex say that it had depended only on his will to mount the throne, he certainly lets him say something that was still far removed from truth. But Voltaire did not on that account need to exclaim, "How? Essex on the throne? And by what right? Under what pretence? How could that have been possible?" For Voltaire should have recollected that Essex descended from the royal house by the maternal side, and that there really were adherents of his foolish enough to count him among those who could lay claim to the throne. When therefore he entered into secret negotiations with King James of Scotland, his first step

was to assure him that he himself did not entertain such
ambitious thoughts. What he thus denied himself is
not much less than what Corneille lets him assume.

While therefore Voltaire finds nothing but historical
perversions throughout the play, he himself is guilty of
no mean distortions. One of these has been already
ridiculed by Walpole.[1]

When for example Voltaire desires to name the old
lovers of Queen Elizabeth, he names Robert Dudley and
the Earl of Leicester. He did not know that both are one
person and that we might as fitly make the poet Arouet
and the Chamberlain de Voltaire into two distinct
persons. His mistake with regard to the box on the
ear given by the queen to Essex is equally unpardonable.
It is not true that he received it after his luckless expedi-
tion to Ireland; he had received it long before; and it is
just as little true that he tried at the time to pacify the
queen's anger by the smallest concession, but on the
contrary he expressed his irritation thereat in the liveliest
and noblest manner both verbally and in writing. Neither
did he take the first step towards reinstatement in the
royal favour; the queen had to take it.

But what does the historical ignorance of M. de
Voltaire concern me? As little as the historical ignorance
of Corneille should have concerned him. And in truth I
only want to defend Corneille against him.

Granted that the whole of Corneille's tragedy is a
romance : if it is pathetic, does it become less pathetic
because the poet has employed real names?

Why does the tragic poet choose real names? Does he
take his characters out of these names, or does he take
these names because the characters that history lends to
them have more or less resemblance to the characters
that he intends to portray in his plot? I do not speak of
the manner in which most tragedies have perhaps arisen,
but how they should arise.

Or to express myself after the usual practice of authors ;
is it the mere facts, the circumstances of time and place,
or is it the characters of the persons that make the facts

---

[1] The Castle of Otranto, Pref.

a reality, that have induced the author to choose this fact
rather than another as the subject of his play? If it
is the characters, then the question is instantly decided
how far the poet may depart from historical accuracy.
In all that does not concern the characters, as far as
he likes. Only the characters must remain sacred to
him. To strengthen these, to depict them in their best
light is all that he may add on his own account : the
smallest essential change would annul the reasons why
they bear these and not other names, and nothing offends
us more than that for which we can find no reason.

No. 24.

If the character of Corneille's Elizabeth is the poetical
ideal of the true character that history has given to this
queen, if we find in it the irresolution, the contradictions,
the anxiety, remorse, despair which did befall or could
really have befallen a proud and tender heart like that of
Elizabeth under this or that circumstance of life ; if these
feelings, I say, have been portrayed with true colours,
then the poet has done all that his duty as poet requires
of him. To examine his work, chronology in hand, to
bring him before the judgment-seat of history that he
may produce testimony for every date, for every casual
allusion even of those persons about whom history itself is
in doubt, is to mistake his calling, while it is mere
cavilling when it proceeds from those to whom we cannot
attribute such misunderstanding.

True, in M. de Voltaire it might easily be neither
misunderstanding nor *chicane.* For Voltaire is himself a
tragic poet and unquestionably a far greater one than the
younger Corneille. Otherwise it would be possible to be
master of an art and yet to have false conceptions concerning that art. And as regards *chicane*, all the world
knows that this is not his manner. What looks like it
occasionally in his works is nothing but waywardness ;
from sheer waywardness he now and then plays the part
of historian in poetics, in history that of philosopher, and
in philosophy that of wit.

Was he to know for nothing that Elizabeth was sixty-

eight years old when she had the earl beheaded?
Jealous, in love in her sixty-eighth year! Added to this,
Elizabeth's large nose, what ludicrous whimsicalities must
arise therefrom! Only after all, these merry drolleries are
to be found in the commentary on the tragedy, just in the
very place where they have no business to be. The poet
would have been justified in saying to his commentator:
"My dear Mr. Annotator, these drolleries belong to your
universal history, not to my text. For it is false that
my Elizabeth is sixty-eight years old. Pray show me
where I have said so. What is there in my play that
hinders you from assuming her to be about the same age
as Essex? You say: But she was not the same age.
Which she? The Elizabeth in your 'Rapin de Thoyras';
that may be. But why did you read 'Rapin de
Thoyras'? Why are you so learned? Why do you
confound that Elizabeth with mine? Do you seriously
believe that the remembrance of what they have read in
'Rapin de Thoyras' at some past time will be more
vividly present to this or that person among the audience,
than the sensuous impression that a well-formed actress
in her prime will make upon him? For he sees my
Elizabeth, and his own eyes convince him that it is not
your sexagenarian Elizabeth. Or will he believe 'Rapin
de Thoyras' more than his own eyes?"

Thus also could the poet explain the part of Essex.
"Your Essex in 'Rapin de Thoyras,'" he could say, "is
only the embryo of mine. What that one assumes to be,
mine is; what that one would perhaps have done for the
queen under favourable circumstances, mine has done.
Why you hear that the queen herself admits this.
Will you not believe my queen as much as 'Rapin de
Thoyras's'? My Essex is a man of worth, a great man,
but proud and inflexible. Yours was in truth neither
great, nor proud, nor inflexible; so much the worse for
him. It suffices for me that he was great and inflexible
enough to justify me in giving his name to the character
I have abstracted therefrom."

In short, tragedy is not history in dialogue. History is
for tragedy nothing but a storehouse of names wherewith
we are used to associate certain characters. If the poet

finds in history circumstances that are convenient for the
adornment or individualising of his subject; well, let him
use them.　Only this should be counted as little a merit
as the contrary is a crime.

Excepting this point of historical accuracy, I am very
ready to subscribe to the rest of M. de Voltaire's criticism.
'Essex' is a mediocre play, both as regards intrigue and
style.　To make the earl the sighing lover of an Ireton;
to bring him to the scaffold more from despair that she
cannot be his, than from a noble pride which will not let
him descend to excuses and prayers: that was the most
unfortunate conception that Corneille ever conceived, but
which, as a Frenchman, he could not help having.　The
style which is weak in the original, has become almost
abject in the translation.　But taken as a whole, the play
does not want in interest, and has here and there some
felicitous lines, that are however happier in French than
in German.　"The actors," adds M. de Voltaire, "particularly the provincial ones, are very fond of playing the
part of Essex, because they can appear with an embroi-
dered ribbon under their knee and a large blue ribbon
over their shoulders.　The earl is a hero of the first
order, who is pursued through envy: this makes an
impression.　Moreover, the number of good tragedies
that exist among all the nations on the globe is so small,
that those which are not quite bad, will still attract
spectators, if only they are supported by good actors."

He confirms this general statement by various separate
observations, that are as acute as they are correct, and
which it might be well to recall at a future representation.　I will therefore retail the chief of these here,
firmly convinced that criticism does not interfere with
enjoyment and that those who have learnt to judge a
piece the most severely are always those that visit the
theatre the most frequently.

"The part of Cecil is a secondary and a very chilly
one.　To paint such fawning flatterers the poet must be
master of those colours wherewith Racine painted his
Narcissus.　The Duchess of Ireton as he paints her is a
sensible, virtuous woman, who neither desired to draw
down on herself the anger of her queen by her love for the

earl, nor wished to marry her lover. This character would
be very fine if it possessed more life and if it at all contri-
buted towards the unravelling of the plot; but here it
only stands in the character of a friend. That is not
sufficient for the stage.

"It seems to me that all that is said and done by the
persons in this tragedy is still lame, confused, and indis-
tinct. Action must be definite, the plot clear and every
sentiment plain and natural; these are the primary and
essential rules. But what does Essex want? What is
Elizabeth's intention? Wherein does the earl's crime
consist? Is he guilty or is he wrongfully accused? If
the queen thinks him innocent she must take his part.
If he is guilty, then it is very absurd to let his confidante
say that he is far too proud even to sue for mercy. This
pride would suit a virtuous innocent hero, but does not
become a man who is convicted of high treason. He is to
humiliate himself, says the queen. Ought that to be her
real disposition if she loves him? If he does humble
himself, if he has accepted her pardon, will he love
Elizabeth more than before? I love him a hundred times
more than myself, says the queen. Ah, Madam, if it has
come to this point, if your passion has become so ardent,
why then do you not examine into your lover's accusa-
tions yourself, instead of permitting his enemies to per-
secute him and oppress him in your name, as is affirmed
though without reason, throughout the whole play.

"Neither is it possible to discern whether the earl's
friend, Salisbury, deems him innocent or guilty. He
represents to the queen that appearances are often deceptive, that everything was to be feared from the party
feeling and injustice of his judges. Nevertheless, he
appeals to the queen's mercy. Why need he do this, if
he did not hold his friend guilty? What is the spectator
to believe? He does not know what to make either of
the earl's conspiracy or of the queen's regard for him.

"Salisbury tells the queen that the earl's signature
has been forged. Yet it does not occur to the queen to
investigate such an important point. Nevertheless as a
queen and as a lover she was bound so to do. She does
not even reply to this suggestion which she should have

seized upon eagerly. She only replies that the earl is too proud and that she insists upon his suing for mercy.

"But why should he sue for mercy if his signature was forged?"

No. 25.

"Essex himself protests his innocence; but why will he die rather than convince the queen? His enemies have calumniated him; he can destroy them by a single word; why does he not do so? Is that in accordance with the character of a proud man? If his love for Ireton makes him act thus unreasonably the poet should have shown him more under the mastery of this passion throughout the play. The heat of passion can excuse everything, but we do not see him in this heat.

"The pride of the queen is in constant opposition to the pride of Essex; such a contest can please cheaply. But if it is only pride that makes them act thus, then both in Elizabeth and in Essex it is mere obstinacy. He is to crave my pardon; I will not crave her pardon; this is the eternal burden. The spectator must forget that Elizabeth is either very absurd or very unjust, when she demands that the earl is to crave pardon for a crime which neither he has committed nor she investigated. He must forget this and he really does forget it, to occupy himself only with the sentiments of pride that are so flattering to the human heart

"In short, no single part in this tragedy is what it should be, all are perverted and yet the play has pleased. Whence this pleasure? Obviously out of the situation of the personages that is touching in itself. A great man who is led to the scaffold will always interest; the representation of his fate makes an impression even without the help of poetry; very nearly the same impression that reality itself would make."

So much is the tragic poet dependent on his choice of subject. Through this alone the weakest and most confused play can achieve a kind of success, and I do not know how it is that in such plays good actors always show themselves to best advantage. A masterpiece is

rarely as well represented as it is written. Mediocrity
always fares better with the actors. Perhaps because
they can put more of themselves into the mediocre; perhaps because the mediocre leaves us more time and repose
to observe their acting; perhaps because in the mediocre
everything turns upon one or two prominent characters,
whereas in a more perfect play every person demands a
first-rate actor, and if they are not this, in spoiling their
part they also help to spoil the whole.

In 'Essex' all these and various other causes combine.
Neither the earl nor the queen is delineated by the poet
with such force that their parts cannot be strengthened
by the actors. Essex does not speak so proudly but that
the actor can show greater pride in every posture, every
look, every situation. Indeed it is essential to pride that
it express itself more by outward bearing than by words.
Essex's words are often modest, and he lets us see rather
than hear, that it is a proud modesty. This *rôle* must
therefore necessarily gain in representation. Neither can
the subordinate parts have an evil influence upon him;
the more subduedly Cecil and Salisbury are performed,
the more prominent will Essex be. I need therefore
not relate in detail, how excellently Eckhof performed
that which even the most indifferent actor cannot wholly
spoil.

This is not quite the case with Elizabeth's part, yet
even she can scarcely fail utterly. Elizabeth is as
affectionate as she is proud, and I willingly believe
that a female heart can be both at once, but how an
actress can represent both well, that I do not properly
comprehend. In nature we do not ascribe much tenderness to a proud woman, nor much pride to a tender
one. We do not ascribe it, I say; for the distinctive
signs of the one contradict the signs of the other. It is
a miracle if both are equally exhibited; and if one of
these is especially in her power, then the passion that expresses itself through the other can be felt, but scarcely
we believe, felt as powerfully as she says. Now how
can an actress go beyond nature? If her figure is majestic, if her voice is full and masculine, if her mien is
bold, if her movements are rapid and decided, then the

proud parts will be rendered admirably by her; but how about the tender ones? If, on the other hand, her figure is less imposing, if her looks speak gentleness, her eyes a modest fire, her voice more melody than majesty, her movements more grace and dignity than power and intellect, then the tender parts will be rendered admirably by her, but how about the proud ones? She will not mar them, certainly not, she will exhibit them sufficiently, we shall see an offended angry lover in her, only no Elizabeth who was masculine enough to send home her general and lover with a box on the ear. I think therefore, that the actresses who could exhibit to us this twofold Elizabeth with equal skill, are even rarer than the Elizabeths themselves, and we can and must be satisfied if one half of the character is played well and the other half is not totally overlooked.

Madame Loewen pleased greatly in the part of Elizabeth, and applying my general remark to her, she let us see and hear more of the tender woman than the proud monarch. Her figure, her voice, her modest action led us to expect nothing else, and I think that our enjoyment lost nothing thereby. For if one part of this character must of necessity obscure the other, if it cannot be but that either the queen or the loving woman must suffer, I think it is preferable that something of the pride of the queen be lost, rather than the tenderness of the loving woman.

It is not only my individual opinion when I judge thus; still less is it my intention thereby to compliment a lady who would still be a great artist, whether or no she had succeeded in this part. I only know one way in which to flatter an artist of my own or of the other sex; and this consists in assuming that they are far removed from all vanity, that art is above all else in their estimation, that they like to be judged openly and freely, and would now and then be criticized falsely rather than seldom. Whoever does not understand such flattery, in him I must confess myself mistaken and he does not deserve that we should study him. The true artist will not even believe that we see and comprehend his perfections, however much noise we may make about them, until he

perceives that we also have an eye and an ear for his
shortcomings. He will smile to himself at our unreserved
admiration, and only the praise of him who also has
courage to blame him, will touch him nearly.

I was about to say that reasons might be assigned why
the actress should emphasize the tender rather than the
proud Elizabeth. She must be proud, that is conceded
and that she is proud, we hear. The question is only,
whether she should appear more tender than proud, or
more proud than tender; whether if we have the choice
between two actresses we should rather elect her as
Elizabeth who can express the offended queen with all
the attributes of vengeful severity and majesty, or her
who can play the jealous loving woman with all her
injured feelings of slighted love, with all her readiness to
pardon the beloved criminal, with all her anxiety at his
obstinacy, her sorrow at his loss? And I say; the latter.

For, in the first place, the repetition of the same
character is thus avoided. Essex is proud, and if Elizabeth
is to be proud also, she must be so in a different way. If
in the earl tenderness is subordinate to pride, in the
queen tenderness must vanquish her pride. If Essex
assumes a higher tone than belongs to him, then the
queen must appear to be something less than she is. To
let both walk on stilts, their noses in the air, looking
down with contempt upon all around them, would be
tedious monotony. We must not be led to think that
Elizabeth, if she were in Essex's place, would act like
Essex. The result shows that she is more flexible, she
must therefore from the beginning be less haughty in
her bearing. The person who is established by external
position in a high place, needs to make less effort than
he who has won this place through his own inner power.
We know for all that, that Elizabeth is the queen, even if
Essex gives himself more royal airs.

Secondly it is more fitting to tragedy that the characters should rise in their sentiments, not descend in them.
It is preferable that a tender character should have
moments of pride, rather than that a proud one should be
carried away by tenderness. The one is elevating, the
other rather the contrary. A grave queen, with wrinkled

brow, a look that intimidates all, a voice that alone would
command obedience, if such a one breaks out into
love-sick moans and sighs for the little satisfactions of
her passions, it is almost, *almost* ludicrous. A lover on
the other hand who is reminded by her jealousy that she
is a queen, raises herself above herself, and her weakness
becomes terrible.

No. 26.

.   .   .   .   .
.   .   .   .   .

The thirty-second evening ' Semiramis ' by M. de
Voltaire was repeated.

Since the orchestra in our dramas in a measure fills the
place of the ancient choruses, connoisseurs have long
desired that the music played before and between and after
the acts, should be more in accord with the substance of
these acts. Herr Scheibe is the first among musicians to
perceive a wholly new field for art in this matter. He has
comprehended that if the emotions of the spectators are
not to be weakened or broken in an unpleasant manner,
every drama requires its own musical accompaniment.
He therefore made the attempt as early as 1738 with
' Polyeucte ' and ' Mithridates ' to compose suitable symphonies to every play, and these were performed in the
company of Neuber both here in Hamburg, and at Leipzig
and elsewhere. Further he treated the subject in detail
in a special journal, the *Critical Musician*, saying what
the composer must observe chiefly who desires to work
successfully in this new *genre.*

" All symphonies," he says, " that are composed to a
drama must relate to its contents and nature. Consequently
a different kind of symphony is required by a tragedy
from that of a comedy. And as various as are tragedies
and comedies among themselves, so varied also must their
music be. Then too especial attention must be bestowed
on the different divisions of the music necessitated by the
play, so that every division corresponds to the nature
of the dramatic divisions. Therefore the opening symphony must refer to the first act; while the symphonies
that occur between the acts must correspond partly with
the close of the foregoing ; partly with the commencement

of the following act, and the last symphony be suited to
the close of the last act.

" All symphonies to tragedies must be grand, vivacious,
suggestive. The characters of the chief personages and
the chief plot must be carefully observed, so that the
composition be arranged to accord. This is of no common
importance. We find tragedies in which this or that
virtue of hero or heroine is the subject-theme. If we
contrast ' Polyeucte ' with ' Brutus,' ' Alzire ' with ' Mithridates,' we shall at once perceive that the same music
by no means suits both. A tragedy in which religion
and piety accompanies the hero through all vicissitudes,
demands symphonies that reflect something of the
solemnity and grandeur of church music. If generosity,
bravery, or endurance in all misfortunes mark the tragedy,
then the music must be more vivacious and fiery. Of
this latter nature are the tragedies ' Cato,' ' Brutus,' ' Mithridates.' ' Alzire,' and ' Zaire,' on the other hand require
a somewhat varied music, because the events and characters of each play are thus constituted and show more
variety of emotion.

"In like manner comedy symphonies must be freer,
more flowing, even playful; and yet in especial must
also conform to the particular tendency of the comedy
in question. As the comedy is now more serious, now
amorous, now farcical, so also must the symphonies be
constituted. . . .

"Opening symphonies must refer to the whole play
and at the same time prepare for its commencement and
thus harmonise with the first act. They can consist of
two or three movements, as may seem good to the composer. But the symphonies between the acts, because
they must refer to the foregoing and the coming act,
should consist most naturally of two movements. The
first can refer to the past, the second to the coming
events. Still even this is only requisite when the
emotions are too diverse, else one movement would
suffice, if only it be of sufficient length to cover the
necessities of the performance, such as snuffing the
candles, changing of dresses, &c. The closing symphony
must accord exactly with the close of the play, to

emphasise the occurrences to the spectators. What can
be more ludicrous, than that the hero loses his life in an
unhappy manner and a merry, lively symphony follows?
And what can be more absurd than that a comedy ends
happily and a sad and solemn symphony follows?

" Since however the music in plays is purely instrumental, a change of instruments is very needful, that the
attention of the audience may be the more surely riveted,
an attention that easily flags if the same instruments are
always heard. It is just as needful though that the
opening symphony should be full and strong and fall
with weight upon the ear. The change in the instruments must therefore chiefly occur between the acts.
Judgment is needed to pronounce which instrument is
best suited to the matter in hand and will express the most
surely the desired emotion. A sensible choice therefore
must be made here also if a good and certain result is to
be attained. It is especially reprehensible to change the
same instruments in successive *entr'actes*. It is always
better and more agreeable to avoid the necessity for this."

These are the chief rules for bringing about a closer relation between music and poetry. I have preferred to give
them in the words of a musician rather than in my own,
moreover in the words of him to whom belongs the honour
of this invention. For poets and art-critics are not rarely
censured by musicians, because they require and expect
far more from them than their art is capable of pro-
ducing. The majority must therefore be told by one of
their own guild, that the matter is feasible before they
will bestow the smallest attention upon it.

True, it would be easy to make the rules; they only
teach what should be, without saying how it can be.
The expression of emotion, which is everything, remains
solely the work of genius. For although there are and
have been musicians who have succeeded marvellously, a
philosopher is unquestionably needed who learns their
method and knows how to deduce general principles
from their examples. And the more frequent these
examples become, the more materials are collected for
these deductions, the sooner may we look for them; and
I am much in the wrong if a great step has not been

taken in this direction by the ardour of composers of
such dramatic symphonies. In vocal music the text helps
the expression too much, the weakest and most vacillating is strengthened and decided by the words. In
instrumental music, on the contrary, this help is completely wanting and it says nothing if it does not say that
which it would express very emphatically. The musician
must employ his best power here, he must choose among
the different successions of tones, only those that express
an emotion most definitely. We shall hear these often,
we shall compare them one with another, and through
observation of what they have in common, we shall discover the secret of expression.

What an additional pleasure we shall thus derive
from the theatre is self-evident. Since the beginning of
the new management of our theatre pains have been taken
with the orchestra and able men have been found willing
to lend their hands and prepare models of this form of
composition, that have succeeded beyond expectation. For
' Olindo and Sophronia,' Herr Hertel composed a special
symphony, and the second representation of ' Semiramis '
was marked by such a one from the hand of Herr
Agricola of Berlin.

No. 27.

I will endeavour to give an idea of Herr Agricola's
music. Not however in its effects ; for the more vivid and
delicate a sensuous pleasure, the less can it be described in
words ; it is not possible to escape falling into general praise,
vague exclamations and shrieking admirations, and these
are as uninstructive to the amateur as they are nauseous to
the master whom we seek to honour. No, I mean to speak
merely of the intentions that the master has had and of
the means he has employed to attain his end.

The opening symphony consists of three movements.
The first movement is a largo with oboes and flutes beside
violins ; the bass part is strengthened by bassoons. The
expression is serious, sometimes wild and agitated ; the
listener is to expect a drama of this nature. But not
of this nature only ; tenderness, remorse, conscience,

humility play their parts also, and the second movement, an andante with muted violins and bassoons, is occupied with mysterious and plaintive tones.   In the third move- ment the emotional and the stately tones are mingled, for the scene opens with unusual splendour; Semiramis is approaching the term of her glory and as this glory strikes the eye, so the ear also is to perceive it.   The character is allegretto and the instruments are the same as in the previous movement, except that oboes, flutes and bassoon have phrases they play together.

The music between the acts has throughout only one single movement, whose expression refers to what has gone before.   A second that refers to the coming does not seem to be approved by Herr Agricola.   I am much of his opinion in this.   For the music is to spoil nothing for the poet; the tragic poet loves the unexpected, the sudden, more than any other; he does not like to betray his design and the music would betray him if it indicated the coming passion.   It is different with the overture, it cannot refer to anything preceding, and even the overture must only indicate the general tendency of the play and not more strongly or decidedly than the title does.   We may show the spectator the goal to which he is to attain, but the various paths by which he is to attain it, must be entirely hidden from him.   This reason against a second movement between the acts is derived from consideration for the poet, and is confirmed by another that belongs to the range of music.   For assuming that the passions which reign in two consecutive acts are opposed one to another, the two movements would naturally have to be of equally opposite character.   Now I can well comprehend how the poet can carry us over from any one passion to its very opposite without unpleasant violence; he does so gradually and slowly, he ascends the ladder rung by rung either up or down, without making any jump.   But can the musician do this?   Granted that he can do this in a piece of sufficient length, can he do so in two distinct, entirely opposed pieces, must not the jump from *e.g.* the calm to the stormy, from the tender to the cruel be necessarily very marked and have all the offensive traits that any sudden transition has in nature, such as from darkness to light,

from cold to heat? Now we melt with sympathy and
suddenly we are to rage. Why? How? Against whom?
Against the person for whom our soul was all pity? or
against another? Music cannot define all this; it only
leaves us in uncertainty and confusion; we feel without
perceiving a correct sequence for our feelings; we feel as
we do in a dream, and all these undefined sensations are
more fatiguing than agreeable. Now poetry never lets us
lose the thread of our sensations, here we know not only
what we are to feel, but also why we are to feel it, and
only this knowledge makes the sudden transition not only
bearable but also pleasant. Indeed this explanation of
sudden transitions is one of the greatest advantages that
music attains from its union with poetry, nay perhaps the
very greatest. For it is not nearly so needful to confine
general sensations in music, such as pleasure, to a certain
individual cause for pleasure, because these dark uncertain
sensations are still very agreeable. But it is needful to
unite opposed and contradictory sensations by those
definite ideas that words alone can convey, so that not
only manifold things may be noticed but also the connexion existing between these manifold things. Now in
the double movement adopted between the acts of a play,
this connexion would only be subsequently explained; we
should only learn afterwards why we must pass from one
passion to another totally opposite, and that is as good as
if we never knew, as far as the music is concerned. The
leap has had its bad effect and has not offended us the less
because we now perceive it ought not to have offended us.
Now it must not be supposed that hence all symphonies
are to be condemned because the whole consists of several
movements that are different one from another, and each of
which expresses something different from the other. They
express something different but not something opposed; or
rather they express the same only in a different manner
A symphony that expresses in its various movements,
opposed passions, is a musical monster. Only one passion
must rule in a symphony and each separate movement
must enunciate and awaken in us the same passion, only
with various modifications, according to the degree of its
strength and vivacity or according to the varied inter-

mixture with cognate passions. The overture was entirely
of this character; the impetuosity of the first movement
melts into the pathos of the second, which is raised to a
solemn dignity in the third. A musician who takes
greater liberties in his symphonies, who breaks off the
emotion in every movement to commence a fresh and
different emotion in the next, and then again lets this go,
in order to throw himself into a third and different movement, may have spent much art, but uselessly; can surprise, confound, tickle, but cannot touch. Whoever would
speak to our hearts and awaken sympathetic emotions
must observe the same sequence of idea as though he
were instructing or enlightening our reason. Music is a
vain sandheap if devoid of sequence and inner connexion
of all and every part; it can make no permanent impression.
Only proper connexion makes it into firm marble upon
which the hand of the artist immortalises himself.

The movement after the first act therefore seeks chiefly
to keep up the anxiety of Semiramis to which the poet
dedicated that act; anxieties that are still mingled with
some hopes; an andante mesto, with muted violins and
bass-viol.

In the second act Assur plays too important a part to
do otherwise than rule the expression of the music. An
allegro assai in G major with French horns, flutes and
oboes, the bass part strengthened by a bassoon expresses
the feelings of fear and doubt, mingled with ever-recur-
ring pride that distinguish this faithless and imperious
minister.

In the third act the ghost appears. At the first performance I remarked how little impression this apparition
of Voltaire's makes on the audience. But the musician
has very properly taken no heed of this, he makes good
what the poet has omitted and an allegro, E minor with
the same instrumentation as the foregoing, only that
E horns vary with G horns, express no mute and indolent
astonishment, but the true dismay which such an apparition
must evoke from the people.

Semiramis's anxiety in the fourth act rouses our pity;
we pity her remorse though we know the full extent of
her guilt. The music also sounds the note of pity and

sympathy in a larghetto A minor, with muted violins and bass-viol and oboes.

At last there follows upon the fifth act one single movement, an adagio in E major, with violins and bass-viol, horns, and increased oboes and flutes and bassoons.

The expression is suited to the personages of the tragedy and characterised by dignity tending to grief, with some due regard, so it seems to me, to the last four lines in which Truth raises her warning voice with might and solemnity against the great ones of the earth.

To perceive the intentions of a musician means to admit to him that he has attained them. His work is not to be a riddle whose solution is as difficult as it is uncertain. Whatever a healthy ear quickly perceives, that and nothing else is what he desired to say; his merit increases with his lucidity; the easier, the more general he is of comprehension, the more he deserves praise. It is not praiseworthy in me that I have heard aright, but it is the greater praise for Herr Agricola that in this, his composition, no one has heard anything different from that which I have heard.

No. 28.

On the thirty-fourth evening Regnard's 'Distrait' was performed.

Regnard first brought out his 'Distrait' in 1697 and it did not meet with the least favour. Thirty-four years later, when the comedians brought it out again, it found great favour. Which public was in the right? Perhaps neither of them were so far wrong. The severe public condemned the piece as no good formal comedy, as which no doubt the author issued it. The other public received it as nothing more than it is; a farce, an absurdity to make them laugh; they laughed and were thankful. The first public thought:—

> " non satis est risu diducere rictum
> Auditoris . . ."

and the second:—

> " Et est quædam tamen hic quoque virtus."

Excepting for the versification, which happens to be very faulty and careless, this comedy cannot have given Regnard much trouble. The character of his chief personage he found fully sketched in La Bruyère. He had nothing to do but to put the chief traits partly into action, partly to recount them. What he has added of his own is insignificant.

There is nothing to object to in this verdict, but against another criticism that attacks the poet on the score of morality, there is the more. An absent-minded person is said to be no *motif* for a comedy. And why not? To be absent, it is said, is a malady, a misfortune and no vice. An absent man deserves ridicule as little as one who has the headache. Comedy must only concern itself with such faults, as can be remedied. Whoever is absent by nature can merit this as little by means of ridicule, as though he limped.

But is it then true that absence of mind is a disease of the soul that cannot be cured with our best exertions? Is it really more a natural defect than a bad habit? I cannot believe it. For are we not masters of our attention? Is it not in our power to exert it, to abstract it, at will? And what else is absent-mindedness than a false use of our attention? The absent person thinks, only he does not think that which he should think in accordance with his present sensuous impressions. His mind is not asleep, not numbed, not inactive, it is only absent, busy elsewhere. But just as well as it can be elsewhere, so it could also be here; it is the mind's proper function to be present at the actual changes of the body. It costs pains to disaccustom the mind of this its proper function, and should it be impossible to accustom it again thereto?

Well, but now granted that absence of mind is incurable, where is it written that comedy should only laugh at moral faults, and not at incurable defects? Every absurdity, every contrast of reality and deficiency is laughable. But laughter and derision are far apart. We can laugh at a man, occasionally laugh about him, without in the least deriding him. Indisputable and well-known as this difference is, yet all the quibbles which Rousseau lately made against the use of comedy only

arose from the fact that he had not sufficiently regarded
it.   He says, for instance, Molière makes us laugh at a
misanthrope and yet the misanthrope is the honest man
of the play, Molière therefore shows himself an enemy to
virtue in that he makes the virtuous man contemptible.
Not so; the misanthrope does not become contemptible, he
remains what he was, and the laughter that springs from
the situations in which the poet places him does not rob
him in the least of our esteem.   The same with the *distrait*,
we laugh at him, but do we despise him on that account?
We esteem his other good qualities as we ought; why
without them we could not even laugh at his absence of
mind.   Let a bad worthless man be endowed with this
absence of mind, and then see whether we should still find
it laughable?   It will be disgusting, horrid, ugly, not
laughable.

No. 29.

Comedy is to do us good through laughter; but not through
derision; not just to counteract those faults at which it
laughs, nor simply and solely in those persons who possess
these laughable faults.   Its true general use consists in
laughter itself, in the practice of our powers to discern
the ridiculous, to discern it easily and quickly under all
cloaks of passion and fashion; in all admixture of good
and bad qualities, even in the wrinkles of solemn earnest-
ness.   Granted that Molière's Miser never cured a miser;
nor Regnard's Gambler, a gambler; conceded that
laughter never could improve these fools; the worse for
them, but not for comedy.   It is enough for comedy that,
if it cannot cure an incurable disease, it can confirm the
healthy in their health.   The Miser is instructive also
to the extravagant man; and to him who never plays the
Gambler may prove of use.   The follies they have not got
themselves, others may have with whom they have to live.
It is well to know those with whom we may come into
collision; it is well to be preserved from all impressions
by example.   A preservative is also a valuable medicine,
and all morality has none more powerful and effective,
than the ridiculous.

.   .   .   .

On the thirty-fifth evening 'Rodogune' by Pierre Corneille was performed in the presence of H.M. the King of Denmark.

Corneille owned that he set most store by this tragedy, that he held it far above his 'Cinna' and 'Cid,' that his other plays had few merits that were not to be found all united in this; a happy theme, a totally new creation, powerful verses, thorough reasoning, strong passions, and interest that increased from act to act.

It is but just that we should linger a while over this great man's masterpiece.

The story on which it is founded is told by Appianus Alexandrinus towards the end of his book on the Syrian Wars. " Demetrius, surnamed Nicanor, undertook a campaign against the Parthians, and lived as captive for some time at the court of the Parthian king, Phraates, with whose sister, Rodogune, he married. Meanwhile Diodotus, who had served the former kings, seized upon the Syrian throne, and placed upon it the son of Alexander Nothus, a mere child, under whose name he ruled as regent. After a while however he made away with the young king, placed himself on the throne and called himself Tryphon. When Antiochus, the brother of the captive king, heard at Rhodes of his fate and of the disorders in his kingdom, he returned to Syria, conquered Tryphon with much difficulty and caused him to be executed. Then he turned his arms against Phraates and demanded the release of his brother. Phraates, who feared the worst, did indeed release Demetrius, but nevertheless Antiochus and he came to a battle in which the latter was overcome and killed himself in despair. Demetrius after his return to his kingdom was murdered by his wife Cleopatra out of hatred against Rodogune, notwithstanding that Cleopatra herself, exasperated at this marriage, had united herself to Antiochus, the brother of Demetrius. She had two sons by Demetrius, of whom the eldest Seleucus, ascended the throne upon the death of his father, and whom she shot to death with an arrow, either because she feared he might avenge the death of his father upon her or because her cruel nature impelled her to this step. Her younger son, Antiochus, followed his brother in the

government and forced his atrocious mother to empty the
poisoned cup she had prepared for him."

In this story lay matter for more than one tragedy. It
would have cost Corneille little more invention to make for
it a ' Tryphon,' an ' Antiochus,' a ' Demetrius,' a ' Seleucus,'
than it cost him to make a ' Rodogune.' What chiefly
interested him therein was the outraged wife who deems
that she cannot avenge too fearfully the usurped rights of
her rank and bed. He therefore selected her and it is
unquestionable that his play ought consequently to have
been named after Cleopatra and not Rodogune. He himself acknowledged this, and it was only that he feared
confusion among his auditors between the Queen of
Syria with that famous last Queen of Egypt of similar
name, that he preferred to take his title from the second
instead of the first character in his play, " I believed
myself," he says, " the more entitled to make use of this
liberty, since I had observed that the ancients themselves
did not deem it necessary to call a play after its hero, but
without scruple would even call it after the chorus, whose
connexion with the action is far less and more episodic,
than that of Rodogune. For instance Sophocles has named
one of his tragedies the Trachiniæ which nowadays we
rarely name otherwise than the dying Hercules." This
observation is in itself quite correct, the ancients considered a title as quite unimportant, they did not deem in
the least that it need indicate the contents, enough if it
served to distinguish one play from another and for this
the smallest circumstance suffices. Yet for all that I
scarcely believe that Sophocles would to-day name
' Deianira ' the play he called the Trachiniæ. He did not
hesitate to give it an insignificant name, but to give it a
deceptive name, a name that draws attention to a wrong
point, he would doubtless have avoided. Corneille's
fears went too far. Whoever knows the Egyptian Cleopatra knows also that Syria is not Egypt, that various
kings and queens have borne the same names, but whoever does not know of the one cannot confound it with
the other. At least Corneille need not have avoided the
name Cleopatra so carefully in the play itself; the first
act loses thereby in lucidity, and the German translator did

well to disregard this.   No writer, and least of all a poet,
must assume his readers to be so very ignorant; he may
even at times think that what they do not know, they
may inquire about.

No. 30.

Cleopatra, in history, murders her husband, shoots one
of her sons and wishes to poison the other.   Beyond question one crime sprang out of another and they all sprang
from one and the same source.   At least it can be assumed
with probability that the jealousy that can make an en-
raged wife can make an equally angered mother.   To see
a second wife placed in the same rank with herself, to share
with such a one the love of her husband and the dignity
of her station, quickly ripened the resolve in a proud and
sensitive heart, not to possess that which it could not
possess alone.   Demetrius must not live because he will
not live for Cleopatra alone.   The guilty husband falls,
but in him falls also a father who leaves avenging sons.
The mother had not thought of these in the heat of her
passions, or only thought of them as *her* sons of whose submission she was assured or whose filial zeal would infallibly choose for the party first offended if they must choose
between the parents.   She did not find it thus.   The son
became king, and the king saw in Cleopatra not the
mother but the regicide.   She had everything to fear from
him and from that moment he had all to fear from her.
Jealousy still boiled in her heart, the faithless spouse still
lived in his sons, she began to hate all that recalled to her
that she ever loved him and self-preservation strengthened
this hate.   The mother was readier than the son, the
offending woman readier than the offended man; she
executed her second murder in order to have executed the
first unpunished; she executed it upon her son and satisfied herself by the representation that she was only ex-
ecuting it upon one who had resolved on her own destruction, that she was not really murdering but only preventing
her own murder.   The fate of the eldest son would also
have been the fate of the younger, only he was readier or
luckier.   He forced his mother to drink the poison she
had prepared for him; one inhuman crime avenges the

other, and it only depends on the circumstances on which side we feel most disgust or sympathy.

This triple murder should constitute only one action, that has its beginning, its centre and its end in the one passion of one person. What therefore does it lack as the subject for a tragedy? Nothing for genius, everything for a bungler. Here there is no love, no entanglement, no recognition, no unexpected marvellous occurrence; everything proceeds naturally. This natural course tempts genius and repels the bungler. Genius is only busied with events that are rooted in one another, that form a chain of cause and effect. To reduce the latter to the former, to weigh the latter against the former, everywhere to exclude chance, to cause everything that occurs to occur so that it could not have happened otherwise, this is the part of genius when it works in the domains of history and converts the useless treasures of memory into nourishment for the soul. Wit on the contrary, that does not depend on matters rooted in each other, but on the similar or dissimilar, if it ventures on a work that should be reserved to genius alone, detains itself with such events as have not further concern with one another except that they have occurred at the same time. To connect these, to interweave and confuse their threads so that we lose the one at every moment in following out the other and are thrown from one surprise into another, this is the part of wit and this only. From the incessant crossing of such threads of opposed colours results a texture, which is to art what weavers call *changeant*: a material of which we cannot say whether it be blue or red, green or yellow; it is both, it seems this from one side, that from another, a plaything of fashion, a juggling trick for children.

Now judge whether the great Corneille has used his theme like a genius or like a wit. For this judgment nothing else is required but the application of the axiom, disputed by none: Genius loves simplicity, and wit complication.

In history Cleopatra murders her spouse from jealousy. From jealousy? thought Corneille: Why that would be quite like a common woman; no, my Cleopatra must be a heroine who would even gladly have lost her husband but on no account her throne. That her husband loves Rodogune must not pain her as much as that Rodogune is to be a queen like herself; this is far more elevated in idea.

Quite true; far more elevated and—far more unnatural. For to begin with, pride is a far more unnatural, a more artificial, vice than jealousy. Secondly the pride of a woman is still more unnatural than the pride of a man. Nature has formed the female sex to love, not to enact violence; it is to awaken tenderness, not fear; only its charms are to render it powerful; it should only rule by caresses and should not desire to rule over more than it can enjoy. A woman who likes ruling merely for its own sake, all of whose inclinations are subordinate to ambition, who knows no other happiness than to command, to tyrannise, to put her foot on the necks of nations; such a woman may have existed once or more than once, but nevertheless she is an exception and whoever paints an exception, unquestionably paints what is against nature. Corneille's Cleopatra who is such a woman, who allows herself every crime to gratify her ambition, her offended pride, who casts about her Machiavellian maxims, is a monster of her sex, and Medea is amiable and virtuous as compared with her. For all the cruelties committed by Medea, she commits from jealousy. I will forgive all to a tender jealous woman, she is what she should be, only to excess. But a woman who commits crimes from deliberate ambition and cold pride revolts our heart and all the art of the poet cannot render her interesting. We gaze at her with wonder as we gaze at a monstrosity and when we have sated our curiosity, we thank Heaven that nature only errs like this once in a thousand years and are vexed with the poet who wishes to pass off such abortions as human beings whom it is good for us to know. If we go through all history, among fifty women who have dethroned or murdered their husbands, there is scarcely one of whom we could not prove that offended love drove her to this step. From mere love of dominion, from mere pride to sway the sceptre that had been borne by a loving husband, scarcely one has so far forgotten herself. It is true that many who have thus usurped government as offended wives have ruled afterwards with all manly pride. They had too well learnt the wounding power of subjection by the sides of their cold, morose, faithless husbands, so that their independence, attained by means of extreme danger, was the more precious to them. But surely none thought or felt within herself what Corneille lets his Cleopatra say of herself; the most senseless bravado of crime. The greatest criminal knows how to excuse himself to himself, tries to persuade himself that the crime he commits is no such great crime, or that unavoidable necessity makes him commit it. It is against all nature that he should boast of vice as vice; and the poet is to be extremely censured who from mere desire to say something that is dazzling or strong, lets us misread the human heart as if its fundamental inclinations could thus turn to evil for evil's sake.

Such distorted characters, such shuddering tirades are more frequent with Corneille than any other poet and it may easily be that he founds his surname the Great, in part on these. It is true, everything with him breathes of heroism, even that which should not be capable of it and is not capable of it, namely vice. The Monstrous, the Gigantic they should call him, not the Great. For nothing is great that is not true.

No. 31.

In history Cleopatra only avenges herself upon her husband, she would not or could not avenge herself on Rodogune. With the poet this vengeance is long past; the murder of Demetrius is only recounted and all the action of the play concerns Rodogune. Corneille will not suffer his Cleopatra to halt half-way; she must deem herself unavenged so long as she has not avenged herself on Rodogune. It is certainly natural to a jealous woman to be still more implacable to her rival than to her faithless husband. But Corneille's Cleopatra, as I said, is little or not at all jealous, she is only ambitious, and the revenge of an ambitious woman should never resemble that of a jealous one. The two passions are too diverse for their expressions to be the same. Ambition is never without a kind of nobility, and revenge is too much opposed to nobility for the revenge of an ambitious person to be without bounds. So long as he pursues his object, it knows no limits; but scarcely has it attained this, scarcely is the passion appeased, than revenge begins to grow colder and calmer. It is proportioned not so much to the disadvantages that have been suffered, as to those that are still to be feared. Whoever can no longer harm the ambitious man, of him he forgets that he has harmed him. Whomsoever he has not to fear, he despises, and he whom he despises is far beneath his revenge. Jealousy on the other hand is a form of envy, and envy is a petty crawling vice that knows no other satisfaction than the total destruction of its object. It is a furious fire, nothing can mollify it, since the offence that has awakened it never can cease to remain the same offence, and as it grows the longer it lasts, so jealousy's thirst for vengeance is never quenched and will be executed late or early with the self-same fury. Just so the vengeance of Corneille's Cleopatra, and the dissonance therefore with which this vengeance appears in her character, can be nothing but highly offensive. Her cunning wrath, her envious vengeance against a person from whom she has nothing further to fear, whom she has in her power, whom she ought to forgive if she had the least spark of generosity, the careless levity with which she not alone commits crimes but with which also she suggests crimes the most senseless and barefaced to others, makes her so petty that we cannot despise her enough. This contempt must at last overpower our admiration and there remains of the whole Cleopatra only an ugly loathsome woman who is for ever raging and reviling and who deserves the first place in a madhouse.

But not enough that Cleopatra revenges herself on Rodogune, the poet decrees that she shall do so in quite an exceptional mode. How does he set about this? If Cleopatra had despatched Rodogune herself the thing would have been too natural, for what is more natural than to kill an enemy? Could it not be brought about that a loving woman were killed in her at the same time? And that she should be killed by her lover? Why not? Let us imagine that Rodogune was not fully married to Deme-

trius; let us imagine that after his death both of his sons
became enamoured of his betrothed; let us imagine that
the sons were twins, that the throne pertains to the
elder and that the mother has ever kept secret which is
the elder of the two; let us imagine that the mother has
at last resolved to reveal this secret, or rather not to
reveal it but to declare instead that that one is the
elder and shall ascend the throne who will consent to a
certain condition; let us imagine that this condition is
the death of Rodogune. We should then have what we
desire to have; both princes are deeply in love with
Rodogune, whoever of them will kill his beloved, he shall
reign.

Very good; but can we not complicate the action yet
farther? Can we not place the good princes in yet
greater straits? We will try. Let us therefore imagine
that Rodogune learns Cleopatra's plan; let us further
imagine that she loves one of the princes, but that she has
not revealed it to him, nor will reveal it to him or any
one; that she is firmly resolved not to choose as her
husband either the beloved one, or the one to whom the
throne shall accrue, but only him who shall prove himself
most worthy. Rodogune must be avenged, avenged on
the mother of the princes; Rodogune must declare to
them, whichever of you desires me, let him murder his
mother!

Bravo! I call that something like an intrigue! These
princes have fared well, they will have much to do to
extricate themselves! The mother says to them: Whoever of you would rule, let him murder his beloved! And
the beloved says: Whoever would have me, let him murder
his mother! It is a matter of course that these princes must
be very virtuous and love one another from the bottom
of their hearts, that they must have much respect for
their devil of a mamma and as much tenderness for their
amorous fury of a mistress. For if they are not both
very virtuous, then the complication is not so bad as it
seems; or it is too bad so that it is not possible to dis-
entangle it. One goes and kills the princess in order to
have the throne and the thing is done. Or the other
goes and kills his mother to have the princess and the

thing is done again. Or they both kill their love and both
want to have the throne; and so the story cannot end.
Or they both kill their mother and both want to have
their love, and again it cannot end. But if they are both
so nice and virtuous, neither of them will kill the one or
the other, they both stand still prettily and gape open-
mouthed and do not know what to do; and that is just
the beauty of it. True the play will thereby assume
the very strange aspect that its women will be worse
than raving men, and the men act more womanishly than
the feeblest woman; but what matters that? Rather it
is an additional merit in the play, far the contrary is so
common, so hackneyed!

But to be serious; I do not know whether it costs much
trouble to make such inventions, I have never attempted
it, it is hardly likely that I shall ever attempt it. But
this I know, it is very hard work to digest such inventions.

Not because they are mere inventions, because not the
faintest trace of them is to be found in history. Corneille might have spared himself this consideration.
"Perhaps," he says, "we may question whether the
liberty of poetry may extend so far as to invent a whole
history under familiar names, as I have done here, where
after the recital in the first act which is the foundation
of the following, up to the effects of the fifth, not the
smallest thing occurs that has any historical veracity.
But," he continues, "it seems to me that if we only
retain the results of a history, all the surrounding
circumstances all the introductions to these results are
in our power. At least I can recall no rule against this,
and the example of the ancients is wholly on my side.
For compare Sophocles's 'Electra' with the 'Electra' of
Euripides and see whether they have more in common
than the mere result, the last occurrence in the history
of their heroine at which each one arrives on a different
path by different means, so that one at least must be the
total invention of their author. Or let us regard 'Iphigenia
in Tauris' which Aristotle names the model of a perfect
tragedy and that yet has greatly the appearance of
being a complete invention, seeing it is only founded

on the circumstance that Diana removes Iphigenia
from the altar on which she is to be sacrificed in a cloud
and places a deer in her stead.   Then the 'Helena' of
Euripides deserves especial comment, where the main
action, as well as the episodes, the entanglement and the
dénouement are entirely fictitious and borrow nothing save
their names, from history."

Certainly it was permissible to Corneille to treat historical events at his discretion.   For instance he might
assume Rodogune to be as young as he pleased, and Voltaire is much in the wrong when he again here reckons
out of history that Rodogune cannot have been so young
because she had married Demetrius when the young
princes, who must now be at least twenty, were in their
infancy.   What does that concern the poet?   His Rodogune
did not marry Demetrius; she was very young when the
father wanted to marry her and not much older when the
sons became enamoured of her.   Voltaire with his historical censorship is quite unbearable.   If only instead he
would verify the dates in his General History of the
World !

No. 32.

Corneille could have gone back still further for
examples from the ancients.   Many really deem that
tragedy in Greece was invented to keep alive the memory
of great and marvellous events, that its first purpose
was to tread carefully in the footprints of history and to
diverge neither to right nor left.   But they are mistaken.
For Thespis already left historical accuracy quite unre-
garded.[1]   He brought upon himself sharp rebuke from
Solon on that account.   But without saying that Solon
understood legislation better than poetics, the conclusions
which might be drawn from his rebuke can be evaded in a
different manner.   Under Thespis art already employed
all privileges before it could prove itself worthy of these
on the score of utility.   Thespis pondered, invented, let
familiar personages say and do what he desired, but he
perhaps did not know how to make his inventions probable

---

[1] Diogenes Laertius, lib. i. § 59.

and instructive. Solon therefore perceived in them only
the untrue, without the least suspicion of their utility.
He was jealous against a poison, which can easily be of
ill effect if it does not bear with it its antidote.

I greatly fear that Solon would also have named
the invention of the great Corneille nothing but miserable lies. For wherefore all these inventions? Do they
render anything more probable in the history wherewith
he overloads them? They are not even probable in
themselves. Corneille boasted of them as very wonderful
exertions of his power of invention, and yet he should
have known that not the mere fact of invention, but
invention conformable to its purpose, marks a creative
mind.

The poet finds in history a woman who murders her
husband and sons. Such indeed can awaken terror and
pity and he takes hold of it to treat it as a tragedy. But
history tells him no more than the bare fact and this is
as horrible as it is unusual. It furnishes at most three
scenes, and, devoid of all detailed circumstances, three
improbable scenes. What therefore does the poet do?

As he deserves this name more or less, the improbability or the meagre brevity will seem to him the
greatest want in this play.

If he be in the first condition, he will consider above all
else how to invent a series of causes and effects by which
these improbable crimes could be accounted for most
naturally. Not satisfied with resting their probability
upon historical authority, he will endeavour so to con-
struct the characters of his personages, will endeavour so
to necessitate one from another the events that place his
characters in action, will endeavour to define the passions
of each character so accurately, will endeavour to lead
these passions through such gradual steps, that we shall
everywhere see nothing but the most natural and common
course of events. Thus with every step we see his
personages take, we must acknowledge that we should
have taken it ourselves under the same circumstances and
the same degree of passion, and hence nothing will repel
us but the imperceptible approach to a goal from which
our imagination shrinks, and where we suddenly find

ourselves filled with profound pity for those whom a fatal
stream has carried so far, and full of terror at the consciousness that a similar stream might also thus have borne
ourselves away to do deeds which in cold blood we should
have regarded as far from us. If the poet takes this line,
if his genius tells him that he cannot ignobly falter in
its course, then the meagre brevity of his fable has vanished
at once, it no longer distresses him how he shall fill his
five acts with so few events, he is only afraid lest five
acts should not suffice for all his material, that enlarges
more and more under his treatment now that he has
discovered its hidden organisation and understands how
to unravel it.

Meantime the poet who less deserves this name, who is
nothing but an ingenious fellow, a good versifier, he, I say,
will find so little obstacle in the improbability of his scheme
that he actually seeks therein its claim to admiration,
which he must on no account diminish if he would not
deprive himself of the surest means to evoke pity and
terror. For he knows so little wherein this pity and
terror really consist that in order to evoke them he thinks
he cannot pile up enough marvellous, unexpected, incredible and abnormal matters and thinks he must ever
have recourse to extraordinary and horrible misfortunes
and crimes. Scarcely therefore has he scented in history
a Cleopatra, the murderess of her husband and sons, than
he sees nothing further to do, in order to form this into a
tragedy, than to fill in the interstices between the two
crimes and to fill it with matter as strange as the crimes
themselves. All this, his invention and the historical
materials, he kneads into a very long, very incomprehensible romance, and when he has kneaded it as well
as flour and straw can be kneaded together, he places his
paste upon the skeleton wires of acts and scenes, relates
and relates, rants and rhymes, and in four to six weeks,
according as rhyming is easy or difficult to him, the
wonderwork is finished; is called a tragedy, is printed
and performed, read and looked at, admired or hissed,
retained or forgotten as good luck will have it. For
et habent sua fata libelli.

May I presume to apply this to the great Corneille?

Or must I still make this application? According to the
secret fate that rules over writings as over men, his
'Rodogune' has been held for more than a hundred years
the greatest masterpiece of the greatest tragical poet of
all France and has occasionally been admired by all
Europe. Can an admiration of a hundred years be
groundless? Where have mankind so long concealed
their eyes, their emotions? Was it reserved from 1644 to
1767 to a Hamburg dramatic critic to see spots in the
sun and to debase a planet to a meteor?

Oh no! Already in the last century a certain honest
Huron was imprisoned in the Bastille at Paris; he found
time hang heavy on his hands although he was in Paris,
and from sheer *ennui* he studied the French poets; and this
Huron could not take pleasure in 'Rodogune.' After this
there lived, somewhere in Italy at the beginning of this
century, a pedant who had his head full of the tragedies
of the Greeks and of his countrymen of the sixteenth
century and he also found much to censure in ' Rodogune.'
Finally a few years ago there was a Frenchman, a great
admirer of Corneille's name, who because he was rich and
had a good heart, took pity on the poor deserted grand-
daughter of the great poet, had her educated under his
eyes, taught her to make pretty verses, collected alms for
her, wrote a large lucrative commentary to the works of
her grandfather as her dowry, and so forth; yet even he
declared ' Rodogune ' to be a very absurd play, and was
utterly amazed how so great a man as the great Corneille,
could write such wretched stuff. Under one of these the
above dramatic critic must have gone to school and most
probably under the last named, for it is always a Frenchman who opens the eyes of a foreigner to the faults of a
Frenchman. Beyond question he repeats after him; or if
not after him, after the Italian, or perhaps even after
Huron. From one of these he must have learnt it. For
that a German should think of himself, should of himself
have the audacity to doubt the excellence of a Frenchman,
who could conceive such a thing? .   .   .

No. 33.

On the thirty-sixth evening (Friday, July 3rd) M. Favart's comedy 'Soliman the Second' was performed, also in the presence of H.M. the King of Denmark.

I do not care to examine how far history confirms that Soliman the Second became enamoured of a European slave, who knew so well how to enchain him and train him to her will that, contrary to all the customs of his realm, he caused himself to be formally united to her and had to declare her as empress. Enough that Marmontel has founded on this one of his moral tales, in which however he changes this slave, said to have been an Italian, into a Frenchwoman, beyond question because he considered it as too unlikely that any other beauty but a French one, could have carried off such a rare victory over a Grand Turk.

I do not know what to say to Marmontel's tale. It is not that it is not told with much wit, and with all the subtle knowledge of the world, its vanities, its absurdities, as well as with the elegance and grace that distinguish this author. From this side it is excellent, charming. But it is intended for a moral tale, and I cannot find where its morality resides. Certainly it is not as licentious and offensive as a tale by La Fontaine or Grécourt; but is it moral because it is not absolutely immoral?

A Sultan who yawns in the lap of luxury, to whom its too easy and every-day enjoyment has made it distasteful and repulsive, whose relaxed nerves must be contracted and irritated by something quite new and peculiar; whom the most subtle sensuality, the most refined tenderness woo in vain; this sick libertine is the suffering hero of the story. I say the suffering because the glutton has impaired his digestion by too many sweets. Nothing more will taste good to him, until at last he discovers something that would revolt every healthy stomach; rotten eggs, rats' tails and *pâté* of caterpillars; those he likes. The noblest, most modest beauty, with a large, blue, languishing eye, with an innocent sensitive soul, commands the Sultan—until he has won her. Another, majestic in form, dazzling in colour, flowery words on her

lips, fascinating tones in her sweet voice, a very muse,
only more seductive is—enjoyed and forgotten. At last
there appears a female thing, flippant, careless, wild, witty
to the verge of immodesty, merry to madness, much
physiognomy, little beauty, a figure more *mignonne* than
well formed; this thing, when the Sultan sees it, tumbles
down upon him with the grossest flattery : Grâce au ciel,
voici une figure humaine! . . . And like this opening
compliment, so all else. Vous êtes beaucoup mieux, qu'il
n'appartient à un Turc; vous avez même quelque chose
d'un Français.—En vérité ces Turcs sont plaisants.—Je me
charge d'apprendre à vivre à ce Turc.—Je ne désespère
pas d'en faire quelque jour un Français.—And the thing
gets its way. It laughs and scolds, threatens and mocks,
ogles and mouths, until the Sultan, after having changed
the whole aspect of the seraglio to please it, further
changes the laws of the realm and runs danger of revolting the clergy and the mob against him, if he insists on
becoming happy with it after the fashion of those others
who have been so, according to its own confession, in
its fatherland. Was it worth all this trouble?

Marmontel begins his tale with the observation that
great changes in a state have often arisen from petty
causes and lets the Sultan conclude with the secret question to himself : how is it possible that a little turned-up
nose could subvert the laws of a kingdom? We are
almost led to believe that he desired to illustrate by
example this observation and this seeming misrelation
between cause and effect. But such a teaching would
unquestionably be too general, and Marmontel discovers
in his preface that he had a far other and more specific
aim in view. "I wished," he says, "to expose the folly
of those who desire to bring a female to complaisance
by force and by looks; I therefore chose as an example a
sultan and a slave as the two extremes of dominion and
dependence." But Marmontel must surely have lost sight
of this intention during his elaboration of the theme, for
nothing aims thither, not the smallest forcible endeavour
is seen on the part of the Sultan. The first insolent
speeches spoken to him by the gay Frenchwoman, reduce
him to the most reticent, obedient, complaisant, yielding,

subservient husband, *la meilleure pâte de mari*, than whom France would scarcely furnish a better. In a word; either there is no moral in this story of Marmontel's, or it is that which I have indicated above in the character of the Sultan, the beetle after he has roamed among all the flowers, at last ends on the dung-heap.

But moral or no moral, it is the same thing to a dramatic poet whether a general truth can be deduced or no from his fable, and Marmontel's story was neither more nor less fitted to be brought out on the theatre on that account. Favart has done this, and very happily. I counsel all who desire to enrich the theatre from similar tales to compare Favart's performance with Marmontel's original matter. If they possess the gift of deduction, the smallest change this has suffered and had to suffer, will prove instructive, and their feelings will lead them to discover many manœuvres which would have remained hidden from mere speculation and which no critic has as yet generalised into rules, though it well merits this, and would often bring more truth and life into their plays, than all the mechanical laws with which the shallow art critic deals. . . .

I will pause over but one of these changes. But first I must quote the judgment given by the French themselves on this play.[1] At first they expressed doubts against Marmontel's foundation. "Soliman the Second," they said, "was one of the greatest princes of his century, the Turks have no sultan whose memory they revere more than that of Soliman; his conquests, his talents and virtues made him respected even by the enemies whom he subjugated. Now what a miserable petty part does Marmontel cause him to play! According to history Roxelane was a cunning ambitious woman, who, to gratify her pride was capable of the boldest blackest deeds, who knew how, by means of wiles and false tenderness, to bring the Sultan so far as to cause him to rage in fury against his own kindred, and stain his fame by the execution of his innocent self. And this Roxelane is, according to Marmontel, a little foolish coquette like any that flutters about

---

[1] Journ. Encyclop., Janvier 1762.

Paris, her head full of wind and a heart rather good than
bad. Are such mummeries permissible? May a poet or a
narrator, if we permit him any amount of liberty, extend
this liberty over well-known characters? If he may
change facts according to his good-will, may he then depict
a Lucretia prostituted and a libertine Socrates?"

Undoubtedly this would be going too far. I should not
like to undertake the justification of Marmontel; I have
further expressed my views that characters must be more
sacred to a poet than facts. For one reason, because if
characters are carefully observed in so far as the facts are
a consequence of the characters, they cannot of themselves
prove very diverse; while the self-same facts can be
deduced from totally different characters; secondly,
because what is instructive is not contained in the mere
facts but in the recognition that these characters under
these circumstances would and must evolve these facts.
Now Marmontel has reversed this. That there was once
in the seraglio a European slave who knew how to raise
herself to be the legal wife of the sultan, that is a fact.
The character of this slave and this sultan denote the
manner how this fact came about, and as it was possible
by means of more than one kind of character, it is certainly
open to the poet, as a poet, to choose which form he wills,
whether that which history ratifies or any other, according
as it be suited to the moral intention he has in his play.
Only if he chooses other and even opposed characters
to the historical, he should refrain from using historical
names, and rather credit totally unknown personages
with well-known facts than invent characters to well-
known personages. The one mode enlarges our knowledge
or seems to enlarge it and is thus agreeable. The other
contradicts the knowledge that we already possess and is
thus unpleasant. We regard the facts as something
accidental, as something that may be common to many
persons; the characters we regard as something individual
and intrinsic. The poet may take any liberties he likes
with the former so long as he does not put the facts into
contradiction with the characters; the characters he may
place in full light but he may not change them, the
smallest change seems to destroy their individuality and

to substitute in their place other persons, false persons, who have usurped strange names and pretend to be what they are not.

No. 34.

And yet it seems to me a far more pardonable fault not to give to personages characters that history has given them than to offend in these freely chosen characters in the point of intrinsic truth or instructiveness. The first fault can exist together with genius, but not the second. It is permitted to genius not to know a thousand things that every schoolboy knows. Not the accumulated stores of his memory, but that which he makes out of himself, which he brings forth out of his own feelings, constitute his riches[1]; what he has heard or read he has either forgotten or does not care to know beyond the point where it suits his end. He blunders therefore now from confidence, now from pride, now with, now without intention, so often, and so grossly, that we other good people cannot marvel enough ; we stand still and wonder and cry out : " But no ! how could a great man not know better? How is it possible he did not remember? did he not think ?" Oh let us be silent; we think that we will humble him and we only make ourselves ridiculous. All we know better than he only proves that we went to school more diligently than he, and that was very needful to us if we were not to turn out complete dunces.

Marmontel's Soliman might for all I cared have been quite another Soliman and his Roxelane quite another Roxelane than history taught me : if only I had found that though they are not of this real world they could have belonged to another world, a world whose events might be connected in a different order but still connected logically as they are here; a world in which cause and effect may follow in a different order but yet follow to the general effect of good ; in short to the world of a genius, a world that endeavours to copy in miniature the Highest Genius and transposes, exchanges, reduces, increases the various particles of the present world in order to form a whole therefrom that should harmonise with his own aims

[1] Pindar, Olymp. II. 10.

and ends. And since I do not find this latter in the work of
Marmontel, I can be content that he should not be allowed
to go scot-free of the former. Whoever cannot, or will
not indemnify us, must not offend us purposely. And here
Marmontel has really offended, it may be that he could
not or would not do otherwise.

For according to the indicated conception that we make
to ourselves of genius, we are justified in demanding
purpose and harmony in all the characters a poet creates;
that is if he demands from us that we should regard him
in the light of a genius.

Harmony; for nothing in the characters must be contradictory; they must ever remain uniform and inherently
themselves; they must express themselves now with
emphasis, now more slightly as events work upon them,
but none of the events must be mighty enough to change
black to white. The Turk despot must, even when he
is in love, remain a Turkish despot. The Turk who only
knows sensual love, must not think of any of the little
refinements that a pampered European imagination connects therewith. "I am weary of these caressing
machines; their soft pliability has nothing attractive,
nothing complimentary; I want to have difficulties to
overcome, and when I have overcome them I want to be
kept in breath by new difficulties." A King of France may
think thus, but no Sultan. It is true, if once we give
a Sultan such a form of thought, the despot is lost to view,
he himself puts off his despotism in order to enjoy a more
spontaneous love; but will he therefore suddenly become
the tame monkey whom a bold acrobat can force to dance
whenever she wills? Marmontel says: Soliman was too
great a man to conduct the little affairs of his seraglio on
the same footing with more important State affairs. Very
good, but then he should not in the end have conducted
great State affairs on the footing of the little affairs of his
seraglio. For to a great man both things are needful;
to treat trifles as trifles and important matters as important
matters. He sought, as Marmontel makes him say, free
hearts who should suffer slavery gladly from mere love for
his person, he had found such a heart in Elmire; but does
he know what he desires? The tender Elmire is set aside

for a voluptuous Delia, until a thoughtless woman entraps
him and makes him into a slave before he has enjoyed the
dubious favour that until now was the death of his desires.
Will it not also be so here? I must laugh at the good
Sultan and yet he deserves my sincere pity. If Elmire
and Delia lose everything after enjoyment that before
charmed him, what will Roxelane retain after this critical
moment? Eight days after her coronation will he hold
it worth while to have made this sacrifice to her? I
greatly fear that after the very first day he will see in his
wedded Sultana nothing save her confident impudence
and her turned-up nose. It seems to me I hear him
exclaim : By Mahomet ! where have my eyes been !

I do not mean to assert that all these contradictions
that make Soliman's character so contemptible and mean,
need prove that such a character could not exist. There
are enough people who combine yet more contemptible
contradictions. But on this very account they must not
be subjects for poetical imitation. They are beneath
poetry, for they lack instructive qualities; unless indeed
we employed their very contradictions, and their absurd or
unhappy consequences as instructive elements, but this was
evidently not Marmontel's design in his Soliman. Now a
character in which the instructive is lacking, lacks purpose.

To act with a purpose is what raises man above the
brutes, to invent with a purpose, to imitate with a purpose, is that which distinguishes genius from the petty
artists who only invent to invent, imitate to imitate.
They are content with the small enjoyment that is connected with their use of these means, and they make
these means to be their whole purpose and demand that
we also are to be satisfied with this lesser enjoyment,
which springs from the contemplation of their cunning
but purposeless use of their means. It is true that genius
begins to learn from such miserable imitations; they are
its preliminary studies. It also employs them in larger
works for amplification and to give resting-places to our
warmer sympathy, but with the construction and elaboration of its chief personages it combines larger and wider
intentions; the intention to instruct us what we should
do or avoid; the intention to make us acquainted with the

actual characteristics of good and bad, fitting and absurd.
It also designs to show us the good in all their combinations and results still good and happy even in misery;
the bad as revolting and unhappy even in happiness.
When its plot admits of no such immediate imitation, no
such unquestionable warning, genius still aims at working
upon our powers of desire and abhorrence with objects
that deserve these feelings, and ever strives to show these
objects in their true light, in order that no false light
may mislead us as to what we should desire, what we
should abhor.

Now what of all this exists in the characters of Soliman and Roxelane? As I have said; nothing. But there
is a great deal of the contrary. A couple of persons
whom we ought to despise, of which one should fill us
with disgust and the other with anger; a blunted
sensualist, a prostitute, are painted in the most seductive
and attractive colours, so that I should not wonder if
many a husband held himself justified in being weary of
his legitimate, lovely and amiable wife because she was
an Elmire and no Roxelane.

•   •   •   •   •   •   •   •

No. 35.

•   •   •   •   •   •   •   •

I have once before, elsewhere, drawn the distinction
that exists between the action in an Æsopian fable
and a drama. What is valid for the former, is valid for
every moral tale that intends to bring a general moral
axiom before our contemplation. We are satisfied if this
intention is fulfilled and it is the same to us whether this
is so by means of a complete action that is in itself a
rounded whole, or no. The poet may conclude wherever he
wills as soon as he sees his goal. It does not concern him
what interest we may take in the persons through whom
he works out his intention; he does not want to interest
but to instruct us, he has to do with our reason, not with
our heart, this latter may or may not be satisfied so long
as the other is illumined. Now the drama on the contrary
makes no claim upon a single definite axiom flowing out of
its story. It aims at the passions which the course and

events of its fable arouse and treat, or it aims at the
pleasure accorded by a true and vivid delineation of
characters and habits. Both require a certain integrity of
action, a certain harmonious end which we do not miss in
the moral tale because our attention is solely directed to
the general axiom of whose especial application the story
affords such an obvious instance.

.   .   .   .

No. 36.

.   .   .   .   .

Let us instance the Matron of Ephesus. This acrid fable
is well known, it is unquestionably the bitterest satire that
was ever made on female frivolity. It has been recounted
a thousand times after Petronius, and since it pleased even
in the worst copy, it was thought that the subject must
be an equally happy one for the stage. Houdar de la
Motte and others made the attempt, but I appeal to all
good taste as to the results of these attempts. The
character of the matron in the story provokes a not unpleasant sarcastic smile at the audacity of wedded love;
in the drama this becomes repulsive, horrible. In the
drama the soldier's persuasions do not seem nearly so
subtle, importunate, triumphant, as in the story.

In the story we picture to ourselves a sensitive little
woman who is really in earnest in her grief, but succumbs
to temptation and to her temperament, her weakness
seems the weakness of her sex, we therefore conceive no
especial hatred towards her, we deem that what she does,
nearly every woman would have done. Even her suggestion to save her living lover by means of her dead
husband we think we can forgive her because of its
ingenuity and presence of mind; or rather its very
ingenuity leads us to imagine that this suggestion may
have been appended by the malicious narrator who desired
to end his tale with some right poisonous sting. Now in
the drama we cannot harbour this suggestion; what we
hear has happened in the story, we see really occur; what
we would doubt of in the story, in the drama the evidence of our own eyes settles incontrovertibly. The
mere possibility of such an action diverted us; its reality

shows it in all its atrocity; the suggestion amused our
fancy, the execution revolts our feelings, we turn our
backs to the stage and say with the Lykas of Petronius,
without being in Lykas's peculiar position: " Si justus
Imperator fuisset, debuit patris familiæ corpus in moni-
mentum referre, mulierem adfigere cruci." And she seems
to us the more to deserve this punishment, the less art the
poet has expended on her seduction, for we do not then
condemn in her weak woman in general, but an especially
volatile, worthless female in particular. In short, in order
happily to bring Petronius's fable on the stage it should
preserve its end and yet not preserve it ; the matron should
go as far and yet not as far. The explanation of this
another time.

On the thirty-eighth evening ' Merope ' by M. de
Voltaire was performed.

Voltaire composed this tragedy at the instigation of
Maffei's ' Merope,' probably in the year 1737, probably at
Cirey when with his Urania, the Marquise du Châtelet.
For already in January 1783 the MS. was at Paris in the
hands of Father Brumoy, who as a Jesuit and the author
of the Théâtre des Grecs was the most fitted to awaken
interest in its favour and to prepare the metropolis to
receive it with due respect. Brumoy showed the MS. to
the author's friends, and among others he sent it to old
Father Tournemine, who greatly flattered at being consulted by his dear son Voltaire, concerning a tragedy and
a matter about which he did not understand much, wrote
a letter full of praise of it, which was then printed in
the preface of the play and serves as a lesson and a warning to all officious art critics. He calls the play one of
the most perfect tragedies, a very model, and we may consequently now make ourselves quite happy that the play
of Euripides on the same theme has been lost, or rather
it is no longer lost for Voltaire has restored it.

Now greatly though all this should have pacified
Voltaire, yet he did not seem to hurry himself with its
representation, which only took place in 1743. He earned
all the full fruits he could have anticipated from his
statesmanlike procrastination. ' Merope ' met with extraordinary success and the pit showed an honour to the poet

of which up till that time there had been no instance. It
is true that the great Corneille was well received by the
public, his chair on the stage was always left unoccupied
even when the crowd was very great and when he came
every one rose up, a distinction which in France is only
shown to princes of the royal blood. Corneille was
regarded as at home in the theatre and when the master of
the house appears, what more becoming than that his
guests show their deference? But quite other honours
were reserved for Voltaire; the pit was anxious to know
in person the man they so greatly admired and, therefore,
when the play was over, they desired to see him, and called
and exclaimed and clamoured until M. de Voltaire had to
come out and allow himself to be gaped at and clapped.
I know not which of the two most perplexed me, the
childish curiosity of the public or the vain complaisance
of the poet. How do people think that a poet looks? Not
like other mortals? And how weak must be the impression made by his work if in the end one desires nothing
more ardently than to see the face of its maker. The
true masterpiece, so it seems to me, fills us so entirely
with itself that we forget its author over his work, that we
do not regard it as the production of a simple being but
as the work of general nature. Young says of the sun
that it would have been a sin in the heathens not to pray
to it. If there is sense in this hyperbole, it is this; the
glory, the majesty of the sun is so great, so imposing, that
savage man can be pardoned, nay that it is natural, that
he can conceive of no greater glory, no higher majesty of
which this is but the reflexion, if he so lose himself in
his admiration of the sun as not to consider its Creator.
I incline to believe that the real reason why we know so
little of the person and the life of Homer is to be
sought in the excellence of his poems. We stand astonished before the broad rushing river and do not think
of its source in the distant mountains. We do not want
to know, we are more content to forget that Homer the
schoolmaster in Smyrna, Homer the blind beggar, is the
same Homer who so delights us in his works. He leads
us among gods and heroes and we must feel great *ennui* in
this society if we want to look round and inquire after the
porter who has admitted us. The deception must be very

slight, we must feel little nature and much art if we are
so curious concerning the artist. So little flattering therefore to a man of genius is the desire of the public to know
him by sight. What advantage has he before any chance
marmot which the public is just as eager to behold? Yet
the vanity of the French poets seems to have been satisfied. For when the Parisian pit saw how easily a Voltaire
was to be tempted into this trap, how tame and pliant
such a man became under doubtful caresses, it often
repeated this amusement, and rarely was a new play performed afterwards, whose author was not likewise called
out and who came out quite willingly. From Voltaire to
Marmontel, and from Marmontel deep down to Cordier,
nearly all have stood in this pillory. How many a poor
contemptible face must have been among them! At last
the farce went so far that the more serious among the
nation grew annoyed. Polichinello's happy thought is
well known. And recently a young poet had the courage
to let the pit call in vain. He would not appear. His
play was mediocre, but his behaviour the more to be
admired and praised. I would rather have aided in
abolishing such an abuse by my example, than have
occasioned it by ten 'Meropes.'

No. 37.

I have said that Voltaire's ' Merope ' was instigated by
Maffei's. But instigated is perhaps saying too little for
it has arisen thence; fable, plan and manner belong to
Maffei, without his aid Voltaire would not have written a
' Merope ' or certainly a very different one.

Therefore to judge the Frenchman's copy correctly we
must first become acquainted with the Italian original,
and to value the latter's poetical merits we must first of
all cast a glance over the historical facts on which he
founded his fable.

Maffei himself thus condenses these facts in the preface
to his play: " Pausanias relates how after the conquest of
Troy the Heraklidæ, *i.e.* the descendants of Hercules,
settled in the Peloponnesus, and how the territory of
Messina fell by lot to Kresphontes. Kresphontes's wife

was named Merope. Now Kresphontes showed himself
too indulgent to his people and he and his sons were
murdered by the nobles of his realm, all excepting the
youngest, named Æpytus who was being educated at a
distance among his mother's relations. This youngest
son when he was grown up reconquered the paternal
kingdom by the aid of the Arcadians and Dorians and
revenged his father's death upon the murderers. Apollodorus relates how after Kresphontes and his two sons
had been murdered, Polyphontes, likewise a Heraklide,
had taken possession of the throne and forced Merope to
be his wife and how the third son whom the mother had
safely concealed, afterwards killed the tyrant and regained
the throne. Hyginus relates that Merope nearly killed
her son unwittingly, but that she was hindered in time by
an old servant who revealed to her that he whom she
deemed the murderer of her son, was her son himself, and
that this now recognised son had on the occasion of a sacrifice been enabled to slay Polyphontes. Hyginus however
names this son Telephontes and not Æpytus."

It would be astonishing if such a story, containing such
peculiar reverses of fortune and recognitions had not been
already treated by the ancient tragedians. And was it
not? Aristotle in his 'Poetics' mentions a Kresphontes
in whom Merope recognises her son just at the moment
when she is about to kill his presumed assassin. Plutarch
in his second treatise on 'Eating of Flesh' beyond doubt
refers to this very play [1] when he recalls the tumult into
which the whole theatre is aroused when Merope lifts the
axe against her son and the fear that seizes each spectator
lest the stroke should fall before the old servant arrives.
Aristotle refers to this Kresphontes without the name of
an author, but as in Cicero and other classics we find
reference to a Kresphontes of Euripides, he can scarcely
have meant any other work than this.

Father Tournemine says in the above-named letter:

---

[1] Assuming this (as we may surely assume with certainty, because
it was not usual with the ancient poets, nor permitted, to steal one
from another) the passage in Plutarch must be a fragment from Euripides. Joshua Barnes has not included it, but another editor of the
poet might do so.

" Aristotle, this wise legislator of the stage, has placed
the fable of Merope in the first rank of tragic fables (a
mis ce sujet au premier rang des sujets tragiques), Euripides
treated it, and Aristotle remarks that as often as the
' Kresphontes ' of Euripides was represented on the stage of
witty Athens, this tragic masterpiece moved, delighted
and touched in a most extraordinary way a public
greatly spoilt by masterpieces ;" pretty phrases, but they
do not contain much truth ! The father was in error on
two points. He confused Aristotle with Plutarch, and
he did not rightly understand Aristotle. The first error
is a trifle, the second merits the trouble of saying a few
words because many have equally misunderstood Aristotle.

The matter lies as follows : Aristotle examines in the
14th chapter of his Poetics by what means fear and pity
are aroused. All events, he says, must occur either
between friends or enemies, or between indifferent persons.
When an enemy kills his enemy neither the attack nor
the execution of the deed awaken other pity than that
common feeling which is connected in general with pain
and destruction. The same is true of indifferent persons.
Consequently tragical events must occur between friends,
a brother must kill, or wish to kill, his brother, a son his
father, a mother a son, or a son a mother, or else desire to
ill-treat them in a painful way. This may occur with or
without intention or knowledge, and since the deed must
be either consummated or not, four kinds of events arise
which more or less express the intentions of tragedy.
The first, when the action is undertaken with the full
knowledge of the personages concerned, and towards whom
it is to be perpetrated, but not carried out. The second,
when it is purposely undertaken and actually carried out.
The third, when the deed is undertaken and carried out
without the knowledge of its object, and the perpetrator
recognises too late the object on whom it is perpetrated.
The fourth when the deed, undertaken in ignorance, is
not carried out, because the persons involved have recognised each other in time. Of these four classes Aristotle
gives the preference to the latter, and since he quotes the
action of Merope in ' Kresphontes,' as an example thereof,
Tournemine and others have accepted this as if he had

thus declared this fable to be the most perfect kind for tragedy.

While in reality Aristotle says, shortly before, that a good tragical fable must not end happily but unhappily. How can these two statements exist together? It is to end unhappily; and yet the events which, in accordance with this classification are preferred to all other tragical events, end happily. Does not the great critic openly contradict himself?

Victorius, says Dacier, was the only person who perceived this difficulty, but since he did not understand what Aristotle really meant in his fourteenth chapter, he did not even try to overcome the difficulty. Aristotle, says Dacier, is not speaking of fable in general, but only wants to teach how the poet should treat tragical events without changing the essential that history relates of them; and which of these kinds is the best. When, for instance, the murder of Klytemnestra by Orestes is to be the subject of the play, there are according to Aristotle four ways of working this material, either as an occurrence of the first, second, third or fourth class; the poet must only consider which is the best and most suited. It cannot be that the murder is treated as an event of the first class because according to history it really took place, and must take place through Orestes. Nor according to the second, because this is too horrible. Nor according to the fourth, because thus Klytemnestra would be saved, and she must on no account be saved. Consequently only the third class remains.

The third! but Aristotle gives the preference to the fourth and not only in individual cases and according to circumstances, but in general. The worthy Dacier often acts thus, Aristotle remains in the right with him, not because he is in the right, but because he is Aristotle. While thus deeming that he is covering some of his faults he makes him commit far worse ones. Now if an opponent should have the prudence to attack the latter instead of the former, then it is all over with the infallibility of his classical author about which he cares more than about truth. If so much depends on coincidence with history, if the poet may soften but not wholly change well-known

incidents, will there not be some among them that must
of necessity be treated according to the first or second
class? Klytemnestra's murder ought to be treated according to the second, for Orestes has committed it knowingly
and designedly; but the poet may choose the third
because it is more tragical and does not totally contradict
history. Well, so be it: but how about Medea who
murders her children? What other plan but the second
can the poet pursue here? For she must murder them
and murder them designedly, both circumstances are
equally historical. Then what order of precedence can
there be among these categories? The one that is the
most excellent in one case cannot be thought of in
another. Or to press Dacier yet harder, let us make the
application not to historical, but to fictitious events.
Granted that the murder of Clytemnestra belonged to the
latter category and it had been open to the poet to perpetrate it or not, to perpetrate it with knowledge or without.
Which mode would he have had to employ in order to
make of it the most perfect tragedy possible? Dacier
himself says the fourth, for if he had preferred the third
it would only have arisen from regard for history. The
fourth therefore? The one therefore which ends happily?
But the best tragedies, says Aristotle, who accords preference to this fourth plan, are those which end unhappily?
And this is just the contradiction which Dacier sought
to remove. Has he removed it? He has rather confirmed it.

No. 38.

Nor am I singular in regarding Dacier's exposition
as inadequate. The German translator of Aristotle's
'Poetics' has found it equally unsatisfactory.[1] He gives
his reasons against it, that do not actually contradict
Dacier's evasions but yet seem to him quite sufficient
to abandon the defence of his author and attempt a new
venture to save something which is not to be saved.
"I leave it to a deeper comprehension to remove these
difficulties, I can find no light towards their explanation,
and it seems to me only probable that our philosopher

[1] Herr Curtius, p. 214.

did not think through this chapter with his wonted care."

I must confess that this seems to me highly improbable. Aristotle is not often guilty of a palpable contradiction. Where I would seem to find one in such a man, I prefer rather to mistrust my own reason. I redouble my attention, I re-read the passage ten times, and do not think that he contradicts himself before I perceive from the entire connexion of his system how and why he has been betrayed into this contradiction. If I find nothing that could so betray him, that must, so to speak, make this contradiction inevitable, then I am convinced that it is only an apparent contradiction. Else it would certainly have occurred first to the author who had to think over his matter so often, and not to me, the unpractised reader who has taken him up for instruction. I therefore pause, retrace the thread of his ideas, ponder every word, and repeat to myself again and again : Aristotle can err and has often erred, but that he should here insist on something which on the next page he contradicts, that Aristotle cannot do. Then at length light will come.

But without further circumlocution, here is the explanation of which Herr Curtius despaired. Nevertheless I make no claim to the honour of a deeper comprehension. I am contented with the honour of evincing more modesty towards a philosopher like Aristotle.

Now Aristotle commends nothing more to the tragic poet than a good conception of his fable, and he has endeavoured to render this easy to him by various and subtle remarks. For it is the fable that principally makes a poet ; ten will succeed in representing customs, reflexions, expressions for one who is excellent and blameless in this. He declares a fable to be an imitation of an action, πράξεως, and an action by a combination of events is σύνθεσις πραγμάτων. The action is the whole, the events are the parts of this whole, and as the goodness of any whole rests on the goodness and connexion of its several parts, so also tragical action is more or less perfect, according as the events of which it is composed separately and collectively coincide with the intentions of the tragedy. Aristotle classes the events that can take place in a tragic

action under three mains heads: change of circumstances,
περιπέτεια; recognition, ἀναγνωρισμός; and suffering, πάθος.
What he means by the two first the names sufficiently
reveal. Under the third he comprehends all that can
occur of a painful and destructive nature to the acting
personages; death, wounds, martyrdom and so forth.
Change of circumstances and recognition are that by which
the more intricate fable, μύθος πεπλεγμένος, is distinguished
from the simple, ἁπλοῦς. They are therefore no essential
part of the fable, they only make the action more varied
and hence more interesting and beautiful, but an action
can have its full unity, completion and greatness without
them. But without the third we can conceive of no
tragical action; every tragedy must have some form of
suffering, πάθη, be its fable simple or involved, for herein
lies the actual intention of tragedy, to awaken fear and
pity, while not every change of outward circumstances,
not every recognition, but only certain forms of these attain
this end, and other forms are rather disadvantageous
than profitable. While therefore Aristotle regards and
examines separately the various parts of tragical action
that he has brought under these three main divisions,
explaining what are the best outward changes, the best
recognition, the best treatment of suffering, he finds in
regard to the former that such changes of fortune are the
best and most capable of awakening and stimulating pity
and fear, which change from better to worse. In regard
to the latter division he finds that the best treatment of
suffering in the same sense is when the persons whom
suffering threatens, do not know each other or only recognise each other at the moment when this suffering is to
become reality and it is therefore stayed.

And this is called a contradiction? I do not understand where can be the thoughts of him who finds the
least contradiction here. The philosopher speaks of
various parts; why must that which he maintains of one
of these parts of necessity apply to the others? Is the
possible perfection of the one also the perfection of the
other? Or is the perfection of a part also the perfection
of the whole? If change of circumstances and that which
Aristotle includes under the word suffering, are two

different things, as they are indeed, why should not something quite different be said of them? Or is it impossible
that a whole should have parts of opposed characteristics?
Where does Aristotle say that the best tragedy is nothing
but a representation of changes of fortunes from pro-
sperity to adversity? Or where does he say that the best
tragedy results from nothing but the recognition of him
on whom a fearful and unnatural deed was to have been
committed? He says neither one thing nor the other of
tragedy generally, but each of these things of an especial
part that more or less concerns the end, which may
or may not have influence. Change of fortune may
occur in the middle of the play, and even if it continues
thus to the end of the piece, it does not therefore constitute its end. For example, the change of fortune in
' Œdipus ' that evinces itself already at the close of the
fourth act, but to which various sufferings, $\pi\acute{a}\theta\eta$, are added
and with which the play really concludes. In the same
manner suffering can attain its accomplishment in the
play and at the same moment be thwarted by recognition,
so that by means of this recognition the play is far from
concluded, as in the second ' Iphigenia ' of Euripides where
Orestes is already recognised in the fourth act by his
sister who was in the act of sacrificing him. And how
perfectly such tragical changes of fortune can be combined
with tragical treatment of suffering in one and the same
fable, can be shown in ' Merope ' itself. It contains the
latter but what hinders it from having the former also, if
for instance Merope, when she recognises her son under
the dagger in her eagerness to defend him from Polyphontes, contributes to her own or to her loved son's
destruction? Why should not this play close as well
with the destruction of the mother as with that of the
tyrant? Why should it not be open to the poet to raise
to the highest point our pity for a tender mother and
allow her to be unfortunate through her tenderness? Or
why should it not be permissible to let the son whom a
pious vengeance has torn from his mother, succumb to the
pursuit of the tyrant? Would not such a ' Merope ' in
both cases combine those two characteristics of the best tragedy, in which the critic has been found so contradictory?

I perceive very well what caused the misunderstanding. It was not easy to imagine a change of fortune from better to worse without suffering, or suffering that has been obviated by recognition otherwise than connected with change of fortune. Yet each can equally be without the other, not to mention that both need not touch the same person, and even if it touches the same person, that both may not occur at the same time, but one follows the other, and one can be caused by the other. Without considering this, people have only thought of those instances and fables, in which both parts either harmonise or in which one of necessity excludes the other. That such exist, is unquestionable. But is the art critic to be censured because he composes his rules in the most general manner, without considering the cases in which his general rules come into collision and one perfection must be sacrificed to another? Does such a collision of necessity bring him into contradiction with himself? He says: This part of the fable, if it is to have its perfection, must be of such and such a constitution, that part of another, a third again of another. But where has he said that every fable must of necessity have all these parts? Enough for him that there are fables that could have them all. If your fable is not among the number of these happy ones; if it only admits of the best changes of fortune, the best treatment of suffering, then examine with which of the two you would succeed best as a whole, and choose. That is all!

No. 39.

Finally Aristotle may or may not have contradicted himself; Tournemine may have understood him rightly or no; the fable of 'Merope' is neither in the one case nor the other to be pronounced at once as a perfect fable. For if Aristotle has contradicted himself, then he maintains just the contrary, and it must first be examined where he is most in the right, here or there. But if he has not contradicted himself, in accordance with my explanation, then the good he says of it does not concern the whole fable but only a separate part thereof. Perhaps the misuse of his authority by Father Tournemine was only a Jesuit's trick, to give us to understand that such a perfect fable, treated by such a great poet as Voltaire, must needs be a masterpiece.

But Tournemine and Tournemine! I fear my readers will ask "Who is this Tournemine? We know no such Tournemine!" For many might really not know him and many might ask thus because they know him too well, like Montesquieu.[1]

Let them have the goodness therefore to substitute M. de Voltaire for Father Tournemine. For he too endeavours to give us the same erroneous impressions of the lost play of Euripides. He too says, that Aristotle in his immortal 'Poetics' does not hesitate to pronounce that the recognition by Merope of her son is the most interesting moment in the whole Greek theatre. He too says that Aristotle accords preference to this *coup de théâtre* before all others. And he even assures us of Plutarch, that he held this play of Euripides to be the most touching of all his plays.[2] This latter statement is wholly fictitious. For Plutarch does not even name the title of the play whence he quotes the situation of Merope; he neither says how it is called nor who was its author; still less does he declare it to be the most touching of Euripides' dramas.

Aristotle should not have hesitated to pronounce that the recognition by Merope of her son is the most interesting moment in the whole Greek theatre! What an expression! "not hesitated to pronounce." What hyperbole: "the most interesting moment of the whole Greek theatre"! Should we not infer herefrom that Aristotle was carefully reviewing all the interesting moments that a tragedy may have, comparing one with another, weighing the various examples that he found in each

---

[1] Lettres familières.

[2] "Aristote, dans sa Poëtique immortelle, ne balance pas à dire que la reconnaissance de Mérope et de son fils était le moment le plus intéressant de toute la scène Grecque. Il donnait à ce coup de théâtre la préférence sur tous les autres. Plutarque dit que les Grecs, ce peuple si sensible, frémissaient de crainte que le vieillard, qui devait arrêter le bras de Mérope, n'arrivât pas assez tôt. Cette pièce, qu'on jouait de son temps, et dont il nous reste très-peu de fragments, lui paraissait la p'us touchante de toutes les tragédies d'Euripide," &c.— *Lettre à M. Maffei.*

poet, or at least in the most famous, and then pronounced boldly and surely his verdict in favour of this moment of Euripides? And yet it is only one single kind of interesting moment that he cites as an example, and besides it is not even the only example of this kind. Aristotle found similar instances in ‘Iphigenia,’ where the sister recognises the brother, and in ‘Helle’ where the son recognises his mother, just as they are about to lift their hands against them.

The second example of ‘Iphigenia’ is truly from Euripides, and if, as Dacier suspects, ‘Helle’ also was the work of this poet, it would be remarkable that Aristotle should have found all three examples of such a fortunate recognition just in the very poet who most employs the unhappy peripeteia.* And yet, why remarkable? We have seen that one does not exclude the other, and although in ‘Iphigenia’ a happy recognition follows upon the unhappy peripeteia and the play therefore ends happily, who knows whether in the two others an unhappy peripeteia did not follow a happy recognition and they therefore concluded quite in the manner by which Euripides has gained for himself the character of the most tragic of all tragic poets?

In ‘Merope’ this was possible in a twofold manner, as I have shown. Whether it really thus occurred or no cannot be conclusively decided out of the few fragments that remain to us of the ‘Kresphontes.’ They contain nothing but moral axioms and reflexions often quoted by later authors and do not throw the smallest light upon the economy of the play.[3] Only from one of these, wherein Polybius appeals to the goddess of Peace, we can infer that the time of action fell before peace had been restored in Messene, and from a few others we may almost conclude that the murder of Kresphontes and his two eldest sons either formed a part of the action or else just preceded it, which does not very well agree with the recognition of the younger son who only came to avenge his father and brothers many years after. But the title

[3] That which Dacier quotes (Poëtique d’Aristote, chap. xv. rem. 23) without remembering where he had read it, is in Plutarch in the essay : “How to make use of one’s enemies.”

[* *i.e.* Change of circumstances, as denoted on p. 110.]

causes me the greatest difficulty. If this recognition and
vengeance of the youngest son formed the main part of
the contents, how came the play to be named 'Kresphontes'? Kresphontes was the name of the father; the
son according to some was called Æpytus, according to
others Telephontes; perhaps because the one was the real
the other the assumed name that he bore in foreign lands,
in order to be safe from the persecutions of Polyphontes.
The father must long have been dead when the son recon-
quers, the paternal kingdom. Is it likely that a tragedy
should be named after a person who does not occur in
it? Corneille and Dacier were able quickly to get over
this difficulty by assuming that the son was likewise
named Kresphontes,[4] but with what likelihood? or what
authority?

If, however, there be truth in a discovery whereupon
Maffei flatters himself, then we can know the plot of
Kresphontes with fair exactitude. He thinks that he has
found it in the 184th fable of Hyginus,[5] and he further
holds Hyginus's fables in great part as nothing but the
arguments of older tragedies, which assumption Reinesius
hold before him, and consequently recommends newer

---

[4] Remarque 22 sur le Chapitre xv de la Poët. d'Arist.: "Une mère,
qui va tuer son fils, comme Mérope va tuer Cresphonte," &c.

[5] "Questa scoperta penso io d' aver fatta, nel leggere la Favola 184
d'Igino, la quale a mio credere altra non è, che l'Argomento di quella
Tragedia, in cui si rappresenta interamente la condotta di essa. Sov-
vienmi, che al primo gettar gli occhi, ch' io feci già in quell' Autore,
mi apparve subito nella mente, altro non essere le più di quelle Favole,
che gli Argomenti delle Tragedie antiche: mi accertai di ciò col con-
frontarne alcune poche con le Tragedie, che ancora abbiamo; ed appunto
in questi giorni, venuta a mano l' ultima edizione d' Igino, mi è stato
caro di vedere in un passo addotto, come fu anche il Reinesio di tal
sentimento. Una miniera è però questa di Tragici Argomenti, che se
fosse stata nota a' Poeti, non avrebbero penato tanto in rinvenir soggetti
a lor fantasia: io la scoprirò loro di buona voglia, perchè rendano col
loro ingegno alla nostra età ciò, che dal tempo invidioso le fu rapito.
Merita dunque, almeno per questo capo, alquanto più di considera-
zione quell' Operetta, anche tal qual l' abbiamo, che da gli Eruditi non
è stato creduto: e quanto al discordar talvolta dagli altri Scrittori
delle favolose Storie, questa avertenza ce ne addita la ragione, non
avendole costui narrate secondo la tradizione, ma conforme i Poeti in
proprio uso convertendole le avean ridotte."

poets rather to search in this disused quarry for the old
tragic fables, than to invent new ones. The advice is not
bad and should be followed, and it has been followed by
many before Maffei gave it or without knowing that
Maffei had given it. Herr Weiss has taken the materials
of his Thyestes thence and many more are still waiting
there for an intelligent eye. Only it might be not the
largest but the very smallest part of Hyginus's work
which could thus be made use of. Nor need it on
that account be composed of the arguments of old tragedies, it can have flowed directly or indirectly from
the same sources to which the tragedians applied. Nay,
Hyginus, or whoever made the compilation, seems to have
regarded the tragedies as diverted and sullied streams, in
that in several places for which we have nothing but the
authority of the tragic poets, he separates them distinctly
from the older genuine tradition. Thus for example, he
first relates the fable of Ino and Antiope according to
tradition, and then, in a separate paragraph, according to
the treatment of Euripides.

No. 40.

I do not mean to say by this that because the name of
Euripides does not head the 184th Fable, it cannot therefore have been deduced from his ' Kresphontes.' Rather I
confess that it really has the manner and entanglement of
a tragedy, so that, if it was not one, it could easily become
one, and one whose plan would far nearer approach to
antique simplicity than all the modern ' Meropes.' Judge
for yourselves. The story of Hyginus that I have only
briefly referred to above, is as follows :—

Kresphontes was king of Messene and had three sons by
his wife Merope, when Polyphontes stirred up a revolt
against him, in which he and his two eldest sons lost
their lives. Polyphontes then took possession of the
kingdom and the hand of Merope, who, during the revolt
found an opportunity to bring her third son, Telephontes,
into the safe keeping of a friend in Ætolia. The older
Telephontes became, the more uneasy grew Polyphontes.

He could expect little good from him and therefore promised a great reward to whoever should put him out of
the way. Telephontes learnt this and since he now felt
himself equal to undertake his revenge, he stole away
secretly from Ætolia, went to Messene, came before the
tyrant and said that he had murdered Telephontes and
therefore demanded the promised reward. Polyphontes
received him hospitably and commanded that he should
be entertained in his palace until he could question him
further. Telephontes was therefore conducted into the
guest-chamber where he fell asleep from weariness.
Meanwhile the old servant whom mother and son had
till now employed to carry their respective messages,
came weeping to Merope and announced that Telephontes
was absent from Ætolia and that none knew whither he
had gone. Merope at once hastens to the guest-chamber,
for she is not ignorant whereof the stranger boasts. Sho
is armed with an axe and would certainly have murdered
her son in his sleep, if the old man who had followed her
in, had not recognised him in time and hindered the
mother from such a deed of horror. Now both make
common cause, and Merope assumes a calm, forgiving
attitude towards her husband. Polyphontes deems all his
wishes gratified and desires to show his thankfulness to
the gods by a solemn sacrifice. But when they are all
assembled around the altar, Telephontes directs the blow
with which he pretended to slay the sacrificial beast,
towards the king; the tyrant falls and Telephontes
succeeds to the possession of his paternal realm.[1]

[1] In the 184th Fable of Hyginus, whence the above tale is extracted
events have palpably been interwoven that have not the smallest connexion among themselves. It begins with the fate of Pentheus and
Agave, and ends with the history of Merope. I cannot comprehend
how the editor could let this confusion stand unnoticed, or is it possible
that it only exists in the edition I have before me (Joannis Schafferi,
Hamburgi, 1674). I leave this examination to those who have the
means at hand. Enough that here with me the 184th Fable must end
with the words "quam Licoterses excepit." The rest either belongs to
a separate fable of which the opening words are lost, or what is more
likely belongs to the 237th, so that, both connected, I have thus read
the fable of Merope, whether it be the 237th or 184th Fable. It is
understood that in the latter the words, "cum qua Polyphontes, occiso

In the 16th century two Italian poets, Gio. Bapt.
Liviera and Pomponio Torelli, had extracted the matter
for their tragedies, 'Kresphontes' and 'Merope,' from this
fable of Hyginus, and were thus according to Maffei,
treading in the footsteps of Euripides without knowing
it. But this conviction notwithstanding, Maffei so little
thought of making his work a mere divination on Euripides, in order to let the lost 'Kresphontes' revive in his
'Merope,' that he rather diverged purposely from the main
outlines of this assumed Euripidean plan, and only employed in all its bearings the one situation that chiefly
touched him therein.

The mother who loves her son so ardently that she
desires to avenge herself on his murderer with her own
hand, suggested to him to picture maternal tenderness
generally and to transfuse his play with this pure and
virtuous passion to the exclusion of all other love. What
did not therefore coincide with this intention, was changed,
and this chiefly regarded the circumstances of Merope's
second marriage and her son's foreign education. Merope
must not be the wife of Polyphontes, for it seemed to the

Cresphonte, regnum occupavit" must fall away as a needless repetition,
together with the following ejus, which is already superfluous.

"Merope.

"Polyphontes, Messeniæ rex, Cresphontem Aristomachi filium cum
interfecisset, ejus imperium et Meropem uxorem possedit. Filium
autem infantem Merope mater, quem ex Cresphonte habebat, abscondite
ad hospitem in Ætoliam mandavit. Hunc Polyphontes maxima cum
industria quærebat, aurumque pollicebatur, si quis eum necasset.
Qui postquam ad puberem ætatem venit, capit consilium, ut exequatur
patris et fratrum mortem. Itaque venit ad regem Polyphontem,
aurem petitum, dicens se Cresphontis interfecisse filium et Meropis,
Telephontem. Interim rex eum jussit in hospitio manere, ut amplius
de eo perquireret. Qui cum per lassitudinem obdormisset, senex qui
inter matrem et filium internuncius erat, flens ad Meropem venit,
negans eum apud hospitem esse, nec comparere. Merope credens eum
esse filii sui interfectorem, qui dormiebat, in Chalcidicum cum securi
venit, inscia ut filium suum interficeret, quem senex cognovit, et
matrem a scelere retraxit. Merope postquam invenit occasionem sibi
datam esse, ab inimico se ulciscendi, redit cum Polyphonte in gratiam.
Rex lætus cum rem divinam faceret, hospes falso simulavit se hostiam
percussisse, eumque interfecit, patriumque regnum adeptus est."

poet at variance with the conscientiousness of a pious mother, to abandon herself to the embraces of a second husband in whom she recognised the murderer of her first, and whose very existence demanded that he should free himself of all those who had any nearer claims to the throne. The son must not be brought up in safety and comfort under the roof of a noble friend of the paternal house, in the full knowledge of his rank and future destiny, for maternal love would grow cold if it were not irritated and developed by incessant pictures of discomfort and ever new dangers that threaten its absent object. Nor must the son arrive with the definite purpose of killing the tyrant, he must not be deemed by Merope the murderer of her son, because he gives himself out as himself, but because a certain connexion of chances has thrown suspicion upon him; for if he knows his mother then her confusion is over after the first verbal explanation, and her touching sorrow, her tender despair, has not play enough.

In accordance with these changes it is easy to imagine Maffei's plan; Polyphontes has been reigning for fifteen years and yet he does not feel the throne a sure one. For the people are still attached to the house of the former king and reckon upon the last branch thereof. To assuage the discontented, it occurs to him to marry Merope. He offers her his hand under the plea of real love. But Merope scorns this plea and he then endeavours to attain by threats and violence what his pretences could not compass. He is just urging her imperatively when a youth is brought before him who has been taken upon the high road connected with a murder. Ægisthus, so the youth is named, has done nothing but defend his own life against a robber, his aspect betrays so much nobility and innocence, his speech so much truth, that Merope, who besides recognises a certain line of the mouth that was peculiar to her husband, is induced to beg the king for his life and the king grants it. Immediately after Merope misses her youngest son, whom she has confided to an old servant, Polydorus, after her husband's death, with the command to educate him as his own son. He has secretly left the old man whom he deems his father, to see the

world and can be found nowhere. The mother's heart
fears the worst, some one has been murdered on the high
road, how if this was her son ? Her fears are strengthened
by various circumstances, the king's willingness to pardon
the murderer, also by the sight of a ring that is found on
Ægisthus and which she is told Ægisthus took from the
murdered man. This is her husband's signet ring which
she had confided to Polydorus to give to her son when he
should have reached man's estate and it should be time
to reveal his rank to him. She at once causes the
youth, whose life she had implored, to be bound to a
column, and intends to pierce his heart with her own
hand. At this moment the youth remembers his parents,
he utters the name Messene and recalls his father's
caution to avoid this spot. Merope demands an explanation of this, meantime the king comes up and the youth
is liberated. So near as Merope was to the recognition
of her error, so deeply she falls back into it, when she
sees how maliciously the king triumphs in her despair.
Ægisthus must inevitably be her son's murderer and
nothing shall save him from her vengeance. At night-
fall she hears that he is sleeping in an ante-room and
goes in with an axe to sever his head and has already
raised the axe for the fatal blow, when Polydorus, who
has shortly before entered the ante-room and recognised
the sleeping Ægisthus, stays her arm. Ægisthus awakes
and flies, and Polydorus reveals to Merope her own son in
the person of his supposed murderer. She wishes to
follow him and would inevitably have revealed his
identity to the tyrant by her wild tenderness, had not the
old man restrained her. Early next day her marriage
with the tyrant was to take place, she must go to the
altar, but she would die sooner than give her consent.
Meantime Polydorus has made himself known to Ægisthus; Ægisthus hurries to the temple, forces his way
through the crowd and the rest is told by Hyginus.

No. 41.

The worse matters looked generally with the Italian
theatre at the beginning of this century, the greater was

the applause and delight wherewith Maffei and Merope
were greeted.

> " Cedite Romani scriptores, cedite Graii,
>   Nescio quid majus nascitur Œdipode,"

cried Leonardo Adami, who had only seen the first two
acts in Rome.   In Venice during the carnival of 1714
hardly any other play but 'Merope' was acted; the whole
world wanted to see the new tragedy again and again, and
even the Opera was neglected for it.   It was printed
four times in one year, and in sixteen years (1714 to
1730) more than thirty editions were issued in and
out of Italy, in Vienna, Paris, London.   It has been
translated into French, English, and German and it was
intended to print it with all these translations.   It had
been twice translated into French, when M. de Voltaire
took possession of it again to bring it upon the French
stage.   But he soon found that this could not be by
means of a real translation, and he gave his reasons for
this at length in a letter to the Marquis afterwards
printed as a preface to his own 'Merope.'

"Tho tone," he says, "of the Italian 'Merope' is too
naive and *bourgeois* and the taste of the French parterre
too delicate and refined for plain simple nature to please
them.   It would not see nature except under certain disguises of art and these disguises must be far other at
Paris than in Verona."   The whole letter is written with
extreme politeness, Maffei has erred in nowise, all his care-
lessness and faults are put to the account of the national
taste, they are even beauties, but alas! only beauties for
Italy.   Indeed it is not possible to criticise more politely.
But this tiresome politeness!   Even a Frenchman soon
finds it burdensome if his vanity suffers thereby in the
very least.   Politeness makes us appear amiable but not
great, and the Frenchman desires to appear great as well
as amiable.

But what follows upon the elegant dedication of M. de
Voltaire?   The writing of a certain De la Lindelle, who
says as many rude things about the good Maffei as Voltaire has said polite.   The style of this De la Lindelle is
about the style of Voltaire; it is a pity that so good a

writer has not written more and is so generally unknown.
But whether Lindelle is Voltaire or really Lindelle; whoever would see a French Janus-head that laughs in front
in the most flattering mode and makes the most malicious
grimaces behind, let him read both letters at one time. I
should not like to have written either, least of all both.
Voltaire remains this side the truth from politeness, while
Lindelle ranges far beyond it on the other side from desire
to depreciate. One should have been more candid, the other
more just, if the suspicion was not to be aroused that the
same author desired to take back under a strange name all
that he had conceded in his own.

Voltaire may reckon it as much as he pleases to the credit
of the Marquis that he was one of the first among Italians
who had courage and strength enough to write a tragedy
without gallantry, in which the whole intrigue rests on
the love of a mother and the tenderest interest springs
from pure virtue. He may lament that the false delicacy
of his nation does not permit him to make use of the
easy natural means offered by the circumstances towards
the *dénouement*, and of the true unstudied speeches which
the matter itself suggests. The Parisian parterre is unquestionably much in the wrong in that it will not hear
of any ring upon the stage since Boileau mocked at the
royal ring in his Satires.[1] It is wrong in forcing its
poet rather to have recourse to every other, even the
most awkward means of recognition, than to employ a
ring, with which all the world, since all time has connected
a kind of recognition, a kind of assurance of personality.
It is wrong in not suffering a young man who deems
himself the son of common parents, who is wandering
about alone in search of adventures, not to be held to
be a robber, after he has committed a murder, because
it foresees that he must become the hero of the play,
and in being offended that such a man should not be
presumed capable of possessing a valuable ring, when
there is no lieutenant in the king's army who does not

---

[1] "Je n'ai pu me servir comme M. Maffei d'un anneau, parce que
depuis l'anneau royal dont Boileau se moque dans ses satyres, cela
semblerait trop petit sur notre théâtre."

own *de belles Nippes*.[2] The Parisian parterre, say I, is
wrong in this and similar cases; but why must Voltaire,
even in other cases where it certainly is not wrong, rather
prefer to make it seem wrong sooner than Maffei? If
French politeness towards strangers consists in making
them seem right even where they should be corrected,
then I do not know what is more offensive and unbecoming a free man, than this French politeness. The
gossip which Maffei puts into the mouth of old Polydorus
about merry weddings, and gorgeous coronations that he
has seen at a moment when our interest is at its height
and the imagination of the spectators is busy with quite
other things; its Nestorian, but misplaced Nestorian
gossip, cannot be excused by any difference of taste
between different cultivated peoples. In this, taste must
everywhere be the same, and the Italian has not his own
taste, but simply none, if he does not yawn and get as
impatient as the Frenchman. "You have been allowed,"
says Voltaire to the Marquis, "to translate and employ
in your tragedy that beautiful and touching comparison
of Virgil's—

"'Qualis populea mœrens Philomela sub umbra
    Amissos queritur fœtus . . .'

If I should take such a liberty I should be referred with
it to the epopee. For you cannot think how severe the
master is whom we must strive to please; I mean our
public. They demand that in a tragedy the hero should
speak everywhere and the poet nowhere, and contend that
at critical junctures in assemblies, at violent scenes, at
a threatening danger, no king, no minister would make
poetical comparisons." Now does such a public demand
anything unfair? Does it not contend the truth? Should
not every public demand this? contend this? A public
that judges otherwise does not merit the name, and must
Voltaire make the whole Italian public such a public,
just because he has not candour enough to say straight

---

[2] "Je n'oserais hasarder de faire prendre un héros pour un voleur,
quoique la circonstance où il se trouve autorise cette méprise.

out to the poet, that here and in several places he has
gone astray and poked his own head through the
curtain?

And leaving out of regard that detailed comparisons
scarcely find a fit place in a tragedy, he should have
noticed that Virgil's was greatly abused by Maffei.   In
Virgil it increases our pity, and that is its purpose, but
Maffei puts it into the mouth of him who rejoices over
the misfortune of which it is a picture, and to be in
accordance with Polyphontes's mood it ought to arouse
more scorn than pity. But Voltaire does not hesitate
to lay even greater faults that exert influence over the
whole play, to the charge of the Italian taste, rather
than to the charge of one poet among them. Voltaire
thinks that he displays the greatest *savoir vivre* when he
consoles Maffei by saying that the whole nation comprehends this no better than he does ; that his faults are the
faults of his nation, but that the faults of a whole nation
really were no faults, since it did not matter what was good
or bad in itself but what a whole nation deemed good or
bad.   " How could I have ventured," he continues, making
a deep bow to the Marquis and sneering at him in secret,
" how could I have ventured to let minor characters speak
so often one with another as you have done!   They serve
with you to prepare for the interesting scenes between
the chief characters ; they are the entrances to a beautiful
palace ; but our impatient public desires to find itself
instantly inside this palace. We must fain submit to
the taste of a people which has become satiated with
masterpieces and hence is spoilt."   What else does this
mean than : " M. le Marquis, your play contains very very
many cold, tedious and useless scenes. But far be it from
me to reproach you with these! Heaven forfend! I am
a Frenchman, I have *savoir vivre*, I should not force something unpleasant upon you. Beyond doubt you wrote
these cold, tedious useless scenes advisedly and with all
care, because they are just what your nation needs.   I
wish that I too could get off as cheaply, but alas! my
nation is so far, so very far ahead that I must be yet
farther to satisfy them.   I will not on that account think
more of myself than of you, but since my nation does so

far over-top yours——" Further I do not venture to
extend my paraphrase, for else—

"Desinit in piscem mulier formosa superne : "

politeness might become *persiflage* (I use this French
word because we Germans know nothing of the matter),
and *persiflage* stupid pride.

No. 42.

It is not to be denied that a goodly portion of the
faults which as idiosyncrasies of Italian taste Voltaire
only seems to excuse in his precursor in order to charge
them upon the whole Italian nation, these faults I say do
exist in the 'Merope' of Maffei, as well as other and far
greater ones. In his youth Maffei had much leaning
towards poetry, he versified with ease in all the various
styles of the famous poets of his country, but this inclination and this facility prove little or nothing in favour of
the peculiar genius that is required for tragedy. Afterwards he devoted himself to history, criticism and archæo-
logy, and I question whether these studies are the fittest
nourishment for a tragic genius. He was buried among
Church fathers and ecclesiastical documents and wrote
against the priests and Basnago, when, incited by social
circumstances, he took up his 'Merope' and finished it in
less than two months. If such a man, amidst such occupations could make a masterpiece in so short a time, he must
have had the most extraordinary head or else a tragedy
is a very slight affair. That however which a scholar of
good classical taste, who looks upon the matter rather
as a recreation than a labour worthy of him, could produce,
that he did produce. His treatment is more mannered
and artificial than felicitous, his characters are more in
accordance with the analysis of moralists, or after well-
known types in books, than drawn from life; his expressions evince more imagination than feeling; the *littérateur*
and the versifier are everywhere discernible, but rarely
the poet and the genius.

As a versifier he hunts greatly after descriptions and
metaphors. He has some most excellent ones, true pic-

tures, that cannot be enough admired if spoken by himself,
but which are quite unendurable spoken by his personages,
and even result in utter absurdities. Thus for example
it is very proper that Ægisthus should describe minutely
his struggle with the robber whom he murders, for on
this rests his defence ; but that when he confesses to have
thrown the corpse into the river, he should paint the
minutest phenomena that accompany the fall of a heavy
body into water, how it shoots down, with what sound
the waters divide, how it splashes up into the air, and how
the floods close up again,[1] this would not be forgiven even
to a cold garrulous lawyer who defends him, much less to
himself. Whoever stands before a judge to defend his
life has far other things near his heart than to be so
childishly accurate in his narrative.

As a literary man Maffei has shown too much reverence
for the simplicity of old Greek habits and costumes, such
as we find them depicted in Homer and Euripides. This
latter must be, I will not say ennobled, but brought
nearer to our costume if it is not to detract from the
pathos of tragedy. Also he has too evidently endeavoured
to imitate fine passages from the ancients, without distin-
guishing from what kind of works he borrows them and
into what kind of work he is transporting them. Nestor
in the epic is a friendly garrulous old man, but Polydorus
in the tragedy who is fashioned after him is a detestable
old chatterer. If Maffei had really followed the supposed
plan of Euripides, then the literary man would certainly
have made us laugh. He would have held it to be his
duty to use all the little fragments preserved of 'Kres-

Atto I. sc. 3 :—

". . . in core
Però mi venne di lanciar nel fiume
Il morto, o semivivo ; e con fatica
(Ch' inutil' era per riuscire, e vana)
L' alzai da terra, e in terra rimaneva
Una pozza di sangue : a mezzo il ponte
Portailo in fretta, di vermiglia striscia
Sempre rigando il suol ; quinci cadere
Col capo in giù il lasciai : piombo, e gran tonfo
S' udì nel profondarsi : in alto salse
Lo spruzzo, e l' onda sopra lui si chiuse."

phontes' and to work them neatly into his play.[2]   Wherever he thought they fitted he would have put them·up
as posts round which his dialogue must twine.   What
pedantic tyranny!   And to what end?   If it is not these
moral axioms with which space is filled up, well then it is
others.

Yet notwithstanding this, there are passages where we
might wish that the literary man had forgotten himself
less.   For instance: after the recognition and Merope's
discovery that she has twice been in danger of murdering
her own son, he makes Ismene exclaim with astonishment:
"What a wonderful event, more wonderful than was ever
conceived of on a stage!"

> "Con così strani avvennimenti uom forse
> Non vide mai favoleggiar le scene."

Maffei did not recollect that his play was laid at a time
when theatres were yet unknown; in the time before
Homer, whose poem scattered the first seeds of the drama.
I would not have laid stress on this heedlessness to any
person but to him who held it needful to excuse himself
in the preface, for employing the name Messene at a time
when beyond doubt no town of this name existed, since
Homer does not mention it.   A poet can treat such trifles
as he likes, we only demand that he should be consistent
and that he should not in one instance have scruples which
in another he boldly disregards, unless we are to believe
that the omission has arisen from ignorance rather than
from designed disregard.   Altogether the lines quoted
would not please me, even if they did not contain an
anachronism.   The tragedian should avoid everything
that can remind the audience of their illusion, for as soon
as they are reminded thereof the illusion is gone.   It almost
seems here as though Maffei sought to strengthen this
illusion by assuming the idea of a theatre outside the
theatre, but the mere words "stage" and "invention"

---

[2] "Non essendo dunque stato mio pensiero di seguir la Tragedia
d' Euripide, non ho cercato per consequenza di porre nella mia que,
sentimenti di essa, che son rimasti quà e là; avendone tradotti cinque
versi Cicerone, e recati tre passi Plutarco, e due versi Gellio, ed alcuni
trovandosene ancora, se la memoria non m' inganna, presso Stobeo."

are so prejudicial to the matter that they carry us straight
thither whence he would divert us. It is sooner permitted
to the comic poet thus to place representation in apposi-
tion to representation; for to rouse our laughter does not
require the same degree of illusion as to arouse our pity.

I have said already how severe De la Lindelle is upon
Maffei. According to him Maffei has been content with
what his material offered without bringing the smallest
art to bear on it; his dialogue is without reality, dignity
or grace; the play is full of petty contemptible matter
that would scarcely be tolerated in a harlequinade; it
overflows with absurdities and schoolboy faults. "In one
word," he concludes, "Maffei's work contains a fine subject, but is a wretched play. Every one in Paris is agreed
that it would not have been possible to sit out its representation, and even in Italy sensible people make small
account of it. In vain has the author on his various
journeys, lured the most miserable writers to translate
his tragedy; he could pay a translator more easily than
improve his piece."

As there are rarely compliments without some lies, so
there are rarely rude speeches without some truth.
Lindelle is right in several points, and he might be rude
or polite, so long as he was content merely to find fault
with Maffei. But he desires to tread him under foot, to
annihilate him, and sets to work blindly and perfidiously.
He is not ashamed to tell downright lies, to commit palpable forgeries, in order to be able to raise most malicious
laughter of contempt. Among three blows that he hits,
one always goes into the air, and of the other two that
should hit or graze his adversary, one infallibly hits
Voltaire also, for whose sake all this boxing match is
undertaken. Voltaire seems to have felt this in part, and
is therefore not slow in his answer to Lindelle, to defend
Maffei in all those points in which he thinks he must also
defend himself. This whole correspondence with oneself
lacks, it seems to me, its most interesting part, Maffei's
reply. If only M. de Voltaire would also communicate this
to us! Or was it perhaps not of the nature he had hoped
to provoke by his flatteries? Did Maffei perhaps take the
liberty to place before him in return the peculiarities of

the French taste? did he venture to show him why the
French 'Merope' could please as little in Italy, as the
Italian in France?

No. 43.

Something of the kind might be surmised. But I will
rather prove what I have said myself than surmise what
others may have said.

To begin with, Lindelle's blame may be mitigated in
almost every point. If Maffei has erred he has not always
erred so grossly as Lindelle would have us believe. For
instance he says that Ægisthus exclaims, "Oh, my old
father!" when Merope is about to smite him, and that
the queen is so touched by these words, "old father,"
that she abandons her purpose and conceives the notion
that Ægisthus might be her son. Is not this, he adds
maliciously, a well-founded conception? For certainly it
is something quite remarkable that a young man should
have an old father! "Maffei," he continues, "sought to
amend by this fault, this lack of art and genius, another
fault that he had committed in the first edition of his
play. In this Ægisthus exclaimed: 'Oh, Polydorus,
my father!' And this Polydorus was the very man to
whom Merope had confided her son. At the name
Polydorus the queen could no longer doubt that Ægisthus
is her son, and the play would have been at an end. Now the
fault is certainly removed, but its place has been occupied
by a more gross one." It is true, in the first edition
Ægisthus calls Polydorus his father; but in the following
editions there is no mention of a father. The queen only
starts at the name of Polydorus who warned Ægisthus not
to set foot in the realms of Messene. She does not on
that account abandon her design, she only demands an
explanation, and before she has obtained this the king
appears. The king causes Ægisthus to be released, and
since he lauds and approves the deed for which Ægisthus
has been condemned, and promises to reward it as an
heroic deed, Merope is obliged to fall back upon her
former suspicion. Can he be her son whom Polyphontes
seeks to reward for murdering this son? This conclusion
must needs weigh more with her than a mere name?

She now regrets that for a mere name's sake, a name many might bear, she hesitated in consummating her vengeance.

> " Che dubitar! misera, ed io da un nome
> Trattener mi lasciai, quasi un tal nome
> Altri aver non potesse——"

The subsequent utterances of the tyrant can only confirm her in her belief that he has the most certain and exact intelligence concerning the death of her son. Now is all this so very absurd? It does not seem so to me. I must rather admit that I do not even think Maffei's amendment was so needful. Let Ægisthus say that his father is named Polydorus. It does not make much difference whether it be his father or his friend who warns him against Messene. Enough that, failing contradiction, Merope must hold what the tyrant thinks of Ægisthus as more probable, since she knows that he has long and ardently pursued her son, than what she can infer from a mere coincidence of name. Certainly, if she knew that the tyrant's idea that Ægisthus is the murderer of her son is founded on nothing save her own suspicion, that would alter the matter. But she does not know this, and further she has every reason to believe that the tyrant is sure of his ground. It must be understood that I do not pronounce everything beautiful that can at need be excused; unquestionably the poet might have arranged his plot with more art. I only wish to say that even so as he has made it, Merope does not act without sufficient cause, and that it is very likely and possible that Merope will continue to harbour designs of vengeance which she will seek to execute at the first opportunity granted. That which would offend me therefore is not that she comes a second time to murder her son as the murderer of her son; but that she is bewildered a second time through a lucky chance event. I would pardon the poet if he did not let Merope decide according to the laws of the greater probability, for the passions that are awakened in her might turn the balance in favour of the weakest reasons. But I cannot pardon him for taking such liberties with accident and being so prodigal of wonderful

chance events as though they were the commonest events,
That chance may once lend pious aid to a mother,
may be; we will believe it the more willingly because
the surprise pleases us. But that the same hastiness is
checked a second time in the same way, this is not like
chance; the surprise repeated ceases to be a surprise, its
monotony offends and we are vexed with the poet who
knows how to be as marvellous but not as varied, as
chance.

Of Lindelle's most conspicuous and designed falsifica-
tions I will only instance two. He says : " The fourth act
begins with a cold and needless scene between the tyrant
and Merope's confidante; hereupon the confidante meets,
I know not how, the young Ægisthus, and persuades
him to repose in the atrium, in order that when he has
fallen asleep the queen may murder him with all ease.
He does indeed go to sleep, as he had promised, very
well; then comes the queen, a second time, axe in hand,
to murder the young man, who expressly sleeps for this
purpose. This same situation, twice repeated, betrays the
extremest poverty of idea, and the sleep of this young man
is so absurd that nothing in the world can be more ludicrous." But is it true that the confidante persuades him
into this sleep ? This is an untruth on Lindelle's part.[1]
Ægisthus meets the confidante and begs her to reveal to him
why the queen is so angered against him. The confidante
replies, she would gladly tell him all, but important business calls her elsewhere, he is to wait here a moment,
she will come back directly. The confidante certainly
intends to deliver him up into the hands of the queen, she
persuades him to remain but not to sleep, and Ægisthus,
who remains in accordance with his promise, falls asleep,
not in accordance with his promise but because he is tired,

---

[1] And M. de Voltaire's also. For not only Lindelle says: "Ensuite
cette suivante rencontre le jeune Égiste, je ne sais comment, et lui
persuade de se reposer dans le vestibule, afin que, quand il sera en-
dormi, la reine puisse le tuer tout à son aise;" but M. de Voltaire
himself says, " la confidante de Mérope engage le jeune Égiste à dormir
sur la scène, afin de donner le temps à la reine de venir l'y assassiner."
What is to be inferred from this unanimity I need not remark. It is
rare for a liar to agree with himself, and if two liars agree it must be a
prearranged concern.

because it is night and because he does not see where
else he should spend the night.[2] .Lindelle's second lie is
of the same kind.   He says : "Merope after she has been
hindered by old Polydorus from murdering her son, asks
him what reward he requires for his services, and the old
fool begs her to rejuvenate him."   Begs her to rejuvenate
him?   "The reward of my services," says the old man
"is to see you happy.   What could you give me?   I
need nothing, I ask nothing.[3]   One thing I might wish,
but that is neither in your power nor that of any mortal,
to grant, that the weight of years under which I groan
be lightened," &c.   Does that mean, "lighten thou
the load? give thou me back my strength and youth?"
I do not say that these complaints about the discomforts
of age are in their most appropriate place here, although
they are quite in keeping with the character of Polydorus.   But is every awkwardness a madness?   And
would not Polydorus and his poet be mad in the truest
sense if the latter really placed this petition in the mouth
of the former, as Lindelle falsely asserts?   Falsely
asserts!   Lies!   Do such trifles merit such hard words?
Trifles?   What Lindelle held important enough to lie

[2] Atto IV. sc. 2.

> EGI. Mà di tanto furor : di tanto affanno
> Qual' ebbe mai cagion? . . .
> ISM.   Il tutto
> Scoprirti io non ricuso : mà egli è d' uopo
> Che qui t' arresti per brev' ora : urgente
> Cura or mi chiama altrove.
> EGI.   Io volontieri
> T' attendo quanto vuoi. ISM. Mà non partire
> E non far sì, ch' io quà ritorni indarno.
> EGI. Mia fè dò in pegno ; e dove gir dovrei?—

[3] Atto IV. sc. 7.

> MER. Ma quale, ô mio fedel, qual potrò io
> Darti già mai mercè, che i merti agguagli?
> POL. Il mio stesso servir fu premio ; ed ora
> M'è, il vederti contenta, ampia mercede.
> Che vuoi tu darmi? io nulla bramo : caro
> Sol mi saria ciò, ch' altri dar non puote ;
> Che scemato mi fosse il grave incarco
> Degli anni, che mi stà sù 'l capo, e à terra
> Il curva, o preme sì, che parmi un monte—

about, should that not be important enough to justify a third person in telling him that he has lied?

No. 44.

I now come to Lindelle's blame which touches Voltaire as well as Maffei for whom it was alone intended.

I pass over the two points where Voltaire himself felt that the missile recoiled on him. Lindelle had said that the signs were weak and ignoble from which Maffei's Merope concluded that Ægisthus was the murderer of her son. Voltaire replied: "I cannot deny to you that I think Maffei has acted more artfully than I, in letting Merope believe that her son is the murderer of her son. He could employ a ring for this purpose and that I might not, for since the royal ring at which Boileau mocks in his 'Satires' that would seem very petty on our stage." But why need Voltaire choose old armour instead of a ring? When Narbas took away the child, what could have induced him to take the armour of the murdered king as well? In order that Ægisthus when grown up need not buy new armour but could use his father's old suit? The prudent old man! Did he not take a few old dresses of the mother's as well? Or did he do it that Ægisthus might some day be known by the armour? Such a suit of armour was probably unique? It was probably a suit of family armour that Vulcan himself had made for the great-grandfather. An impenetrable suit of armour? Or perchance embellished with beautiful figures and symbols at whose aspect Eurykles and Merope would recognise it after fifteen years? If this be so, then the old man certainly had to take it, and M. de Voltaire has cause to be grateful to him that, amidst the bloody confusion when another would only have thought of the child, he also thought of so useful a commodity. For if Ægisthus had to lose his father's kingdom, he need not lose his father's armour in which he might reconquer it. Secondly Lindelle has commented upon Maffei's Polyphontes who insists on wedding Merope. As if Voltaire's did not insist on this too! Voltaire therefore replies to him: "Neither Maffei nor I have made the reasons urgent enough why Polyphontes insists on having Merope as his spouse. It is perhaps a fault in the subject, but I acknowledge to you that I hold this fault very small if the interest it awakens be considerable." No, the fault is not in the subject. For in this respect Maffei changed the subject. Why need Voltaire have adopted this change if he did not see his advantage therein?

There are several points which Voltaire might have applied to himself; but what father sees all the faults of his child? The stranger who perceives them all at once, need not therefore be more observant than the father; sufficient that he is not the father. Let us assume that I am this stranger!

Lindelle objects in Maffei that he often leaves his scenes disconnected, the stage empty, that his personages often enter and exeunt without cause! all radical faults which we do not pardon nowadays in the most wretched poet. Radical faults these? But this is the French critic's mode of speaking, and I must allow him this if I do not want to begin with him from the very beginning. But radical or not as they may be, must we believe Lindelle's assertion that such are so rare among the poets of his nation? It is true it is they who boast of most obedience to rules, but it is they also who give to these rules such extension that it scarce repays the labour to bring them forward as rules; or else regard them in such a left-handed and forced manner, that it generally offends more to see them observed thus instead of not at all.[1] Voltaire especially is a master in the art of making the

---

[1] This was in part also Schlegel's verdict. "To tell the truth," he said, in his 'Thoughts for the Institution of a Danish Theatre,' "the English who boast of no unity of place, generally observe this better than the French, who give themselves many airs about following the rules of Aristotle so closely. Now it matters least that the picture of the scenes remains unaltered. But if there is no reason why the acting personages should be at one place instead of having stayed at another where they were before; if one person acts as master and inmate of a room in which shortly before another person acted as if he were master of the house, talking with all ease with himself or a confidante without this circumstance being excused on the score of probability; in short if the persons only come into this garden or room in order to enter on the stage, then the author of the

chains of rule so easy that he retains full freedom to
move about as he likes; and yet he often moves so
awkwardly and heavily and makes such vexatious gyra-
tions that we might almost believe every one of his limbs
was fastened to a different block. It costs me some
self-sacrifice to regard a work of genius from this point
of view; but as it is still so fashionable among the
commoner class of art critics to regard it from scarcely
any other; as it is that about which the admirers of the
French theatre make the most noise, I will look at it more
closely before I join their outcries.

I. The scene is at Messene in the palace of Merope.
This to begin with is not the stern unity of place,
which in accordance with the rules and examples of the
ancients, a Hedelin deemed he could demand. The scene
must not be the whole palace, but only a portion of
the palace, which the eye can overlook from one and
the same point of view. Whether it be a whole palace,
a whole town, or a whole province it is thus the same
impossibility. But Corneille already gave extension to
this rule, of which in any case there is no express mention among the ancients, and decreed that a single town
was sufficient for unity of place. If he wished to justify
his best pieces from this point of view, he was obliged
to relent so far. What was permitted to Corneille was
right for Voltaire. I therefore do not object that the
scene must be imagined now in the room of the queen,
now in this chamber, now in that atrium, now on this
side, now on that. Only in these changes he should have
taken the precaution that Corneille recommended; they
must not be employed in the same act, still less in the same
scene. The place where the act opens must remain through
the act, and to change it in one scene or to enlarge or

---

play would have done better to place the words 'the scene of action
is the theatre' upon his playbill, instead of 'the scene is a room in
the house of Climenes'; or, to speak more seriously, it would have
been far better if the author had followed the custom of the English
to change the scene from one house into another, and thus allow his
spectators to follow his hero, instead of giving the hero the trouble to
go to a place where he has nothing to do in order to please the
spectators."

contract it, is the greatest absurdity conceivable. The
third act of 'Merope' may occur out of doors, under
a corridor, in a saloon, in whose depths the monument
of Kresphontes is seen, at which the Queen intends to
slay Ægisthus with her own hand; but what can be
imagined more paltry than that, in the middle of the
fourth scene when Eurykles leads off Ægisthus, he must
close this background behind him. How does he close it?
Does a curtain fall over it? If ever what Hedelin says
of such curtains applied at all, it must apply to this one [2]
particularly if we also weigh the reasons why Ægisthus
is led away so suddenly, why he must be instantaneously
taken out of sight by means of this machinery whereof
later on. Just such a curtain is raised in the fifth act.
The first six scenes are laid in a hall in the palace and
with the seventh we suddenly have an open view into the
temple, in order that we may see a dead body in a bloody
robe. By what miracle this? And was the sight worth
the miracle? We may think that the doors of this temple
are suddenly opened, that Merope rushes out with the
whole people, and that we thus attain a look into it. I
understand; this temple was her widowed majesty's
private chapel that abutted on the hall and was in com-
munication with it, in order that her gracious highness
might always go dry-footed to her devotions. Only then
we ought not only to see them go out that way, but also see
them enter; at least we ought to see Ægisthus do so, who
at the end of the fourth scene is obliged to run and must
be sure to take the shortest road if eight lines farther
on he is already to have accomplished his deed.

No. 45.

II. Nor has M. de Voltaire made matters less easy to
himself in regard to the rules of unity of time. If we
consider all the events occurring in his 'Merope,' as occur-

---

[2] "On met des rideaux qui se tirent et retirent, pour faire que les
acteurs paroissent et disparoissent selon la nécessité du sujet—ces
rideaux ne sont bons qu'à faire des couvertures pour berner ceux qui
les ont inventés, et ceux qui les approuvent."—Pratique du Théâtre,
liv. ii. chap. 6.

ring on one day, what a number of absurdities we must
conceive. Let us assume a full, natural day, let us even
accord to it thirty hours, the limit to which Corneille
deemed it might be extended. It is true, I see no
physical hindrances why all the events could not have
occurred in this space of time, but I see the more moral
obstacles. It is certainly not impossible that a woman
should be wooed and married within twelve hours,
especially if we drag her by main force before the priests.
But if it occurs do we not require the most cogent and
urgent reasons for such forcible speed? And then if
not even a shadow of such reasons exist, how is that
which is only possible by physical means to appear
probable to us? The state desires to choose a king;
Polyphontes and the absent Ægisthus can alone come into
consideration; in order to nullify the claims of Ægisthus
Polyphontes seeks to marry his mother; on the very day
of the election he sues for her, she refuses him, the
election proceeds and results in his favour, Polyphontes
is now king and we should suppose that Ægisthus might
now appear whenever he willed, the newly elected king
would tolerate him awhile. Nothing of the sort; he insists
on the marriage, insists it should take place that very
day, the very day on which he has first offered his hand
to Merope, the very day on which the people have elected
him king. Such an old soldier and so fiery a wooer!
But his wooing is nothing save diplomacy. The worse
therefore to treat so harshly those whom he would entangle in his interests. Merope refused his hand when
he was not yet king, when she was forced to believe
that he principally sought her hand to help him upon
the throne, but now he is king and has become so without founding his claim on the score of being her husband;
he may renew his suit, perhaps she may yield, he should
leave her time to forget the social rank that once divided
them, to accustom her to look on him as her like, perchance it only needs a short time for this. If he cannot
win her, what boots it him to force her? Will it remain
a secret to her adherents that he forced her? Will they
not think they will have to hate him also for this? Will
they not therefore join themselves to Ægisthus whenever

he appears and regard themselves bound to fight in his
cause the cause of his mother? In vain that fate which
has been so dilatory the past fifteen years, now delivers
Ægisthus into the tyrant's hands and offers him a means
whereby he can possess the throne free from other claims,
a means far shorter and more infallible than the marriage
with the mother. He will and must be married, and
married to-day, this very evening, the new king will
claim the old queen to-night or he is not satisfied. Is
anything more comic conceivable! In the representation
I mean; for that a man with only a spark of sense could
act thus, is obviously out of the question. What good
does it do the poet, that the particular actions that occur
in every act would not require much more time for their
real occurrence than is occupied by the representation of
each act; and that this time, including what is absorbed
between the acts, would not nearly require a complete revolution of the sun; has he therefore regarded the unity of
time? He has fulfilled the words of the rule, but not
their spirit. For what he lets happen in one day, can
be done in one day it is true, but no sane mortal would
do it in one day. Physical unity of time is not sufficient,
the moral unity must also be considered, whose neglect is
felt by every one, while the neglect of the other, though
it generally involves an impossibility, is yet not so
generally offensive because this impossibility can remain
unknown to many. If, for instance, in a play a person
must travel from one place to another and this journey
alone would require more than a day, the fault is only
observed by those who know the distance of the locality.
Not everybody knows geographical distances, while
everybody can feel in him for what actions he would
allow himself one day, for what several. The poet
therefore who does not know how to preserve physical
unity of time except at the expense of moral unity,
who does not hesitate to sacrifice the one to the other,
consults his own interests badly and sacrifices the
essential to the accidental. Maffei at least, takes a
night to his aid, and the marriage which Polyphontes
suggests to-day is solemnised to-morrow. With him too
it is not the day on which Polyphontes ascends the throne,

hence circumstances press less closely, they hurry but they do not overhurry themselves. Voltaire's Polyphontes is an ephemeron of a king, who does not deserve to reign a second day, because he began so stupidly and badly on the first.

III. Lindelle says that Maffei often does not connect the scenes and leaves the theatre empty; a fault that nowadays would not be pardoned to the meanest poet. "The connexion of scenes," says Corneille, "is a great ornament to a poem and nothing can better assure us of the continuity of action than the continuity of representation. Still it is an ornament and no rule, for the ancients did not always submit to it," &c. How! has tragedy become so much more perfect with the French since the days of their great Corneille, that the lack of that which he held but an ornament, has now become an unpardonable fault? Or have the French since his time forgotten yet more the essential of tragedy, that they lay so much stress on matters that in the main have no value? Until this question is decided we may at least consider Corneille as trustworthy as Lindelle, and what, according to him, is no decided fault in Maffei may be placed against the less questionable one of Voltaire that he often leaves the stage much fuller than need be. When, for instance, in the first act, Polyphontes comes to the queen, and the queen goes out with the third scene, with what right can Polyphontes linger in the rooms of the queen? Is this room the place in which he should speak freely with his confidantes? The need of the poet is betrayed yet more in the fourth scene, in which we learn, it is true, matters which we must learn, but which we learn in a place where we should never have expected so to do.

IV. Maffei often does not justify the exits and entrances of his personages: Voltaire often justifies them falsely, which is far worse. It is not enough that a person says why he comes on, we ought also to perceive by the connexion that he must therefore come. It is not enough that he says why he goes off, we ought to see subsequently that he really went on that account. Else that which the poet places in his mouth is mere excuse and no cause. When for example, Eurykles goes off in the third scene of

the second act in order, as he says, to assemble the friends of
the queen, we ought to hear afterwards about these friends
and their assemblage.   As however we hear nothing of
the kind, his assertion is a schoolboy "Peto veniam ex-
eundi," the first falsehood that occurs to the boy.   He does
not go off in order to do what he says, but in order to return
a few lines further on as the bearer of news which the
poet did not know how to impart by means of any other
person.   Voltaire treats the end of whole acts yet more
clumsily.   At the close of the third act Polyphontes says
to Merope that the altar awaits her, that all is ready for
the solemnization of their marriage and he exits with a
Venez Madame.   But Madame does not come, but goes off
into another *coulisse* with an exclamation, whereupon Poly
phontes opens the fourth act, and instead of expressing
his annoyance that the queen has not followed him into
the temple (for he had been in error, there was still time
for the wedding) he talks with his Erox about matters
he should not ventilate here, that are more fitting conversation for his own house, his own rooms.   Then the
fourth act closes, closes exactly like the third.   Polyphontes again summons the queen into the temple, Merope
herself exclaims:—

"Courons tous vers le temple où m'attend mon outrage;"

and says to the chief priests who come to conduct her
thither:—

" Vous venez à l'autel entraîner la victime."

Consequently we must expect to see them inside the
temple at the beginning of the fifth act, or are they
already back again?   Neither; good things will take
time, Polyphontes has forgotten something and comes
back again and sends the queen back again.   Excellent!
Between the third and fourth, and between the fourth
and fifth acts nothing occurs that should, and indeed
nothing occurs at all, and the third and fourth acts only
close in order that the fourth and fifth may begin.

No. 46.

It is one thing to circumvent the rules, another to observe them. The French do the former, the latter was only understood by the ancients.

Unity of action was the first dramatic law of the ancients; unity of time and place were mere consequences of the former which they would scarcely have observed more strictly than exigency required had not the combination with the chorus arisen. For since their actions required the presence of a large body of people and this concourse always remained the same, who could go no further from their dwellings nor remain absent longer than it is customary to do from mere curiosity, they were almost obliged to make the scene of action one and the same spot and confine the time to one and the same day. They submitted *bonâ fide* to this restriction; but with a suppleness of understanding such that in seven cases out of nine they gained more than they lost thereby. For they used this restriction as a reason for simplifying the action and to cut away all that was superfluous, and thus, reduced to essentials, it became only the ideal of an action which was developed most felicitously in this form which required the least addition from circumstances of time and place.

The French on the contrary, who found no charms in true unity of action, who had been spoilt by the wild intrigues of the Spanish school, before they had learnt to know Greek simplicity, regarded the unity of time and place not as consequences of unity of action, but as circumstances absolutely needful to the representation of an action, to which they must therefore adapt their richer and more complicated actions with all the severity required in the use of a chorus, which however they had totally abolished. When they found however, how difficult, nay at times how impossible this was, they made a truce with the tyrannical rules against which they had not the courage to rebel. Instead of a single place, they introduced an uncertain place, under which we could imagine now this, now that spot; enough if the places combined were not too far apart and none required special scenery, so that the same scenery could fit the one about as well as the other. Instead of the unity of a day they substituted unity of duration, and a certain period during which no one spoke of sunrise or sunset, or went to bed, or at least did not go to bed more than once, however much might occur in this space, they allowed to pass as a day.

Now no one would have objected to this, for unquestionably even thus excellent plays can be made, and the proverb says; cut the wood where it is thinnest. But I must also allow my neighbour the same privilege. I must not always show him the thickest part, and cry, "There you must cut! That is where I cut!" Thus the French critics all exclaim, especially when they speak of the dramatic works of the English. What an ado they then make of regularity, that regularity which they have made so easy to themselves! But I am weary of dwelling on this point!

As far as I am concerned Voltaire's and Maffei's 'Merope' may extend over eight days and the scene may be laid in seven places in Greece! if only they had the beauties to make me forget these pedantries!

The strictest observation of the rules cannot outweigh the smallest fault in a character. How tamely Polyphontes talks and acts in Maffei's play has not escaped Lindelle. He is right to mock at the needless maxims that Maffei places in the tyrant's mouth. To remove the best and noblest in the state; to sink the people in sensuality that should sap its strength and make it effeminate; to leave unpunished the greatest crimes under the guise of pity and mercy, etc.; if there be tyrants who reign in this silly mode, will they boast of their method? Thus tyrants are depicted in a schoolboy's essay, but they never speak thus themselves.[1] It is true that Voltaire

---

[1] Atto III. sc. 2 :—

> ". . . Quando
> Saran da poi sopiti alquanto, e queti
> Gli animi, l' arte del regnar mi giovi.
> Per mute oblique vie n' andranno a Stige
> L' alme più audaci, e generose. A i vizi
> Per cui vigor si abbatte, ardir si toglie
> Il freno allargherò. Lunga clemenza

does not suffer his Polyphontes to declaim in so chilly and insane a manner, but occasionally he lets him say things that certainly no man of his kind would speak. For example :—

"Des Dieux quelquefois la longue patience
Fait sur nous à pas lents descendre la vengeance "—

A Polyphontes ought to make this reflexion, but he never does. Still less would he make it at a moment when he encourages himself to new crimes.

"Eh bien, encore ce crime !"   .   .   .

How absurdly he acts towards Merope I have already indicated. His behaviour towards Ægisthus is still less like a cunning and resolute man such as the poet depicted him at first. Ægisthus ought not to have appeared at the sacrifice. What was he to do there? To swear obedience? Before the people? Amid the cries of his despairing mother? Must not that inevitably occur which Polyphontes feared befoıe ?[2]   He has every thing to fear for his person from Ægisthus ; Ægisthus only

---

Con pompa di pietà farò, che splenda
Su i delinquenti ; a i gran delitti invito,
Onde restino i buoni esposti, e paghi
Renda gl' iniqui la licenza ; ed ondo
Poi fra se distruggendosi, in crudeli
Gare private il lor furor si stempri.
Udrai sovente risonar gli editti,
E raddopiar le leggi, che al sovrano
Giovan servate, e transgredite.   Udrai
Correr minaccia ognor di guerra esterna
Ond' io n' andrò su l' atterrita plebe
Sempre crescendo i pesi, e peregrine
Milizie introdurrò. . . ."

[2] **Acte I. sc. 4:**—

"Si ce fils, tant pleuré, dans Messène est produit,
De quinze ans de travaux j'ai perdu tout le fruit.
Crois-moi, ces préjugés de sang et de naissance
Revivront dans les cœurs, y prendront sa défenso.
Le souvenir du père, et cent rois pour ayeux,
Cet honneur prétendu d'être issu de nos Dieux ;
Les cris, le désespoir d'une mère éplorée,
Détruiront ma puissance encor mal assurée."

demands his sword back in order to decide the whole
quarrel between them, and this madly bold Ægisthus he
suffers to come near him at the altar where the first
implement he seizes upon, may be a sword.   Maffei's
Polyphontes is free from this absurdity, for he does not
know Ægisthus and deems him his friend.   What then
was to hinder Ægisthus from approaching him at the
altar?   No one observed his movements, the blow was
struck, the second ready before it occurred to any one to
avenge the first.

"Merope," says Lindelle " when Maffei lets her know that
her son is murdered, desires to tear the heart of the murderer from his body and to rend it with her teeth.[3]   That
is expressing oneself like a cannibal and not like a sorrow-
ing mother ; *bienséance* must everywhere be observed."
Quite true; but though the French Merope is too refined to
desire to eat such a raw heart without salt or dripping, yet
it seems to me that she is at bottom as much of a *cannibal*
as the Italian.

No. 47.

And how so?   If it is unquestionable that we must
judge men more by their deeds than by their words ; if a
hasty word spoken in the heat of passion proves little for
their moral character, but a deliberate cool action proves
all, then I am right.   Merope who abandons herself to
anxious sorrow while uncertainty reigns regarding her
son's fate, and who extends her pity to all unfortunates in
the remembering how unhappy her absent son may be, is
the beau ideal of a mother.   Merope who at the moment
that she hears of the loss of the object of all this tenderness, sinks down staggered and then rouses herself and
raves and threatens and intends to execute the most bloody,
most terrible vengeance on him who is in her power ; this

---

[3] Atto II. sc. 6:—

> " Quel scelerato in mio poter vorrei
> Per trarne prima, s' ebbe parte in questo
> Assassinio il tiranno ; io voglio poi
> Con una scure spalancargli il petto,
> Voglio strappargli il cor, voglio co' denti
> Lacerarlo, o sbranarlo. . . ."

Merope remains the same ideal, only in the condition of
violent action in which she gains in strength and expression what she has lost in beauty and tenderness. But
Merope who takes time for her revenge, prepares for it,
arranges solemnities for it, desires herself to be executioner,
not to kill but to torture, not to punish but to gloat over
the punishment, is this one a mother? Even so, but a
mother as we imagine her among cannibals, a mother such
as every she-bear is. This action of Merope may please
whom it lists, only let him not tell me that it pleases him, if
I am not to despise as well as loathe him. Perhaps M. de
Voltaire would put this down also to a fault in the subject; perhaps he would say Merope must kill Ægisthus
with her own hand or the whole *coup de théâtre* so praised
by Aristotle, which the sensitive Athenians so delighted
in, would fall away. But M. de Voltaire would be wrong
again, and again have confounded the arbitrary deviation
of Maffei with the subject itself. It is true the subject
demands that Merope should kill Ægisthus with her own
hand, but it does not demand that she should do so
upon reflexion. And without reflexion she must have
done it in Euripides if we are to regard Hyginus's fable as
the abstract of his play. The old man comes weeping to
the queen and says that her son has disappeared; she has
just heard that a stranger has arrived who boasts that he
has murdered him and that this stranger is sleeping
quietly under her roof; she seizes the first thing that
falls to hand, tears angrily into the room of the sleeper,
the old man follows her and the recognition occurs at the
moment in which the crime was to be perpetrated. That
was very simple and natural, very touching and human.
The Athenians trembled for Ægisthus without being
obliged to loathe Merope. They trembled for Merope
herself whose noble precipitancy made her run the risk of
being her son's murderer. Now Maffei and Voltaire only
make me tremble for Ægisthus, for I am so out of patience
with their Merope that I should almost like to see her execute her deed. Would that she might have this satisfaction!
If she can take time to execute her revenge she ought also
to have found time for investigation. Why is she such
a bloodthirsty animal? He has murdered her son; very

good, she may do with the murderer what she will in the
first heat of passion; I forgive her, for she is a mortal and
a mother. I will willingly weep and despair with her if
she should find how much cause she has to regret this
first rash heat. But madam, a young man who shortly
before interested you so much, in whom you recognised so
many signs of candour and innocence, need you slaughter
him with your own hand on the tomb of his father as the
murderer of your son, need you call priests and guards to
your aid because you find him in posession of an old
suit of armour that only your son should wear? Oh! fie!
madam. 1 am greatly mistaken if you would not have
been hissed in Athens.

That the maladroitness with which after fifteen years
Polyphontes demands the aged Merope as his wife is as
little a fault of the subject, I have mentioned before.
For according to Hyginus's fable Polyphontes married
Merope immediately after the murder of Kresphontes and
it is quite conceivable that Euripides should have assumed
this circumstance. And why not? The very reasons
with which Voltaire's Eurykles urges Merope after fifteen
years to bestow her hand upon the tyrant would have
been as valid fifteen years earlier.[1]   It was quite in

---

[1] Acte II. sc. 1:—

    " MER. Non, mon fils ne le souffrirait pas.
L'exil où son enfance a langui condamnée
Lui serait moins affreux que ce lâche hyménée.
    EUR. Il le condamnerait, si, paisible en son rang,
Il n'en croyait ici que les droits de son sang;
Mais, si par les malheurs son âme était instruite,
Sur ses vrais intérêts s'il réglait sa conduite,
De ses tristes amis s'il consultait la voix,
Et la nécessité souveraine des loix,
Il verrait que jamais sa malheureuse mère
Ne lui donna d'amour une marque plus chère.
    MER. Ah que me dites-vous?
    EUR.   De dures vérités
Qui m'arrachent mon zèle et vos calamités.
    MER. Quoi! Vous me demandez que l'intérêt surmonte
Cette invincible horreur que j'ai pour Polifonte!
Vous qui me l'avez peint de si noires couleurs!
    EUR. Je l'ai peint dangereux, je connais ses fureurs,
Mais il est tout-puissant; mais rien ne lui résiste;
Il est sans héritier, et vous aimez Égiste."

character with the ancient Greek women that they
conquered their abhorrence against the murderers of
their husbands and accept them in their place if they
thought that the children of their first marriage would
gain advantage thereby : I remember to have read something similar in the Greek novel of Chariton published
by D'Orville in which a mother very touchingly takes her
unborn child to judge between them. I think the passage
deserves to be quoted but I have not the book at hand.
Enough that that which Voltaire puts into the mouth of
Eurykles would have been sufficient to justify Merope's
conduct if he had introduced her as the wife of Polyphontes. The cold scenes of political love-making would
thereby have fallen away and I see more than one method
by which this might have heightened the interest and
made the situations yet more involved.

But Voltaire insisted on remaining on the road that
Maffei had levelled for him ; and because it never occurred
to him that there could be a better and that this better
was the one that had already been traversed in ancient
times, he satisfied himself with removing a few sand-
stones out of the path over which he thought his prede-
cessor had nearly capsized. Would he otherwise have
retained the circumstance that Ægisthus, ignorant of his
own identity, should accidentally have come to Messene,
and there have aroused the suspicion that he was his
own murderer owing to petty dubious indications? In
Euripides, Ægisthus knew himself perfectly, came to
Messene for the express purpose of revenging himself,
and gave himself out to be the murderer of Ægisthus.
He did not discover himself to his mother, be it from
suspicion, from caution, or from whatever cause, it is
certain that the poet did not let him lack for reasons. I
have above lent some of my own reasons to Maffei to account
for the changes he has made with Euripides' plot, but I
am far removed from regarding the reasons as sufficient,
the changes felicitous ; I rather assert that every step that
he ventured aside from the footprints of the Greeks
became a false step ; that Ægisthus does not know himself,
that he chances to come to Messene and " per combinazione
d' accidenti " (as Maffei expresses it) is regarded as the

murderer of Ægisthus, not only gives to the whole story
a very confused, dubious and romance-like aspect but
greatly weakens the interest. With Euripides the spectators knew from Ægisthus himself that it was Ægisthus,
and the more certainly they knew that Merope was coming
to murder her own son, the greater necessarily must be
the horror that possessed them on this account, the more
torturing the pity which befell them lest Merope should
not be hindered in time from the execution of her deed.
Now Maffei and Voltaire, on the contrary, only let us
suspect that the assumed murderer of the son may be the
son himself and our greatest terror is therefore reserved
for the sole moment in which it ceases to be terror. And
the worst is this, that the reasons which lead us to
suppose that the young stranger is the son of Merope are
the very reasons from which Merope should suppose this,
and we do not know him, especially in Voltaire, more
closely and certainly than she ought to know him herself.
We either trust as much to these reasons as Merope trusts
to them or we trust more. If we trust as much, we
must with her deem the youth a deceiver, and the fate
that she intends for him touches us very little. If we
trust more, we must censure Merope that she is not more
observant and lets herself be carried away by such
shallow reasons. Neither case is desirable.

No. 48.

It is true our surprise is greater if we do not know
with certainty that Ægisthus is Ægisthus before Merope
knows it. But what a poor amusement is this surprise!
And why need the poet surprise us? He may surprise
his personages as much as he likes. We shall still derive
our advantage therefrom, even if we have long foreseen
what befalls them so unexpectedly. Nay our sympathy
will be the more vivid and the stronger, the longer and
more certainly we have foreseen it.

On this point I will allow the best French art critic to
speak for me. " In involved plays," says Diderot,[1] " the

---

[1] In his dramatic poetics after the ' Père de famille.'

interest is owing more to the plot than to the words, while in simple plays, the effect rests on the words rather than on the plot. But to what is this interest to refer? To the personages? to the spectators? the spectators are only witnesses, of whom we know nothing, consequently it is the personages whom we must consider. Unquestionably. Let these knot the complication without knowing it, let it be impenetrable for them, bring them without their knowledge nearer and nearer to the *dénouement*. If the personages feel emotion we spectators shall yield to the same feelings, shall feel them also. I am far removed from believing with the majority of those who have written on the dramatic art that the *dénouement* should be hid from the spectator. I rather think it would not exceed my powers to rouse the very strongest interest in the spectators even if I resolved to make a work where the *dénouement* was revealed in the first scene. Everything must be clear for the spectator, he is the confidant of each person, he knows everything that occurs, everything that has occurred and there are hundreds of instances when we cannot do better than to tell him straight out what is going to occur.

"O ye manufacturers of general rules, how little do ye understand art, how little do ye possess of the genius that brought forth the masterpieces upon which ye build and which it may overstep as often as it lists!

My thoughts may appear as paradoxical as they like, yet so much I know for certain, that for one instance where it is useful to conceal from the spectator an important event until it has taken place there are ten and more where interest demands the very contrary. By means of secrecy a poet effects a short surprise, but in what enduring disquietude could he have maintained us if he had made no secret about it! Whoever is struck down in a moment, I can only pity for a moment. But how if I expect the blow, how if I see the storm brewing and threatening for some time about my head or his? For my part none of the personages need know each other if only the spectator knows them all. Nay I would even maintain that the subject which requires such secrecy is a thankless subject, that the plot in which we must have recourse

to it is not as good as that in which we could have done
without it.   It will never give occasion for anything
great.   We shall be obliged to occupy ourselves with
preparations that are either too dark or too clear, the
whole poem becomes a collection of little artistic tricks
by means of which we effect nothing more than a short
surprise.   If on the contrary everything that concerns
the personages is known, I see in this knowledge the
source of the most violent emotions.   Why have certain
monologues such a great effect?   Because they acquaint
me with the secret intentions of the speaker and this
confidence at once fills me with hope or fear.   If the
condition of the personages is unknown, the spectator
cannot interest himself more vividly in the action than
the personages.   But the interest would be doubled for
the spectator if light is thrown on the matter, and he
feels that action and speech would be quite otherwise if
the personages knew one another.

"Only then I shall scarcely be able to await what is to
become of them when I am able to compare that which
they really are with that which they do or would do."

On applying this to Ægisthus it is evident to which of
the two plots Diderot would incline: to the old one of
Euripides where the spectators know Ægisthus from the
beginning as well as he knows himself, or to the new one
of Maffei so blindly accepted by Voltaire where Ægisthus
is a riddle to himself and the spectators; and the whole
play is thus made into a collection of little artistic tricks
that effect nothing but a short surprise.

Diderot is not wrong in pronouncing his thoughts on
the superfluity and poverty of all uncertain expectations
and sudden surprises to be as new as they are valid.
They are new in regard to their abstraction, but very old
in regard to the patterns from which they are abstracted.
They are new in consideration that his predecessors have
always insisted on the contrary, but neither Horace nor
Aristotle belong to these predecessors, they never uttered
anything that could confirm their expounders and suc-
cessors in their predilection for this contrary method the
good effects of which they could not have perceived from
the greater number or from the best plays of the ancients.

Among these Euripides was so certain of himself that he
almost always showed his spectators the goal whither he
would lead them.   Nay, his prologues, which so grievously
offend modern critics, I should be greatly disposed to essay
a defence of, from this point of view.   "Not enough," says
Hedelin, " that he generally lets one of his chief characters
narrate to the spectators what has preceded the action of his
play in order to give them comprehension for what follows ;
he often employs a god for this purpose, of whom he may
assume that he knows everything and through whom he
acquaints us not only with what has occurred but with what
will occur.   We are thus initiated at the beginning into
the plot and the whole catastrophe, and foresee every
event.   This is a very serious fault, totally opposed to
that uncertainty and expectancy that should always reign
on the stage; it destroys all the pleasure of a play, that
should rest simply and solely on novelty and surprise."[2]
No, the most tragic of all tragic poets did not think so
meanly of his art, he knew it was capable of yet greater
perfection and that the gratification of a childish curiosity
was the least of the pretensions it set up.   He therefore
deliberately let his spectators know as much of the coming
action as any god might know, and promised to awaken
their emotions, not so much by that which should occur,
as by the mode in which it should occur.   Consequently
the art critics ought to find no stumbling-block here
except this, that he did not seek to convey to us the
necessary knowledge of the past and the future by a
more subtle mode, but that he had to employ for this a
Higher Being who probably had nothing to do with the
action, and that this Higher Being manifestly addressed the
spectators, by which means the dramatic genus was confounded with the narrative.   But if they restricted their
blame to this, what then is their blame?   Is the useful and
necessary never welcome to us except when it is secretly
forced upon us?   Are there not matters, especially in the
future, which no one but a god can know, and if the
interest rests on such matters, is it not better we should
know them beforehand through the intervention of a god

---

[1] Pratique du théâtre, liv. 3, chap. i.

than not at all? And finally what do we mean by the
mixtures of genres? In our primers it is right we should
separate them from one another as carefully as possible,
but if a genius, for higher purposes amalgamates several
of them in one and the same work, let us forget our primer
and only examine whether he has attained these higher
purposes. What do I care whether a play of Euripides
is neither wholly a narrative nor wholly a drama, call it a
hybrid, enough that this hybrid pleases me more, edifies me
more, than the most rule-correct creations of your correct
Racines or whatever else they may be called. Because
the mule is neither a horse nor an ass, is it therefore the
less one of the most useful beasts of burden?

No. 49.

In a word, where the detractors of Euripides see
nothing but a poet who from indolence or incapacity, or
both causes, endeavours to make his work as easy to himself
as possible; where they think that they discover dramatic
art in its cradle, I think I see it in its perfection, and
admire in Euripides the master who is in reality as correct as they demand, and only seems to be less correct
because he wished to impart to his plays one beauty more
for which they have no comprehension.

For it is clear that all the plays whose prologues annoy
them so much would be completely and entirely comprehensible without these prologues. Erase for instance from
'Ion' the prologue of Mercury, from 'Hecuba' the prologue of Polydorus, let the one begin with the morning
devotions of Ion, the other with the complaints of Hecuba,
is either of them therefore in the least mutilated? How
could you miss that which you have erased if it was not
there at all? Does not everything maintain the same sequence, the same connexion? You must even confess that
the plays would be more beautiful according to your mode
of thought if we did not know from the prologues that Ion,
whom Creusa intends to poison, is the son of this Creusa,
that this Creusa whom Ion wishes to tear from the altar to
a shameful death is the mother of this Ion: if we did not
know that on the very day on which Hecuba must

abandon her daughter for sacrifice the unhappy old
woman is also to hear of the death of her last surviving
son. For all these would bring about excellent surprises,
and these surprises would be sufficiently prepared without
your being able to say they suddenly broke out like
lightning from a white cloud; they do not follow,
they arise, it is not intended to disclose something to you
but to impose something upon you, and yet you still quarrel
with the poet? You still reproach him with want of art.
Forgive him a fault that a single stroke of the pen can
make good; a gardener quietly lops off the superfluous
branch, without scolding at the healthy tree that has
brought it forth. Now if you would assume for a moment
—it is true I am going to ask you to assume a great deal
—that Euripides had as much insight, could have as much
taste as you, and you wonder the more how with so much
insight, so refined taste, he yet could commit so grave a
fault, come over to me and regard what you call his faults
from my point of view.   Euripides knew as well as we
that his 'Ion' for instance could stand without the prologue, that without this it was a play which sustained
the interest and uncertainty of the spectator to the close,
but he did not care for this uncertainty and expectation.
For if the spectator only learned in the fifth act that Ion
was the son of Creusa, then it is not for them her son,
but a stranger, an enemy, whom she seeks to make away
with in the third act; then it is not for them the mother
of Ion on whom Ion seeks to avenge himself in the fourth
act, but only a murderess.   Whence then should fear and
pity arise?   The mere presumption that could be deduced
from coincident circumstances that Ion and Creusa might
have some connexion would not be sufficient for this,
this assumption must become a certainty, and if the
spectator could only receive this certainty from outside,
if it was not possible for one of the acting personages to
initiate him, was it not better that the poet should
initiate him in the only possible way rather than not at
all? Say of this method what you will, enough if it has
helped him to attain his goal, his tragedy is throughout
what a tragedy should be, and if you are still dissatisfied
that the form should give place to the essential then

supply your learned criticism with nothing but plays
where the essential is sacrificed to the form, and you are
rewarded. Let Whitehead's 'Creusa' please you henceforth, in which no god predicts, in which you learn everything from an old garrulous confidante who is questioned
by a cunning gipsy, let these please you better henceforth
than Euripides' 'Ion,' I shall not envy you.

When Aristotle speaks of Euripides as the most tragic
of all tragic poets he did not merely mean that most of
his plays end with an unhappy catastrophe, although I
am aware that many thus interpret the Stagyrite. For
this trick could easily be copied, and the bungler who
murders and slaughters right and left, and allows none of
his personages to leave the stage whole or alive, would
then be permitted to think himself as tragic as Euripides.
Unquestionably Aristotle had various qualities in mind
when he accorded him this epithet. No doubt the above-
named quality belonged to those by means of which the
author let the spectators foresee all the misfortunes that
were to befall his personages, in order to gain their
sympathy while these were yet far removed from
deeming that they required sympathy. Sokrates was the
master and friend of Euripides, and hence how many
might imagine that the poet owed to this friendship with
the philosopher all the wealth of splendid maxims that
he has scattered so profusely throughout his plays! I
think that he owed far more to him; he might have been
just as rich in maxims without him, but he would
scarcely have been as tragic without him. Fine sentences
and moral maxims are just what we are likely to hear
least from a philosopher like Sokrates, his life was the
only moral that he preached. But what we learn in his
society is to know man and ourselves; to be observant of
our emotions; to search for and to love the smoothest and
shortest paths of nature; to judge each matter according
to its intention; this was what Euripides learned from
Sokrates and what made him the first in his art. Happy
the poet who has such a friend and can consult with him
every day, every hour.

Even Voltaire seems to have felt that it would be well
if he could acquaint us from the beginning with the son

of Merope, if we could start with the knowledge that the amiable unhappy youth whom Merope shields at first, and whom she afterwards desires to kill as the murderer of her Ægisthus, is Ægisthus himself. But the youth does not know himself, and there is no one there who knows him better and through whom he could learn it. What then does the poet do? How does he provide that we should know with certainty that Merope is raising the dagger against her own son, even before old Narbas calls to her? Oh! he sets about this most cunningly! Only a Voltaire could have thought of such an artistic trick. As soon as the unknown youth enters, he places the name Ægisthus in large, distinct beautiful letters over the first speech he has to make, and so on over all the following. Now we know it, for Merope has in the preceding scenes named her son more than once, and even if she had not done so we need only refer to the list of *Dramatis personæ* printed at the commencement, to find it there in full! It is certainly rather comic when the person above whose speeches we have a dozen times read the name Ægisthus, on being asked:—

"Narbas vous est connu?
Le nom d'Égiste au moins jusqu'à vous est venu?
Quel était votre état, votre rang, votre père?"

replies:—

"Mon père est un vieillard accablé de misère;
Polyclète est son nom; mais Égiste, Narbas,
Ceux dont vous me parlez, je ne les connais pas."

It is also remarkable that we hear no other name from this Ægisthus who is not called Ægisthus; that when he replies to the queen that his father is called Polycletus, he does not add, and I am called so and so. For a name he must needs have, and M. de Voltaire could surely have invented that also, seeing he has invented so much! Readers who are not well acquainted with the tricks of a tragedy, could easily go astray here. They read that a youth is brought in who has committed murder on the highway; this youth they see is named Ægisthus, but he says he is not called so, and yet does not say what he is called. Oh! this youth, they presume, is not all right, he is an accomplished highwayman, young though he is, and innocently though he poses. Thus, I say, inexperienced readers are in danger of concluding; and yet I believe seriously speaking, that it is better that the experienced reader should learn even in this wise from the beginning who the unknown youth is, than not at all. Only do not tell me that this method of informing them is in the least bit more artistic and subtle than a prologue after the manner of Euripides.

No. 50.

Maffei gives the youth his two names, as is due: he is called Ægisthus as the son of Polydorus and Kresphontes as the son of Merope. In the list of personages he is only introduced under the former name, and Becelli took no small credit to himself for the fact that in his edition of the play, the true identity of Ægisthus could not be guessed.[1] For the Italians are even greater friends to surprises than the French.

But Merope for ever! In truth I pity my readers who promised to themselves in this journal a theatrical newspaper as varied and manifold, as amusing and comical as a theatrical newspaper should be. Instead of containing the story of the plays performed, told in short lively and touching romances, instead of detailed biographies of absurd, eccentric, foolish beings, such as those must be who concern themselves with writing comedies, instead of amusing, even slightly scandalous anecdotes of actors and especially actresses, instead of all these pretty things which they expected, they get long, serious, dry criticisms of old well-known plays; ponderous examinations of what tragedy should or should not be, at times even expositions of Aristotle. And they are to read this? As I say, I pity them; they have been grievously deceived. But let me add in confidence, better they,

---

[1] " Fin ne i nomi de' Personnaggi si è levato quell' errore, comunissimo alle stampe d' ogni drama, di scoprire il secreto nel premettergli, e per conseguenza di levare il piacere a chi legge, overo ascolta, essendosi messo Egisto, dove era, Cresfonte sotto nome d'Egisto."

than I. And I should be much deceived if I made their
expectations my law. Not that their expectations
would be very difficult to fulfil; no indeed, I should
rather find them very easy, if only they agreed better
with my intentions.

But I must indeed try to get over the subject of
' Merope.' I really only wished to show that Voltaire's
' Merope' was *au fond* nothing but the ' Merope' of Maffei,
and I think I have proved this. Aristotle says that it is
not the same subject, but the same treatment and *dénouement* that make two or more plays to be held one and
the same. Therefore it is not because Voltaire has
treated the same story as Maffei, but because he has
treated it in the same way, that I here pronounce him
nothing but the translator and imitator of Maffei; Maffei
did not merely reconstruct the ' Merope' of Euripides, he
made a ' Merope' of his own; for he departed utterly from
the plan of Euripides, and in the intention to write a play
without love, in which the whole interest hinges on
maternal affection, he subverted the entire fable; whether
for good or evil is not in question here, he subverted it
totally. Voltaire took from Maffei this whole subverted
fable; he took from him the fact that Merope is not married to Polyphontes; he took from him the political reasons
for which the tyrant thinks he must, after fifteen years,
insist on this union; he took from him the fact that the
son of Merope does not know himself; he took from him
the cause and manner of his leaving his reputed father;
he took from him the incident that Ægisthus is brought
to Messene as a murderer; he took from him the misunderstanding by means of which he is held to be his
own murderer; he took from him the vague emotions of
maternal love when Merope sees Ægisthus for the first
time; he took from him the reason why Ægisthus was to
die before Merope's eyes, by her hand; he took from him
the discovery of his accomplices; in short Voltaire took
from Maffei the whole plot. And did he not further
borrow from him the whole *dénouement*? did he not learn
from him to connect the sacrifice at which Polyphontes is
to be murdered with the entire action? Maffei made it a
marriage-feast, and perhaps he only let his tyrant at last

think of this union with Merope, in order that the sacrifice might be brought in more naturally, What Maffei invented, Voltaire copied.

It is true that Voltaire has given a different turn to some of the events that he took from Maffei. For instance, instead of Polyphontes having already reigned fifteen years, he allows disorder to have existed in Messene for fifteen years and thus leaves the state in probable anarchy for this long time. Instead of making Ægisthus be attacked on the high-road by a robber, he makes him be attacked in the temple of Hercules, by two unknown personages who are offended at his invoking the aid of Hercules for the Heraclidæ, the god of the temple for his descendants. Instead of letting suspicion be aroused by a ring, as in Maffei, Voltaire arouses this by armour, and so on. But all these changes only regard trifles, that are nearly all beside the play and have no influence on its economy. And yet I would allow these changes to Voltaire as expressions of his creative genius if I could only discover that he had understood how to alter that which he thought required alteration. I will explain myself by one of the quoted examples. Maffei makes his Ægisthus be attacked by a robber who seizes the moment when he sees him alone on the high-road, near to a bridge over the Pamisus. Ægisthus overcomes the robber and throws his body into the river, out of fear that if the body be found in the road, the murderer may be pursued and he be recognised as such. A robber who wishes to rob a prince of his coat and purse is far too common a picture for my noble, delicate *parterre*, thought Voltaire; it would be better to make out of this robber a malcontent who desires to put Ægisthus out of the way as a follower of the Heraclidæ. And why only one? Better two, that makes Ægisthus's heroic deed the greater, and the one who escapes of these two, if I make him much older, can afterwards be regarded as Narbas. Very good, my dear compiler, but now farther, what next? When Ægisthus has killed one of these malcontents, what does he do then? He also carries the dead body to the water. What? and how? and why? From the deserted road to the near river, that is comprehensible; but from the temple

to the river? Was no one then in the temple except
these three? Granted even this, for even this is not the
greatest absurdity. The *how* could be yet imagined, but
not the why. Maffei's Ægisthus bears the body to the
river because he fears to be pursued and recognised,
because he thinks that if he has made away with the
body, nothing can reveal his deed, that this will be
buried in the river with the corpse. But can Voltaire's
Ægisthus imagine this? Never more, or the second man
ought not to have escaped. Will this one be satisfied that
he has escaped with his life? Will he not observe him
from afar, however affrighted he may be? Will he not
pursue him with cries until others detain him? Will he
not indict him and bear witness against him? What will
it then avail the murderer that he has borne the *corpus
delicti* out of the way? Here is an eye-witness who can
prove all. He might have saved himself this useless
trouble and rather have hurried to get across the
boundary. It is true that the body had to be thrown
into the water because of what was coming after; it was
as needful for Voltaire as for Maffei that Merope should
not be undeceived by its aspect; only that what in the
one case Ægisthus does for his own benefit, he does for
the benefit of the poet in the other. For Voltaire
corrected away the cause without reflecting that he
needed the effect of this cause, which henceforward
depended on nothing but his necessity.

One single change made by Voltaire in Maffei's plan
deserves the name of an improvement; namely that of
suppressing Merope's repeated attempts to avenge herself
on her son's presumed murderer, and letting the recognition on the part of Ægisthus take place in the presence
of Polyphontes. Herein I recognise the poet, and especially the second scene of the fourth act is excellent. I
only wish that the general recognition that must follow
in the fourth scene of the third act had been managed
with more art. For that Ægisthus is suddenly led away
by Eurykles and that the depth of the scene closes behind
him, is a very forced method. It is not a hair's-breadth
better than the precipitate flight by which Ægisthus
saves himself in Maffei and concerning which Voltaire

lets Lindelle speak so mockingly. Or rather this flight
is more natural if only the poet had afterwards brought
mother and son once together and had not entirely kept
from us the first touching expressions of their mutual
emotions. Perhaps Voltaire would not have separated
the recognition scene if he had not been forced to expand
his material in order to make five acts of it. He com-
plains more than once about " cette longue carrière de
cinq actes qui est prodigieusement difficile à remplir sans
episodes."—And now for the present enough of ' Merope.'

Nos. 54 and 55.

[Lessing treats at great length the source and subject of
an English tragedy by John Banks : ' The Earl of Essex.'
Referring to the box on the ear given by the Queen to
Essex, he proceeds to treat of this in general.]

A box on the ear in a tragedy! How English, how
unbecoming! But before my over-refined readers mock at
this too much, I beg to remind them of a similar act in
the ' Cid.' M. de Voltaire's commentary concerning this
is curious in many respects. " Nowadays," he says, " we
should not dare to allow our heroes to have their ears
boxed. The actors themselves would not know how to
set about this, they only make believe to give one. Not
even in comedy is such a thing allowed any longer, and
this is the only example we have of it on the tragic stage."
" It is possible that this among other reasons may explain
why the ' Cid ' has been named a tragi-comedy, and at
that time nearly all the plays of Scuderi and Boisrobert
were tragi-comedies. We had long been of opinion in
France that uninterrupted tragedy, without any intermixture of common traits, was not to be borne. The
word tragi-comedy itself is very old. Plautus employs it to
define his ' Amphitryon,' because though the adventure of
Sosia is comic, Amphitryon himself is seriously distressed
thereby." What things M. de Voltaire does write! How
gladly he turns on a little learning and how ill it
generally becomes him!

It is not true that the box on the ear in the ' Cid ' is
the only one on the tragic stage. Voltaire either did not

know the Essex of Banks or he assumed that the tragic
stage of his nation alone deserved the name. Either
hypothesis betrays ignorance, and the latter yet more
vanity than ignorance. What he adds about the name of
tragi-comedy is equally false. Tragi-comedy is the representation of an important action that takes place among
noble persons and has a happy end. Such is the ' Cid '
and the box on the ear did not come into consideration, for
notwithstanding this box on the ear, Corneille afterwards
called his play a tragedy, as soon as he had put aside the
prejudice that a tragedy must of necessity have an unhappy catastrophe. Plautus does employ the word *tragico-
comœdia*, but he only uses it in fun and not to define
a special genus. Neither has any one borrowed it of him
in this sense, until it occurred to the Spanish and Italian
poets of the sixteenth century thus to name certain of
their dramatic abortions. But even if Plautus had seriously
named his ' Amphitryon ' thus, it would yet not have arisen
from the cause invented by Voltaire. It is not because
Sosia's share in the action is comic, Amphitryon's tragic,
that Plautus would have named his play a tragi-comedy.
For his play is altogether comic and we as much enjoy
Amphitryon's perplexity as Sosia's. It must have been
because this comic action passes chiefly among nobler
personages than it was usual to see in a comedy. Plautus
himself clearly expresses this.

" Faciam ut commixta sit Tragico-comœdia :
  Nam me perpetuo facere ut sit Comœdia
  Reges quo veniant et dî, non par arbitror.
  Quid igitur? quoniam hic servus quoque partes habet,
  Faciam hanc, proinde ut dixi, Tragico-comœdiam."

No. 56.

But to return to the box on the ear. It is the case that a
box on the ear received by a man of honour from his equal
or superior, is held to be a grave offence, so that all the
satisfaction that the laws could give are held vain. It
cannot be punished by a third person, it requires the
personal revenge of the offended party and demands to be

avenged as arbitrarily as it was offered. Whether it is
true or false honour that requires this, that is beside our
present question. As I have said, so it is.

And if it is so in the world, why should it not be
so on the stage? If a box on the ear can occur in the
one, why not in the other?

"The actors do not know how to set about it," says M.
de Voltaire. They know quite well, but even as an
assumed person no one likes to have a box on the ear.
The blow excites them, the assumed character receives it,
but they feel it; the feeling destroys the deception, they
lose their composure, shame and confusion shows itself in
their faces against their will; they should look angry and
they look ridiculous; and thus every actor whose own
feelings come into collision with his *rôle* makes us laugh.

This is not the only instance in which we might regret
the abolition of masks. The actor can unquestionably
better command his countenance under a mask; his personality finds less opportunity to break forth and if it
does break forth we are less aware of this.

But the actor may act under the box on the ear as he
wills; the dramatic poet works for the actor it is true, but
he must not therefore deny himself everything that does
not suit or is not easy to the actor. No actor can blush
when he likes, and still the poet may prescribe it; still he
may let one person say that he sees the other changing
colour. The actor does not want to be struck in the face,
he thinks it makes him contemptible, it confuses him, it
pains him: very good. If he has not got so far in his art
that such a thing cannot confuse him; if he does not love
his art so much that for its sake he can bear a little hurt
to his dignity; then let him try to get over the passage
as well as he can, let him avoid the blow, ward it off with
his hand, only do not let him demand that the poet should
take more concern for him than he takes for the person
whom he represents. If the true Diego, the true Essex
must bear a box on the ear, what have their representatives
to say against it?

Perhaps the spectator does not want to see a box on the
ear given? or at most given to a servant whom it does not
especially offend and for whose position it is a proper

chastisement, while a hero—to give a hero a box on the
ear! how petty, how unbecoming! And what if that is just
its very purpose? If this very breach of the decorous is
to be the source of violent resolutions, bloody revenge? If
every other less petty offence could not have provoked this
terrible result? Should that which can become so tragical
in its consequences, which among certain persons necessarily must become tragical, should that be excluded from
tragedy because it finds a place also in comedy, in farce?
Can we not be terrified at one time by that which another
time makes us laugh?

If I should like to banish the box on the ear from any
sort of drama it would be from comedy. For what consequences can it have there? Sad ones? they are beyond
its sphere. Ridiculous ones? they are beneath it and
belong to farce. None? then it was not worth while to
introduce the element. Whoever gives it will only betray
vulgar passion and whoever receives it, nothing but
slavish pusillanimity. It remains consequently to the
two extremes; tragedy and farce, that have more of such
things in common over which we either tremble or jeer.

Now I ask every one who has seen the 'Cid' represented
or who has read it with attention, whether a shudder did
not take hold of him when the boastful Gormas ventures
to strike the old venerable Diego; whether he did not
feel the deepest pity for the one, the bitterest anger
against the other? I ask him whether it did not at once
flash through his brain what sad and bloody consequences
this shameful offence must bring with it, and whether
this did not fill him with fear and expectation? And such
an incident, which has such an effect, should not be
tragical.

If ever any one laughed at this box on the ear, it was
certainly one of the gallery who was too familiar with
boxes on the ear and deserved one at that moment from
his neighbour. And whoever felt inclined to smile
against his will, on account of the awkward manner in
which the actors set about it, certainly bit his lips and
made haste to fall back again into the illusion out of
which every violent action is apt more or less to tear the
spectator.

Moreover I ask, what other offence could so well fill the place of the box on the ears? For every other it would be in the power of a king to give satisfaction to the offended; for every other the son might refuse to sacrifice his father to the father of his beloved. For this alone excuse or pardon cannot avail the *pundonor*, and all legitimate means that the monarch himself would employ are fruitless. In this frame of mind Corneille lets Gormas reply to the king, who urges him to satisfy Diego :—

> " Ces satisfactions n'apaisent point une âme :
> Qui les reçoit n'a rien, qui les fait se diffame,
> Et de tous ces accords l'effet le plus commun,
> C'est de déshonorer deux hommes au lieu d'un."

At that time the edicts against duels, to which such maxims were utterly opposed, had not been long promulgated in France. Corneille received an order to omit the lines, and they were banished out of the mouth of the actor. But every spectator supplemented them from memory and from his own feeling.

In 'Essex' the box on the ear becomes the more critical in that it is given by a person who is not bound by the laws of honour. She is a woman and a queen, what is the offender to do with her? He would ridicule the impetuous, pugnacious woman, for a woman can neither shame us nor beat us. But this woman is at the same time a sovereign, whose indignities cannot be expunged, since they receive a kind of authority from her rank. What therefore can be more natural than that Essex revolts against this rank itself and rages against the eminence that removes the offender from his revenge.

.   .   .   .

No. 59.

.   .   .   .

Many hold pompous and tragic to be much the same thing. Not only many of the readers but many of the poets themselves. What! their heroes are to talk like ordinary mortals! What sort of heroes would those be ? " Ampullæ et sesquipedalia verba," sentences and bubbles

and words a yard long, this constitutes for them the true
tone of tragedy.

Diderot says,[1] " We have not omitted anything that
could spoil the drama from its very foundations." (Observe that he speaks especially of his countrymen.) " We
have retained the whole splendid versification of the
ancients that is really only suited to a language of very
measured quantities and very marked accents, for very
large stages and for a declamation fitted to music and
accompanied with instruments. But its simplicity in
plot and conversation and the truth of its pictures we
have abandoned."

Diderot might have added another reason why we
cannot throughout take the old tragedies for our pattern.
There all the personages speak and converse in a free public place, in presence of an inquisitive multitude. They
must therefore nearly always speak with reserve and due
regard to their dignity; they cannot give vent to their
thoughts and feelings in the first words that come, they
must weigh and choose them. But we moderns, who have
abolished the chorus, who generally leave our personages
between four walls, what reason have we to let them
employ such choice stilted rhetorical speech notwithstanding? Nobody hears it except those whom they
permit to hear it; nobody speaks to them but people
who are involved in the action, who are therefore themselves affected and have neither desire nor leisure to control expressions. This was only to be feared from the
chorus who never acted, however much they might be
involved in the play, and always rather judged the acting
personages than took a real part in their fate. It is as
useless to invoke the high rank of the personages;
aristocratic persons have learned how to express themselves better than the common man, but they do not affect
incessantly to express themselves better than he. Least
of all in moments of passion; since every passion has its
own eloquence, is alone inspired by nature, is learnt in no
school and is understood by the most uneducated as well
as by the most polished.

[1] Second conversation following 'The Natural Son.'

There never can be feeling with a stilted, chosen, pompous, language. It is not born of feeling, it cannot evoke it. But feeling agrees with the simplest, commonest, plainest words and expressions. . . .

Nothing is more chaste and decent than simple Nature, coarseness and confusion are as far removed from her as pomposity and bombast from the sublime. The same feeling which makes the boundary there, makes it here. The most pompous poet is therefore infallibly the most vulgar. Both faults are inseparable, and no species gives more opportunities of falling into both than tragedy.

[Lessing now devotes many pages to a detailed account of an old and anonymous Spanish play dealing with the subject of Essex.]

No. 69.

Although Lope de Vega is regarded as the creator of the Spanish theatre, it was not he who introduced its hybrid tone. The people were already so accustomed to it, that he had to assume it against his will. In his didactic poem concerning the art of making new comedies he greatly laments the fact. As he saw that it was not possible to work to the satisfaction of his contemporaries according to the rules and example of the ancients, he strove at least to put limits to their irregularities ; that was the intention of his poem. He thought, wild and barbaric as the taste of the nation was, it must yet have its principles, and it was better to act according to these with constant uniformity than with none. Plays which do not observe the classical rules may yet observe rules, and must observe something of the kind, if they are to please. These rules deduced from the national taste he wished to establish, and the combination of the serious and the ludicrous was the first.

He said, "You may let kings appear in your comedies. It is true I hear that our wise monarch (Philip II.) did not approve of this, either because he recognised that it was against the rules, or because he deemed it beneath the dignity of a king to be mixed up with the populace. I am willing to admit that this leads back to the oldest comedies, which even introduced gods ; as may be seen amongst others in the ' Amphitryon ' of Plautus and I know well that Plutarch, when he speaks of Menander does not praise the old comedy very much. It is therefore somewhat difficult to me to approve our fashion. But since we in Spain do so far diverge from art, the learned must keep silent on this point. It is true that the tragic fused with the comic, Seneca mingled with Terence, produces no less a monster than was Pasiphae's ' Minotaur.' But this abnormity pleases, people will not see any other plays but such as are half serious, half ludicrous, nature herself teaches this variety from which she borrows part of her beauty."[1]

It is on account of these last words that I quote this passage. Is it true that nature sets us an example of the common and sublime, the farcical and serious, the merry and sad ? It seems so. But if it is true Lope has done more than he intended, he has not only glossed over the faults of his stage, he has really proved that these are no faults, for nothing can be a fault that is an imitation of nature.

[1] " Elígese el sujeto, y no se mire,
  (Perdonen los preceptos) si es de Reyes,
  Aunque por esto entiendo, que el prudente,
  Filipo Rey de España, y Señor nuestro,
  En viendo un Rey en ellos se enfadava,
  O fuesse el ver, que al arte contradize,
  O que la autoridad real no deve
  Andar fingida entre la humilde plebe,
  Este es bolver á la Comedia antigua,
  Donde vemos, que Plauto puso Dioses,
  Como en su Anfitrion lo muestra Jupiter,
  Sabe Dios, que me pesa de aprovarlo,
  Porque Plutarco hablando de Menandro,
  No siente bien de la Comedia antigua,
  Mas pues del arte vamos tan remotos,
  Y en España le hazemos mil agravios,
  Cierren los Doctos esta vez los labios.
    Lo Trágico, y lo Cómico mezclado
  Y Terencio con Seneca, aunque sea,
  Como otro Minotauro de Pasife,
  Harán grave una parte, otra ridícula
  Que aquesta variedad deleyta mucho
  Buen ejemplo nos da naturaleza,
  Que por tal variedad tiene belleza."

One of our modern writers says,[2] "Shakespeare, of all poets since Homer the one who has known men best, who has looked them through and through with a kind of marvellous intuition, from the king to the beggar, from Julius Cæsar to Jack Falstaff, Shakespeare has been blamed that his plays have a very faulty, irregular or badly devised plot; that comic and tragic are thrown together in the strangest manner; that often the very same person that has called up our tears by his touching language, will a few moments afterwards by a strange fancy, a quaint expression of his emotions, chill us, nay even make us laugh, so that afterwards it is difficult for him to get us back into the mood in which he would have us. People blame this and do not consider that just on this account his plays are such natural representations of human life.

" The life of most people and, if we may say so, the life-course of the bodies politic themselves, in so far as we regard it as so many ethical beings, resembles in so many respects the blood-and-thunder tragedies ('Haupt- und Staatsactionen') of old Gothic taste, that we could almost imagine the inventors of these had been wiser than we commonly think, and even if they had not the secret intention of making human life ridiculous, had at least intended to imitate nature as faithfully as the Greeks strove to beautify it. Not to speak of the accidental resemblance that in these plays, as in life, the most important parts are often played by the worst actors, what can be more alike than the two kinds of blood-and-thunder tragedies, in their plan, in the division and disposition of the scenes in their entanglement and their catastrophe? How rarely do the authors of the one or the other ask themselves why they have made this or that just so and not otherwise; how often do they surprise by events for which we were not in the least prepared. How often do we see persons come, enter and exeunt without comprehending why they came and why they have disappeared again. How much in both is left to chance; how often we see the greatest consequences

---

[2] [The following quotation is from the 'Agathon' of Wieland.--Tr.]

provoked by the most petty causes. How often we see
the most serious and important actions treated carelessly
and the insignificant treated with absurd gravity. And
when at last in both everything is so miserably involved
and complicated that we begin to despair of the possibility of disentanglement how happily we suddenly see
the Gordian knot, not unravelled it is true, but hewn
through by a brave dagger-thrust, or by some god who
jumps out of paper clouds amid thunder and lightning.
This cutting open comes to the same thing as unravelling,
in one way or the other the play has an end, and the spectators can applaud or hiss as they will or may. We know
what an important person the noble harlequin represents
in our comic tragedies, who it seems is determined to
maintain himself on the stage of our metropolis ; perhaps
as an eternal monument to our ancestors' taste. Would
to heaven that his person were alone represented on the
theatre. But how many great acts on the theatre of the
world have been acted together with, or what is worse, by
means of a harlequin. How often has all the wisdom and
valour of the very greatest men ; men who have been born
to be the sheltering genius of the throne, the benefactors
of whole peoples and ages, been frustrated by means of
some little whimsical, practical joke of a harlequin, or of
such who, if they do not wear harlequin's jacket and his
yellow hose, certainly bear his whole character. How
often in both kinds of tragi-comedy the complication
arises from some stupid mischievous act by which
harlequin spoils the labour of wise people before they are
aware of it." . . . . .

No. 70.

If in this comparison of the great and small, the
original and counterfeit heroic farce, the satirical mood
were not so prominent, it could be held to be the best
apology for the comi-tragic or tragi-comic drama (mixed
plays I have seen them called somewhere), the most
conscientious deduction of Lope's thoughts, while at the
same time it would confute them. It would prove that just
the example of nature which is to justify the combination
of solemn gravity with farcical merriment can justify as

well every dramatic monster that has neither plan, nor connexion, nor common-sense. Imitation of nature would consequently either be no principle of art, or if it still remain so, it would by means of art cease to be art. At least it would be no higher art than that art which imitates the coloured veins of marble in plaster of Paris; their direction and course may go as they like, the strangest cannot be so strange but that it might seem natural; only that does not seem natural in which too much symmetry, proportion and equality is shown, in which too much is seen of that which in every other art, constitutes art. In this sense the most laboured is the worst, the most arbitrary the best.

Our author might have spoken quite differently as critic. What he here seems to support so elaborately, he would beyond doubt have condemned as a monstrosity of barbarous taste; or at least as the first attempts of an art reviving among an uncultivated people, the form of which has been determined by a combination of some accidental causes or by chance, but in which reason and reflexion have taken little or no part. He would hardly say that the first inventors of mixed plays (since the word is once there, why should I not use it?) "strove to imitate nature as faithfully as the Greeks sought to beautify it."

These words "faithful" and "beautiful," applied to the imitation of nature as the object of imitation, are subject to many misconceptions. There are persons who will not admit of any nature which we can imitate too faithfully, they insist that even what displeases us in nature, pleases us in a faithful imitation, by means of imitation. There are others who regard beautifying nature as a whim; a nature that intends to be more beautiful than nature is just on that account not nature. Both declare themselves to be admirers of the only nature such as she is, the one sees nothing to avoid, the other nothing to add. The former would necessarily admire the Gothic mixed plays, and the latter would find it difficult to take pleasure in the masterpieces of the ancients.

But suppose this were not the consequence? If those persons, great admirers though they are of common every-day nature, should yet declare themselves against the mixture of the farcical and interesting. If these others, monstrous as they deem everything that desires to be better and more beautiful than nature, can yet wander through the whole Greek theatre without finding the least obstacle on this account, how should we explain this contradiction?

We should necessarily have to retrace our steps and retract that which we insisted on before concerning the two species, but how must we retract without involving ourselves in new difficulties? The comparison of such blood-and-thunder tragedies concerning whose worth we dispute, with human life, with the ordinary course of the world, is still so correct.

I will throw out a few thoughts, which if they are not thorough enough may suggest more thorough ones. My chief thought is this : it is true and yet not true that the comic tragedy of Gothic invention faithfully copied nature. It only imitates it faithfully in one half and entirely neglects the other, it imitates the nature of phenomena without in the least regarding the nature of our feelings and emotions.

In nature everything is connected, everything is interwoven, everything changes with everything, everything merges from one into another. But according to this endless variety it is only a play for an infinite spirit. In order that finite spirits may have their share of this enjoyment, they must have the power to set up arbitrary limits, they must have the power to eliminate and to guide their attention at will.

This power we exercise at all moments of our life, without this power there would be no life for us; from too many various feelings we should feel nothing, we should be the constant prey of present impressions, we should dream without knowing what we dream. The purpose of art is to save us this abstraction in the realms of the beautiful, and to render the fixing of our attention easy to us. All in nature that we might wish to abstract in our thoughts from an object or a combination of various objects, be it in time or in place, art really abstracts for us, and accords us this object or this combination of various objects as purely and tersely as the sensations they are to provoke allow.

If we are witnesses of an important and touching event, and another event of trifling import traverses it, we seek and evade the distractions of our attention thus threatened. We abstract from it, and it must needs revolt us to find that again in art which we wished away in nature.

Only if this event in its progress assumes all shades of interest and one does not merely follow upon the other, but of necessity evolves from it, if gravity provokes laughter, sadness pleasure or *vice versâ*, so directly that an abstraction of the one or the other is impossible to us, then only do we not demand it from art and art knows how to draw a profit from this impossibility.

But enough of this, it is evident whither I am tending.

On the forty-fifth evening Romanus's play of ' The Brothers ' and St. Foix's ' Oracle ' were played.

The former play may pass as a German original, although it is mainly taken from the ' Brothers ' of Terence. It has been said that Molière also drew from this source and notably in his ' École des Maris ' ! M. de Voltaire makes his comments on this fact and I gladly quote M. de Voltaire's comments! Something may be learnt from the most trifling, if not always that what he says therein, at least that which he should have said. " Primus sapientiæ gradus est, falsa intelligere " (I cannot remember at this moment where this adage is written) and I know of no author in the world on whom to try whether we have attained to this first rung of wisdom, so well as on M. de Voltaire, and for the same reason I know no other who could less help us to attain the second rung : " secundus vera cognoscere." I think that a critic would best arrange his method according to this adage. First let him search for some one from whom he can differ, he will then gradually approach his subject and the rest will follow of its own accord. I confess that to this end, I have in the present work mainly chosen the French writers', and among these M. de Voltaire especially. Whoever deems this method more superficial than thorough, let him know that even the thorough Aristotle nearly always employed it. " Solet Aristoteles, quærere pugnam in suis libris," says one of his expositors who happens to lie under my hand. " Atque hoc facit non

temere et casu, sed certa ratione atque consilio: nam
labefactatis aliorum opinionibus," &c. Out upon the
pedant! M. de Voltaire would exclaim. Now I am a
pedant only from want of self-confidence.

.   .   .   .   .

No. 73.

On the forty-eighth evening Herr Weiss's tragedy of
'Richard III.' was performed. . . . .

This play is unquestionably one of our most important
original dramas. It is rich in beauties which sufficiently
prove that it would not have been beyond the power of
the poet to avoid the faults with which they are inter-
mingled, had he but had sufficient confidence in himself.

Shakespeare had already brought the life and death of
the third Richard upon the stage, but Herr Weiss did not
recollect this until his own work was already completed.
He says: "Although I shall lose much by this comparison,
it will at least be found that I have not been guilty of
plagiarism. But perhaps it would have been a merit to
commit a plagiarism on Shakespeare."

For this end we must suppose such an act to be possible.
What has been said of Homer, that it would be easier to
deprive Hercules of his club, than him of a verse, can be
as truly said of Shakespeare. There is an impress upon
the least of his beauties which at once exclaims to all the
world: I am Shakespeare's—and woe to the foreign beauty
who has the self-confidence to place itself beside it?

Shakespeare must be studied, not plundered. If we
have genius, Shakespeare must be to us what the *camera
obscura* is to the landscape-painter. He must look into it
diligently to learn how nature reflects herself upon a flat
surface, but he must not borrow from it.

Now in Shakespeare's whole play I do not know one
single scene, not even a single speech which Herr Weiss
could have used as it stands. Even the smallest portions
of Shakespeare are cut according to the great measure of
his historical plays, and these stand to the tragedies of
French taste much as a large fresco stands to a miniature
painting intended to adorn a ring. What material can we
then take from the former to use in the latter? Perchance

a face, a single figure, at most a little group, which must
then be worked out into a whole.. In the same manner
single Shakespearian thoughts must become entire scenes,
and entire scenes whole acts.   For rightly to use a giant's
sleeve for the dress of a dwarf, we must not employ it as
a sleeve but make a whole coat out of it.

If this is done, then the author may feel quite at ease
on the score of plagiarism.   Few persons will be able to
recognise the wool from which the threads have been spun.
Those few who comprehend the art will not betray the
maker, for they know that a grain of gold may be wrought
so skilfully that the value of the form far surpasses the
value of the material.

I, for my part, sincerely deplore that our poet recollected Shakespeare's Richard too late.   He might have
known him and yet remained as original as he now is; he
might have used him without a single borrowed thought
convicting him.

Now if the same thing had occurred to me, I should at
least have afterwards employed Shakespeare's work as a
mirror to wipe from my work all those blemishes which
my eye had not been able to perceive immediately.   How
do I know that Herr Weiss has not done this ?   And why
should he not have done this ?

May it not be that what I consider blemishes he holds
to be none ?   And is it not very probable that he is more
in the right than I am ?   I am convinced that in most
instances the eye of the artist is more penetrating than
that of the most keen-sighted of his observers.   Among
twenty objections made by the latter, the artist will
remember that nineteen of these were made and answered
by himself while at work.

Nevertheless he will not be annoyed at hearing them from
others also, for he likes his work to be criticised.   Whether
it be judged profoundly or superficially, justly or unjustly,
benevolently or satirically, it is all the same to him.   Even
the most superficial, the most unjust, the most awkward
judgment is of more worth to him than tame admiration.
In some form or other he may make use of the former to
his advantage ; but what is he to do with the latter ?   He
does not like to despise the good honest souls who look up

to him as to something extraordinary, and yet he must shrug his shoulders at them. He is not vain, but he is usually proud, and from mere pride he would ten times rather bear an unmerited censure than unmerited praise.

.   .   .   .   .

No. 74.

It is notably Richard's character about which I should like to have the poet's explanation. Aristotle would have rejected it unconditionally. Now as far as Aristotle's authority is concerned I could easily get over that point if I could as easily set aside his reasons.

Aristotle assumes that a tragedy must evoke our terror and pity and from this he infers that the hero must be neither a wholly virtuous nor a wholly vicious man, for by the ill-fortunes of neither can this aim be attained.

If I grant this definition, 'Richard III.' is a tragedy that has missed its aim. If I do not grant it, then I no longer know what a tragedy is.

For Richard III. as represented by Herr Weiss is unquestionably the greatest, most loathsome monster that ever trod the stage. I say the stage, for that the earth ever bore such a monster I greatly doubt.

Now what pity can the destruction of such a monster excite in us? But stay, he is not intended to do this, the poet has not designed this; there are other personages in his work whom he has made the objects of our pity.

Now as to terror? Should not this villain arouse the utmost limits of our terror, a man who has filled up the chasm that separated him from the throne, with the corpses of those who ought to have been to him the dearest in all the world; a blood-thirsty demon who boasts of his blood-thirstiness and rejoices at his crimes.

Most certainly he awakens our terror, if we understand by terror, amazement at such inconceivable crimes, horror of such wickedness as surpasses our comprehension, if we are to understand by it the shudder that seizes us at the sight of terrible deeds that are executed with glee. Of this terror I experienced my fair share at the performance of 'Richard III.'

But this form of terror is so little one of the aims of

tragedy that the old poets sought by all possible means to diminish it whenever their heroes were compelled to commit some great crime. They preferred rather to blame Fate, to make the crime the inevitable curse of an avenging deity, they preferred to change man from a creature of free-will to a machine, rather than to suffer the horrible idea to linger among us that man could by nature be capable of such corruption.

Crébillon is known among the French as the "Terrible." I greatly fear he is so nicknamed more on account of the terror which ought not to be in tragedy, than on account of the legitimate terror which the philosopher reckons as essential to tragedy.

And this ought not to have been named terror at all. The word which Aristotle uses [1] means fear; fear and pity, he says, should be evoked by tragedy, not pity and terror. It is true that terror is a species of fear, it is a sudden overwhelming fear. But this very suddenness, this surprise which is included in the idea of terror, plainly proves that those who here substituted the word terror for fear, did not comprehend at all what kind of fear Aristotle meant. . . .

Aristotle says: "Pity demands a person who suffers undeserved calamity and fear requires him to be one of ourselves. The villain is neither the one nor the other; hence his misfortunes can excite neither the one nor the other."

Fear has, as I have said, been interpreted as *terror* by our modern translators and expositors, and by this substitution they succeed in picking the strangest quarrel imaginable with the philosopher.

One of this herd speaks thus: [2] "It has not been possible to agree about the explanation of terror, and indeed it contains in every respect a link too many which hampers its universality and limits it. If Aristotle understands by his addition 'one of ourselves' merely the similarity of mankind, merely that both the spectator and the actor are human beings, even supposing that their

---

[1] In Cap. xiii. Poetics.
[2] Herr Schmidt in his preface to 'The Comic Theatre.'

character, worth, and social standing were widely different,
this remark was needless since it followed as a matter of
course. But if he was of opinion that only virtuous persons, or such as were afflicted by a pardonable fault could
excite terror, then he was in the wrong, for reason and
experience are opposed to him.   Terror springs incontestably from our feelings of humanity, for every human
being is subject to it and every human being is by means
of this feeling touched at the adverse fortunes of another
man.   It is possible that there may be persons who deny
this of themselves, but such a denial would be a renuncia-
tion of their natural sensibility and hence a mere boast
that springs from perverted principles, but no refutation.
Now therefore if a dreadful event should unexpectedly
befall even a vicious person who has shortly before
engaged our attention, we should immediately forget his
vices and see in him merely the human being.   The mere
aspect of human misery in general makes us sad, and the
sudden, sad emotions that would be thus evoked, these are
terror."

Quite true, only not rightly placed.   For what does this
prove against Aristotle?   Nothing at all.   Aristotle does
not think of this terror when he speaks of fear which can
be excited in us only by the misfortunes of our equals.
This terror which seizes us at the sudden sight of a
suffering that threatens another, is a compassionate terror
and therefore comprehended under the term of pity.
Aristotle would not say pity and fear, if under fear he
understood nothing more than a mere modification of
compassion.

The author of the ' Letters on the Emotions ' [3] says " Pity
is a complex emotion, composed out of love for an object
and displeasure caused by its misery.   The movements by
which compassion evinces itself are distinguishable from
the simple symptoms of love as well as from those of displeasure, for compassion itself is a mere manifestation.   But
how varied can this manifestation be !   Let us change the
one limitation of time in a commiserated misfortune, and
compassion will be shown by totally different signs.   We

[3] Moses Mendelssohn.

feel a compassionate mourning with Electra weeping over her brother's urn, for she thinks the misfortune has taken place and bewails the loss she has sustained. What we feel at the sight of Philoktetes' suffering is likewise compassion, but of a different nature, because the torments sustained by this virtuous man are present and befall him before our eyes. But when Œdipus is terrified at the sudden *dénouement* of the great secret, when Monime is alarmed at seeing the jealous Mithridates grow pale, when virtuous Desdemona is afraid on hearing threatening speech from her Othello who was wont to be so tender, what is it we feel then? Always the same compassion; but compassionate terror, compassionate alarm, compassionate fear. The movements are various, but the essence of the emotion is in all cases the same. For as all love is connected with a willingness to put ourselves in the place of the beloved object, so we must share all kinds of suffering with them, which is very expressively termed compassion. Why then should not fright, terror, rage, jealousy, revenge, in fact all forms of unpleasant emotions, even envy not excepted, spring from compassion? We may see hereby how awkwardly the greater part of the art critics have divided tragic passions into terror and compassion. Terror and compassion! Is then theatrical terror no compassion? For whom does the spectator start when Merope draws the dagger upon her own son? Surely not for himself but for Ægisthus, whose preservation we so sincerely desire; for the deluded queen who regards him as the murderer of her son. But if we only intend to call compassion the displeasure felt at the present misfortunes of another, it will be needful to distinguish from compassion properly so called, not only terror but all other feelings communicated to us by another person."

No. 75.

These ideas are so correct, so clear, so luminous that it seems to us every one might and ought to have had them. Nevertheless I will not attribute the acute observations of the new philosopher to the ancient one; I am too well acquainted with the merits of the doctrine of mixed sensations enunciated by this modern philosopher and for the true theory of which we are indebted to him alone. But of that which he has explained so excellently Aristotle may have been on the whole sensible, at least it is quite undeniable that Aristotle must either have believed that a tragedy could or should excite nothing but genuine compassion, nothing but displeasure at the present misfortunes of another, which we can hardly suppose, or he must have comprehended under the word compassion all passions in general that can be communicated to us by another.

For it is certainly not Aristotle who has made the division so justly censured of tragic passions into terror and compassion. He has been falsely interpreted, falsely translated. He speaks of pity and *fear*, not of pity and *terror;* and his fear is by no means the fear excited in us by misfortune threatening another person. It is the fear which arises for ourselves from the similarity of our position with that of the sufferer; it is the fear that the calamities impending over the sufferers might also befall ourselves; it is the fear that we ourselves might thus become objects of pity. In a word this fear is compassion referred back to ourselves.

Aristotle always requires to be interpreted through himself. Whoever intends to furnish us with a new commentary to his 'Poetics,' which shall distance that of Dacier, him I would advise before all else to read the complete works of the philosopher from beginning to end. He will find explanations of Poetics where he least expects them, most especially must he study the books of Rhetoric and Ethics. Now we imagine that the schoolmen so well versed in the writings of Aristotle would have found these explanations long ago. But his 'Poetics' was the very work of which they took the least notice. Then also they were wanting in other knowledge without which these explanations could not have borne fruit; they were not acquainted either with the theatre or its masterpieces.

The correct explanation of this fear with which Aristotle combines the tragic pity is to be found in the fifth and eighth chapter of the second book of Rhetoric. It would not have been very difficult to have recalled these chapters and yet not one of his expositors seems to have recollected them, at least not one of them has made that use of them which they afford. For even those who without them perceived that this fear could not be compassionate terror, might yet have learnt an important fact therefrom, namely, the reason why the Stagyrite added fear to compassion, why fear alone and no other passion, and why not several passions. Of this reason they know nothing, and I should like to hear what answer their own intelligence would suggest to them if they were asked, for instance, why tragedy could not and should not excite in us compassion and admiration as well as compassion and fear?

All this depends on the conception Aristotle had of compassion. It was his opinion that the misfortune that becomes the object of our compassion must necessarily be of such a nature that we can fear it might happen as well to us or ours. Where this fear is not present compassion does not arise. For neither he whom misfortune has oppressed so heavily that he no longer sees any cause to be afraid of any further ills, nor he who believes himself so fortunate that he cannot comprehend whence any misfortune could befall him, neither the desperate man, nor the arrogant one, is in the habit of feeling compassion for others. Therefore Aristotle explains that which is fearful and that which merits pity by means of one another. All that, he says, is fearful to us, which if it had happened to another, or were to happen to him, would excite our pity ;[1] and we find all that worthy of our compassion, which we should fear if it were threatening us. It would not therefore be enough that the unfortunate person who excites our compassion does not deserve his misfortunes ; he may have drawn them down upon himself by his own weakness, his tortured innocence or rather his too severely punished guilt would lose its

---

[1] Ὡς δ᾽ ἁπλῶς εἰπεῖν, φοβερά ἐστιν, ὅσα ἐφ᾽ ἑτέρων γινόμενα ἢ μέλλοντα ἐλεεινά ἐστιν. I do not know what came to Æmilius Portus in his edition of the Rhetoric (Spiræ, 1598,) when he rendered this : " Denique ut simpliciter loquar, formidabilia sunt, quæcunque simulac in aliorum potestatem venerunt, vel ventura sunt." It ought simply to read, " quæcunque aliis evenerunt, vel eventura sunt."

effect upon us, would be incapable of awakening our pity if we saw no possibility that his sufferings might ever befall us. But this possibility arises, and becomes the more probable, if the poet does not make him out to be worse than mankind in general, if he lets him think and act as we should have thought and acted in his position, or at least as we might have thought and acted ; in short, if he portrays him as one of ourselves. From similarity arises the fear that our destiny might as easily become like his as we feel ourselves to be like him, and this fear it is which would force compassion to full maturity.

Such was Aristotle's conception of compassion, and only thence can the true reason be deduced why next to compassion he only mentioned fear in his definition of tragedy. It is not that this fear is a passion independent of pity, which might be excited now with pity and now without it in the same way as pity can be excited now with and now without fear. This was Corneille's error, but this was not Aristotle's reason ; according to his definition of compassion it of necessity included fear, because nothing could excite our compassion which did not at the same time excite our fear.

Corneille had already written all his plays before he sat down to annotate Aristotle's 'Poetics.'[2] For more than fifty years he had laboured for the stage and after such experience he might unquestionably have given us much valuable information concerning the ancient dramatic code if he had only studied it a little more diligently during the time of his labour. He appears to have done this only in so far as the mechanical rules of dramatic art were concerned. He left essential points disregarded and when he. found at the end that he had sinned against Aristotle, which nevertheless he had not wished to do, he endeavoured to absolve himself by means of explanations and caused his pretended master to say things which he never thought.

[2] He says: "Je hasarderai quelque chose sur cinquante ans de travail pour la scène," in his dissertation on Drama. His first play, 'Mélite,' dates from 1625, and his last, 'Surena,' from 1675, which makes exactly fifty years, so that it is certain that in his exposition of Aristotle he was able to have an eye to all his plays.

Corneille had brought martyrs upon the stage and had
represented them as the most perfect, blameless beings : he
had produced the most loathsome monsters in Prusias,
Phocas, and Cleopatra and of both these species Aristotle
has maintained they are unsuitable for tragedy, because
neither can excite pity nor fear. What does Corneille say
to this? How does he manage that neither his own dignity
nor the authority of Aristotle has to suffer from such a
contradiction? [3]

" We can easily come to terms with Aristotle. We
need only presume that he did not mean to maintain
that both means, terror and compassion, were required at
the same time to effect the purification of our passions,
which according to him is the chief aim of tragedy, but
that one of these means would be sufficient. We may
confirm this explanation from his own works, if we rightly
weigh the reasons he gives for the exclusion of such events
as he censures in tragedies. He never says this or that is
not suited to tragedy because it only excites compassion
and no fear, or that such a thing is insupportable because
it only excites fear without awakening compassion. On
the contrary he rejects them on that account because as
he says they neither produce compassion nor fear, and he
thus shows us that they displeased him because they
lacked both, and that he would not deny them his approval
if they effected only one of these."

No. 76.

Now this is utterly false. I cannot marvel enough how
Dacier who is usually very observant of the distortions
that Corneille practised on Aristotle's text for his own
ends could overlook this, the greatest of all. True how
could he avoid overlooking it since he never consulted the
philosopher's own explanation of compassion? As I have
said what Corneille imagines is utterly false. Aristotle
cannot have meant this, or we should have to believe
that he could forget his own explanation, we should have
to believe he could contradict himself in the most flagrant

---

[3] " Il est aisé de nous accommoder avec Aristote," &c.

manner. If, according to his doctrine, the misfortunes of
another which we do not fear for ourselves cannot awaken
our pity, he could not be satisfied with any tragedy which
excites pity alone and no fear, because he deemed such a
matter an impossibility; such actions did not exist for
him. He believed that events capable of awakening our
compassion, must at the same time awaken our fear, or
rather, by means of this fear, they awaken compassion.
Still less could he have conceived the action of a tragedy,
which might excite our fear without awakening our compassion, for he was convinced that all which excited fear
for ourselves must awaken our compassion too as soon as
we saw it threaten or befall others, and this is the case in
tragedy, where we see all the evils which we fear, happening to others and not to ourselves.

It is true that when Aristotle speaks of the actions that
are not suited to tragedy, he several times uses the
expression that they excite neither compassion nor fear,
but so much the worse for Corneille if he was misled by
this *neither, nor*. These disjunctive particles do not
always express what he makes them express. For if we
deny two or more qualities to an object by means of these
particles, the existence of the object, notwithstanding that
one or the other of the things are wanting to it, depends
on whether these things can be separated in nature as we
separate them in the abstract and by means of the symbolic
expression. For example, if we say of a woman that she
is neither handsome nor witty, we certainly mean to say
that we should be satisfied if she possessed either of these
attributes; for wit and beauty can be separated not only
in thought but they are separated in reality. But if we
say, this man believes neither in heaven, nor in hell, do we
mean to say thereby that we should be satisfied if he
believed in one of them, if he only believed in heaven and
no hell, or in hell and no heaven? Surely not, for whoever believes the one, must needs believe the other;
heaven and hell, punishment and reward are relative
terms; if the one exists, so does the other. Or to draw
an illustration from an allied art, when we say, this
picture is good for nothing, it has neither outline nor
colour, do we mean to say by this that a good painting

could exist with either of the two alone? This is very clear.

But how if the definition that Aristotle gives of compassion were false? How if we could feel compassion with evils and misfortunes that we have in no wise to fear for ourselves?

It is true we do not require the element of fear to feel displeasure at the physical sufferings of a person whom we love. This displeasure arises merely from our perception of the imperfection, as our love arises from the perception of the perfections of the individual, and from this fusion of pleasure and displeasure arises the mixed sensation we call compassion.

But granting this I do not believe that I shall be obliged to forsake Aristotle's cause.

For if we can feel compassion for others without fear for ourselves it remains incontestable that our compassion, strengthened by this fear, becomes far more vivid and intense than it would be without it. Then what hinders us from assuming that the mixed sensation evoked by the physical sufferings of a beloved object can alone be elevated to that height where it deserves to be called affection by adding to it the element of fear for ourselves.

This was what Aristotle really assumed, he did not regard compassion according to its primary emotions, he regarded it merely as an effect. Without mistaking the former he only denies to the spark the name of flame. Compassionate emotions unaccompanied by fear for ourselves, he designates philanthropy, and he only gives the name of compassion to the stronger emotions of this kind which are connected with fear for ourselves. Now though he maintains that the misfortunes of a villain excite neither our compassion nor our fear, he does not therefore deny that the spectacle could awaken emotion in us. The villain is still a man, a human being who for all his moral imperfections possesses perfections enough to raise the wish in us not to witness his ruin and destruction, and arouses in us an emotion nearly allied to compassion, the elements as it were of compassion. But as I have said Aristotle does not call these emotions allied to compassion, compassion, but philanthropy. He says: "We must not permit a villain to pass from unfortunate to fortunate circumstances, for nothing can be more untragical; it then has nothing of all that it ought to have, it awakens neither philanthropy, pity, nor fear. Neither must it be an utter villain who passes from happy to unhappy conditions. Such an event may indeed excite philanthropy, but neither compassion nor fear." I know of nothing more bald and absurd than the common rendering of the word philanthropy. Its adjective is usually translated into Latin by "hominibus gratum;" into French by "ce qui peut faire quelque plaisir"; and into German by "what may give pleasure" (*was Vergnügen machen kann*). So far as I can discover, only Goulston appears not to have mistaken the philosopher's meaning; he translated φιλάνθρωπον by "quod humanitatis sensu tangat." For under this meaning of philanthropy is comprehended the feeling that even the misfortunes of a criminal can evoke, it is not joy at his merited punishment that is understood, but the sympathetic feeling of humanity which is awakened in us at the moment of his suffering in spite of our consciousness that his sufferings are nothing but his desert. Herr Curtius indeed would limit these compassionate emotions felt for a suffering villain to a certain species of evils. He says: "Those accidents to the vicious which excite neither pity nor fear in us, must be the consequences of their vices; for if they happened to them by chance, or innocently, they still retain in the hearts of the spectators the privileges of humanity which does not deny its compassion to a villain who suffers innocently." But he does not seem sufficiently to have considered this. For even when the misfortune befalling a villain is the immediate consequence of his crimes, we still cannot help suffering with him at the sight of his punishment.

The author of the 'Letters on the Sensations' says: "Behold yonder multitude that crowds around a condemned criminal. They have heard of all the horrors, the vices he has committed, they have detested his wicked course of life, they have probably hated him himself. Now he is dragged pale and fainting to the terrible scaffold. The people press through the crowd, stand on tiptoe, climb the roofs to see how his features become distorted in death. The verdict is spoken, the hangman approaches, one moment more will decide his destiny. How earnestly do all the hearts now wish him pardoned. What! pardoned? he, the object of their detestation? he, whom a moment before they would themselves have sentenced to death? Whereby has a spark of humanity been rekindled in them? Is it not the close approach of punishment, the sight of the most terrible physical ill that reconciles us again even with this vile wretch and wins him our affection? Without love it would be impossible to have compassion on his fate."

And it is this love, say I, which we can never entirely lose towards our fellow-creatures, which smoulders inextinguishably beneath the ashes by which our stronger emotions are covered, and which only awaits a favourable gust of wind from misfortune, grief and crime to be blown into the flame of compassion; it is this love which Aristotle understands under the name philanthropy. We are right when we comprehend it as included under the name of compassion. But Aristotle was not wrong when he assigned to it a distinct name, to distinguish it from the highest grade of compassionate emotions in which they become affections by the addition of a possible fear for ourselves.

No. 77.

We must here meet an objection. If Aristotle's conception of the effect of compassion was that it was necessarily connected with fear for ourselves, why was it requisite to have mentioned fear by itself? The word compassion includes it already and it would have sufficed if he had merely said, tragedy is to effect the purification of our passions by the excitation of our pity. The addition of the word fear says nothing more and makes that which he says, ambiguous and uncertain.

I reply, if Aristotle had merely intended to teach us which passions tragedy could and should excite, he then could certainly have spared himself the addition of fear and would beyond doubt have done so, for never was there philosopher who so spared words as he did. But he desired to teach us at the same time which of the passions excited in us by tragedy should be purified and in this intention he was obliged to mention fear separately. For although according to him the sensation of compassion cannot exist either in or out of the theatre without fear for ourselves, although fear is a needful ingredient of compassion yet this does not hold good conversely, and pity for others is no ingredient of fear for ourselves. When once the tragedy is ended, our pity ceases, and nothing remains in us of all the experienced emotions but the possible fear for ourselves which the misfortunes we have pitied have awakened in us. This fear we carry away with us, and as it helps as an ingredient of pity to purify our pity, it now helps to purify itself as a passion capable of independent continuous existence. Consequently to show that it could do this and really does it, Aristotle deemed it necessary to name it separately.

It is incontestable that Aristotle never contemplated giving a sharp logical definition of tragedy, for without limiting himself to its merely essential qualities, he admitted several accidental ones that had become necessary by the customs of his day. But when we deduct these and reduce the other distinctive features, there remains a perfectly accurate definition, namely this, that a tragedy is a poem which excites compassion. According to its genus it is the imitation of an action, like the epopee and comedy, but according to its species, the imitation of an action worthy of compassion. From these two definitions all the rules can be perfectly deduced and even its dramatic form may be determined.

This latter statement may be doubted. At least I know no art critic who ever dreamed of attempting this. They all regard the dramatic form of tragedy as something traditional, which is so nowadays because it is so, and which is left so because it is held to be good. Aristotle alone has penetrated to the cause, but in his explanation he has rather presupposed it than clearly explained it. He says : "Tragedy is the imitation of an action—which not by the means of narration but by the means of pity and fear effects the purification of these and similar passions." It is thus that he expresses himself, word for word. Who is not struck by this curious antithesis : " not by the means of narrative but by the means of pity and fear." Pity and fear are the means employed by tragedy to attain its end, a narrative can only refer to the manner how to employ or not to employ these ways and means. Does it not seem as if Aristotle had left a hiatus here? Does it not seem as if the proper antithesis of narrative, which here is dramatic form, is lacking? But what is it the translators do with the hiatus? One of them carefully walks round it, the other fills it in, but merely with words. None of them see anything further in it than a careless construction of words to which they do not deem it necessary to pay any attention, provided they can render the meaning of the philosopher. Dacier translates *d'une action—qui sans le secours de la narration, par le moyen de la compassion et de la terreur,* &c., and Curtius " of an action which not by the relation of the poet but by the representation of the action itself purifies us from the faults of the represented passions, by means of terror and pity." Very good; both say what Aristotle means to say, only they do not say it *as* he said it. And all depends upon this *as,* for it is not merely a careless construction of words. Briefly the matter stands thus. Aristotle perceived that pity necessarily required a present evil, that evils which happened long ago or threaten in the distant future are not at all commiserated by us or at any rate not as much as present ones and that it was consequently necessary to represent the action which is to arouse our pity not as past but as present—that is to say, not in the narrative but in the dramatic form. This alone that our pity is excited little or not at all by narrative and solely and alone by the actual sight, this justifies him in substituting in his definition the thing itself in place of the form of the thing, because the thing itself is only capable of this form. Had he deemed it possible that our pity could be excited by narration it would indeed have been a very faulty leap, when he said "not by narrative but by pity and fear." But since he was convinced that pity and fear could alone be excited in imitation by means of the dramatic form, he was fully justified in taking this leap

for the sake of brevity. For this I refer to the before-
mentioned ninth chapter of the second book of Rhetoric.[1]

Now with reference to the moral aim accorded to tragedy
by Aristotle, and which he deemed needful to include in
his definition, it is well known what controversy has been
occasioned by it, especially in modern times.

I venture to undertake to prove that all who have declared themselves against it have not understood Aristotle.
They have all substituted their own ideas for his before
they knew for certain what they were. They quarrel
about whims, which they create themselves, and imagine
they have indisputably confuted the philosopher when
they have merely confuted the cobwebs of their own brains.
I cannot enter just now into a more detailed discussion of
this matter, only in order that I may not appear to speak
without proof, I will make two observations:—

1. They make Aristotle say " tragedy is to purify us by
means of terror and pity from the faults of the passions
represented." The passions represented? Then I suppose
if the hero is rendered unhappy by curiosity and ambition,
by love or anger, it is our curiosity, our ambition, our
love, our anger, that tragedy is meant to purify? This
never entered Aristotle's mind; in this manner these
gentlemen have good fighting ground; their imagination
changes windmills into giants, they tilt towards them
in the certain hope of victory, and pay no attention to
Sancho who has nothing further than sound common-
sense, and ambling on his peaceable animal calls after
them not to be in such a hurry and just open their eyes
a little. Τῶν τοιούτων παθημάτων says Aristotle, and that
does not mean the represented passions; they ought to
have translated this by " these and such like," or by the
awakened passions. This τοιούτων refers only to the preceding pity and fear; tragedy should excite our pity and
fear to purify these and such like passions, but not all
passions without distinction. But he says τοιούτων and
not τούτων, these and such like, and not only these, to show

[1] 'Επεὶ δ' ἐγγὺς φαινόμενα τὰ πάθη, ἐλεεινά εἰσι, τὰ δὲ μυριοστὸν ἔτος
γενόμενα, ἢ ἐσόμενα, οὔτ' ἐλπίζοντες, οὔτε μεμνημένοι, ἢ ὅλως οὐκ ἐλέουσιν
ἢ οὐχ ὁμοίως, ἀνάγκη τοὺς συναπεργαζομένους σχήμασι καὶ φωναῖς καὶ
ἐσθῆτι, καὶ ὅλως τῇ ὑποκρίσει, ἐλεεινοτέρους εἶναι.

that he comprehended by pity not merely pity properly
so called but all philanthropic emotions in general, and
by fear not merely the displeasure at impending evil, but
every kind of displeasure related to it, thus the displeasure
experienced from a past evil as well as from a present one,
sorrow and grief.   In this large compass the pity and fear
excited by tragedy is to purify our pity and fear, but only
these and no other passions.   Beyond doubt tragedy may
furnish other useful lessons and examples besides these,
and purify other passions, but these are not its aim ; these
it has in common with the epopee and comedy, in so far as it
is a poem, the imitation of an action in general, but not in
so far as it is a tragedy, the imitation of an action worthy
of pity.   All species of poetry are intended to improve us ;
it is sad that it should be necessary to have to prove this,
still sadder that there are poets who even doubt it.   But
all species of poetry cannot improve all things, at least
not everyone as perfectly as another, but what each can
improve most perfectly, and better than any other species
—that alone is its peculiar aim.

No. 78.

2. As the adversaries of Aristotle paid no attention to
what kind of passions he meant to purify in us by the
means of pity and fear in tragedy, it was very natural
that they should be in error as to the purification itself.
At the close of his Politics, when Aristotle is speaking of
the purification of passions by means of music he promises
to treat of this purification in detail in his Poetics. Corneille
says, " Because we find nothing at all about this matter in
the Poetics the greater part of his commentators have conceived the idea that it has not come down to us complete."
What, nothing at all about this ? I, for my part, believe that
I have found among that which remains to us of his Poetics
it may be much or little, but any way all that he deemed
necessary to say about this matter to any one not wholly
unacquainted with his philosophy.   Corneille himself
observed one passage which according to him afforded sufficient light to discover the means by which the purification

of the passions was effected in tragedy; that namely where Aristotle says "pity demands one who suffers undeservedly, and fear one of ourselves." This passage is truly very important, only Corneille has employed it erroneously. He could hardly do otherwise, because he had got his head full of the purification of passions in general. " Pity for the misfortunes which we see befalling one of ourselves awakens fear in us lest a similar misfortune befall us; this fear awakens the desire to avoid it and this desire an endeavour to moderate, to improve, even to exterminate the passion, by means of which the person is suffering whose misfortunes we pity, for reason tells every one that we must cast off the cause if we wish to avoid the effect." Now this mode of reasoning makes fear a mere tool by means of which pity effects the purification of the passion. This is false and cannot possibly have been Aristotle's meaning, because tragedy could then purify all the passions; not only those two that Aristotle expressly desired to see purified by it. It might purify our anger, our curiosity, our envy, our ambition, our hatred, and our love, just as it is the one or the other passion by means of which have arisen the misfortunes of the commiserated person, but our pity and fear we should have to leave unpurified. Pity and fear are those passions which we, not the acting personages, feel in tragedy; they are those passions through which the acting personages touch us, not those which draw upon them their own misfortunes. There might be a play in which they both exist. But as yet I know no play, in which the commiserated person has been plunged into misfortune by the means of misconceived pity and misconceived fear. Nevertheless such a work would be the only one in which that happens which Aristotle desires according to Corneille, and even in this it would not happen according to the method he demands. This single play would be, as it were, the point at which two inclined straight lines meet, never to touch again in all eternity. Even Dacier could not so grossly miss the drift of Aristotle. He was obliged to be more attentive to his author's words, and these say too positively that our pity and fear are purified by the pity and fear of tragedy. Since he believed however that the benefits of tragedy would be too small if it was merely limited to this, he let himself be led astray on the strength of Corneille's explanation to accord to tragedy purification of all other passions. When Corneille on his part denied this and showed by examples that he held it more as a beautiful thought than as a thing generally attainable, Dacier was obliged to enter into these examples whereby he found himself reduced to such straits that he was forced into making the most violent turns and twists to save his Aristotle and himself. I say *his* Aristotle, for the genuine one is far removed from requiring such turns and twists. He, to repeat it again and again, thought of no other passions which were to be purified by tragic pity and fear than our own pity and our own fear, and it is quite indifferent to him whether tragedy contributes much or little to the purification of the other passions. Dacier should have rested on this purification, only in that case he ought to have connected it with a more complete conception, he says "how tragedy evokes pity and fear, to purify pity and fear, is not very hard to explain. It evokes them by placing before our eyes the misfortunes that have befallen our fellow-creatures by unpremeditated faults, and it purifies them by making us acquainted with these misfortunes and thus teaches us, neither to fear them too much nor to be moved too much if they should really happen to ourselves. It prepares men to bear bravely the greatest calamities and inclines the most wretched to deem themselves happy by enabling them to compare their misfortunes with the far greater ones represented in tragedy. For in what circumstances could any one be who would not recognise at sight of an Œdipus, a Philoktetes, an Orestes, that all the evils that he has to bear are not to be compared with those which these men bear." Well, this is true, and this explanation cannot have cost Dacier many headaches. He found it almost word for word in one of the Stoics who always had an eye to apathy. Without objecting that the feeling of our own misery does not permit of much compassion beside it, that consequently this pity is not to be awakened in a wretched man, that the purification or modification of his sorrows cannot be effected by pity, I will suffer all to stand as he has said it, only I must ask how much has he said thereby?

Has he in any way asserted more than that pity purifies
our passions? Certainly not, and this is scarcely the
fourth part of Aristotle's demand, for when Aristotle maintains that tragedy excites pity and fear to purify pity and
fear, who does not see that this comprehends far more
than Dacier has deemed good to explain? For according to
the different combinations of these conceptions he who
would exhaust Aristotle must prove separately—1. How
tragic pity purifies our pity.   2. How tragic fear purifies
our fear.   3. How tragic pity purifies our fear.   4. How
tragic fear purifies our pity.   Dacier rested at the third
point only and he only explained this badly and partially.
For whoever has endeavoured to arrive at a just and complete conception of Aristotle's doctrine of the purification
of the passions will find that each of these four points
includes in it a double contingency, namely, since (to put
it briefly) this purification rests in nothing else than
in the transformation of passions into virtuous habits,
and since according to our philosopher each virtue has
two extremes between which it rests, it follows that if
tragedy is to change our pity into virtue it must also be
able to purify us from the two extremes of pity, and the
same is to be understood of fear.   Tragic pity must not
only purify the soul of him who has too much pity, but
also of him who has too little; tragic fear must not simply
purify the soul of him who does not fear any manner of
misfortune but also of him who is terrified by every misfortune, even the most distant and most improbable. Likewise tragic pity in regard to fear must steer between this
too much and too little, and conversely tragic fear in
regard to pity.   Dacier as I have said has only shown how
tragic pity may moderate excessive fear but not how its
entire absence may be remedied, nor how it may whole-
somely increase fear in him who has too little; not to
mention that of the rest he has shown nothing at all.
Those who followed after him have not in the least supplied what he has left undone.   But in order to set at rest
the contest about the utility of tragedy according to their
opinion they have drawn matters into it which belong
to poetry in general but in no wise to tragedy as tragedy
in particular; for instance tragedy is intended to nourish

and strengthen the feelings of humanity ; it is to produce
a love for virtue, a hatred for vice &c.,[1] but, my good sir,
what poem should not do the same? Then if this is the
intention of every poem it cannot be the distinctive
feature of tragedy, and therefore this cannot be what we
are seeking.

No. 79.

Now to return to our Richard. Richard arouses in us
as little fear as pity ; neither fear in the misused application of that term for the sudden surprise of pity, nor in
the real meaning of Aristotle of a wholesome fear lest a
similar misfortune befall us. For if he awakened this fear,
he would also excite our pity as certainly as he would on
the other hand excite our fear if we in the least deemed
him worthy of our pity. But he is such an abominable
rascal, such an incarnate devil, in whom we cannot find
the least trait resembling ourselves, that I firmly believe
if he were delivered over to all the tortures of hell before
our very eyes we should not have the smallest pity for
him, nor the least fear that such punishments could be in
store for ourselves, if they are the inevitable consequences
of such crimes only. Now finally what is the misfortune,
the punishment that befalls him ? After being obliged to
witness him committing frightful crimes, we hear that he
died sword in hand. When the queen is told this the
poet makes her say " This is something." I could never
refrain from saying to myself; no this is nothing ! many
a good king died thus defending his crown against a
powerful rebel. Richard dies like a man on the battle-
field of honour, and such a death is to indemnify me for
the displeasure I felt throughout the play at the triumph
of his crimes. (I believe the Greek language is the only
one which possesses a distinct word to express this displeasure at the good fortune of a villain, νέμεσις, νεμεσᾶν.[2])
This death which ought to have gratified my love of
justice only feeds my Nemesis. You escape cheaply—
think I, it is well that there is yet another justice than
the poetic one.

[1] Curtius in his Dissertation on the Intention of Tragedy, appended
to Aristotle's Poetics.   [2] Arist. Rhet. lib. ii. cap. 9.

It may perhaps be said; agreed, we will give up Richard; true the play is called after him but he is not on that account the hero, nor the person through whose means the purposes of tragedy are to be attained, he is only to be the means of exciting our pity for others; do not the queen, Elizabeth, the princes excite this pity?

To avoid all verbal disputes, I say yes. But what strange, harsh sensation is it that has mixed itself up with my pity for these persons; what is it that makes me wish I could spare myself this pity? I do not generally wish this with tragic pity—I linger over it willingly and thank the poet for this sweet torture.

Aristotle has well said it and it will certainly be true, he speaks of a μιαρόν of something terrible, which we experience at sight of misfortunes of wholly good, wholly innocent persons; and are not the queen, Elizabeth, and the princes such persons? What have they done? How have they drawn it down upon themselves that they are in the clutches of this monster? Is it their fault that they have a better right to the throne than he? How about the little moaning victims who can scarcely distinguish right from left; who will deny that they deserve our whole sorrow? But is this sorrow that causes me to think with a shudder of the destiny of these people, with a shudder to which a murmur against Providence is added which is followed afar by despair; is this sorrow? I will not ask—pity? but call it as we may, is it that meant to be excited by an imitative art?

Let no one say history evokes it, that it is founded upon something that really occurred. That really occurred? Granted; then it has its good reason in the eternal and infinite connexion of all things. In this connexion all is wisdom and goodness which appears to us blind fate and cruelty in the few links picked out by the poet. Out of these few links he ought to make a whole, rounded in itself, that is fully explained out of itself, where no difficulty arises, a solution of which is not found in his plan and which we are therefore forced to seek outside of it in the general plan of all things. The whole of this earthly creator should be a mere outline of the whole of the eternal Creator, should accustom us to the thought that as in Him all things are resolved for the best so also it will be here; and the poet forgets his most noble calling when he forces into a narrow circle the incomprehensible ways of Providence and advisedly awakens our shudder thereat. O spare us ye that have our hearts in your power! To what end these sad emotions?—to teach us submission? Cool reason alone could teach us this and if the teachings of reason are to have any hold on us, if we for all our submission are to retain confidence and joyful courage, it is most necessary that we should be reminded as little as possible of the perplexing instances of such unmerited terrible fates. Away with them from the stage, away with them if it might be from all books. Now if not one of the personages in Richard possesses the necessary qualities which they ought to have were this work a real tragedy, how has it nevertheless come to be considered an interesting play by our public? If it excites neither pity nor fear, what does it effect? It must produce some effect, and it does, and if it does produce an effect, is it not indifferent whether it produces this kind or that? If it occupies the spectators, if it amuses them what more do we want? Must they needs be amused and occupied according to the rules of Aristotle?

This does not sound unreasonable but there is an answer to it. Even if 'Richard' is no tragedy, it remains a dramatic poem, even if it lacks the beauties of tragedy it may yet have other beauties: poetical expressions, metaphors, tirades, bold sentiments, the spirited dialogue, fortunate situations for the actor to display the whole compass of his voice, the whole strength of his pantomimic art, &c.

Of these beauties 'Richard' has many, and also has some others that are more nearly related to the genuine beauties of tragedy.

Richard is an abominable villain, but even the exercise of our disgust, especially upon imitation, is not wholly without its pleasures. Even the monstrous in crime participates in the emotions awakened in us by sublimity and audacity; everything that Richard does is horrible, but all these horrors are committed for a purpose; Richard has a plan, and wherever we perceive a plan our curiosity is excited and we willingly wait to see whether and how it will be executed; we so love anything that has an aim that it affords us pleasure quite regardless of the morality of this aim.

We wish that Richard should attain his aim and we wish that he should not attain it. If he attains it, we are spared displeasure at means uselessly employed, if he does not attain it, then so much blood has been shed in vain, and since it has once been shed we would rather it had not been shed for the sake of pastime. On the other hand this attainment would be the triumph of malignity and there is nothing we less like to hear. The aim interested us as an aim to be attained but as soon as it is attained we only see in it all its abominable features and we wish it had not been attained. This wish we foresee and we shudder at the accomplishment of his aim.

We love the good personages of the play, such a tender vivacious mother, sisters and brothers who live for each other; such objects always please us, always excite our sweetest and most sympathetic emotions wherever we encounter them. To see them suffering innocently is harsh and not adapted to awaken emotions conducive to our peace and improvement, but still it does evoke emotions.

Thus the play occupies us throughout and pleases us by this occupation of our mental powers. This is true; only the inference is not true that is thought to be drawn from it, namely, that we should therefore be satisfied with the play.

The poet may have done much and yet have accomplished nothing. It is not enough that his work has an effect upon us, it must have that effect upon us which belongs to its species, and it must have that above all others. The lack of that can be in no wise replaced by other effects, especially if the species is of that importance, value and difficulty that all trouble and exertions would be in vain if it produced nothing but such effects as could be attained by an easier species requiring less preparation. We must not set machines in motion to raise a bundle of straw; I must not blast what I can turn over with my foot; I must not set fire to a funeral pile in order to burn a gnat.

No. 80.

To what end the hard work of dramatic form? Why build a theatre, disguise men and women, torture their memories, invite the whole town to assemble at one place if I intend to produce nothing more with my work and its representation, than some of those emotions that would be produced as well by any good story that every one could read by his chimney-corner at home?

The dramatic form is the only one by which pity and fear can be excited, at least in no other form can these passions be excited to such a degree. Nevertheless it is preferred to excite all others rather than these;—nevertheless it is preferred to employ it for any purpose but this, for which it is so especially adapted.

The public will put up with it; this is well, and yet not well. One has no special longing for the board at which one always has to put up with something.

It is well known how intent the Greek and Roman people were upon their theatres; especially the former on their tragic spectacles. Compared with this, how indifferent, how cold is our people towards the theatre! Whence this difference if it does not arise from the fact that the Greeks felt themselves animated by their stage with such intense, such extraordinary emotions, that they could hardly await the moment to experience them again and again, whereas we are conscious of such weak impressions from our stage that we rarely deem it worth time and money to attain them. We most of us go to the theatre from idle curiosity, from fashion, from ennui, to see people, from desire to see and be seen, and only a few, and those few very seldom, go from any other motive.

I say we, our people, our stage, but I do not mean the Germans only. We Germans confess openly enough that we do not as yet possess a theatre. What many of our critics who join in this confession and are great admirers of the French theatre think when they make it I cannot say, but I know well what I think. I think that not alone we Germans, but also that those who boast of having had a theatre for a hundred years, ay, who boast of having the best theatre in all Europe, even the

French have as yet no theatre, certainly no tragic one. The impressions produced by French tragedy are so shallow, so cold.—Let us hear a Frenchman himself speak of them.

M. de Voltaire says: "Combined with the surpassing beauties of our theatre is connected a hidden fault which remained unobserved because the public of its own accord could have no higher ideas than those imparted to it by the models of the great masters. Only Saint-Evremond has discovered this fault, he says that our dramatic works do not make sufficient impression, that that which should excite our pity only awakens tenderness, that emotion takes the place of agitation, and surprise the place of fear, in short, that our impressions do not penetrate deeply enough. It cannot be denied that Saint-Evremond has put his finger to the secret sore of the French theatre. Let no one rejoin that Saint-Evremond is the author of a miserable comedy, 'Sir Politic Wouldbe,' and of another equally miserable one called 'The Operas'; that his small social poems are the shallowest and commonest we possess of this kind, that he is nothing but a phrase-monger; one may have no spark of genius and yet possess much wit and taste. His taste was unquestionably very subtle, since he accurately hit the cause why most of our plays are weak and cold; we have always lacked a degree of warmth, but we possess everything else." Which means we possessed everything only not that which we ought to have had, our tragedies were excellent, only they were no tragedies. How was it that they were none? Voltaire continues: "This coldness, this monotonous weakness arose in part from the petty spirit of gallantry that reigned at that time among our courtiers and ladies, and transformed tragedy into a succession of amorous conversations after the taste of Cyrus and Clelie. The plays that may be excepted therefrom consisted of long political reasonings such as have spoilt Sertorius, made Otho cold and Surena and Attila wretched. There was yet another cause that kept back high pathos from our stage and prevented the action from becoming truly tragic, and that was the narrow miserable theatre with its poor scenery. What could be done on a few dozen boards that were besides filled with spectators! How could the eyes of the spectators be bribed and enchained, deceived by any display of pomp, by any artifice? What great tragic action could be performed there? What liberty could the imagination of the poet have there? The plays had to consist of long narratives and they thus became rather dialogues than plays. Every actor wished to shine in a long monologue and every play that did not contain these was rejected. In this form all theatrical action, the great expressions of passion fell away, there were no powerful pictures of human misery, all traits of the terrible that could penetrate to the innermost soul were absent, the heart was scarcely touched instead of being torn."

The first cause alleged is very true; gallantry and politics always leave us cold, and as yet no poet in the world has succeeded in combining with them the excitation of pity and fear. The former only exhibits the *fat* or the schoolmaster, the latter requires that we should have nothing but the human being.

But the second cause, how about that? is it possible that the want of a large theatre and good scenery should have such an influence on the genius of the poet? Is it true that every tragic action demands pomp and display; ought not the poet rather so to arrange his play, that it can produce its full effect without these appendages?

It certainly ought to do so, according to Aristotle. The philosopher says: "Pity and fear may be excited by vision, they may also be produced by the connexion of the events themselves, the latter plan is more excellent and after the manner of the best poets. The fable must be so arranged that it must excite pity and fear in him who merely listens to the relation of its events; such is the fable of 'Œdipus' that only requires to be heard to produce this effect. To attain this aim by the organs of sight requires far less art and is the business of those who have undertaken the business of the representation of the play."

Shakespeare's plays are said to afford a curious proof how needless are scenic decorations. We are asked what plays could more need the assistance of scenery and the whole art of the decorator than these with their constant interruptions and change of scene; yet there was a time when the stages on which they were performed consisted of nothing but a curtain of poor coarse stuff which when it was drawn up showed either the walls bare or else hung with matting or tapestry. Here was nothing for the imagination, nothing to assist the comprehension of the spectator or to help the actor and yet it is said, that notwithstanding, Shakespeare's plays were at that time more intelligible without scenery than they became afterwards with it.[1]

If therefore the poet need take no notice of decorations, if the decorations may be omitted even where they appear necessary without any disadvantage to his play, why should the narrow miserable theatre be the reason that the French poets have furnished us with no touching plays? Not so, this was not the cause, the cause lay in themselves.

And experience has proved this. Nowadays the French have a beautiful roomy stage, no spectators are tolerated on it, the *coulisses* are empty, the scene-painter has a free field; he paints and builds all the poet requires of him, yet where are they now, those warmer plays which they have attained since? Does M. de Voltaire flatter himself that his 'Semiramis' is such a play? It contains pomp and decoration enough; a ghost into the bargain, and yet I know no chillier play than his 'Semiramis.'

No. 81.

Nor do I mean to assert by all this that no Frenchman is capable of writing a really touching tragical play; that the volatile spirit of the nation is unable to grapple with

---

[1] Cibber's 'Lives of the Poets of Great Britain and Ireland,' vol. ii. pp. 78, 79: "Some have insinuated that fine scenes proved the ruin of acting. In the reign of Charles I. there was nothing more than a curtain of very coarse stuff, upon the drawing up of which the stage appeared, either with bare walls on the sides, coarsely matted, or covered with tapestry; so that for the place originally represented, and all the successive changes in which the poets of those times freely indulged themselves, there was nothing to help the spectator's understanding, or to assist the actor's performance, but bare imagination. The spirit and judgment of the actors supplied all deficiencies and made, as some would insinuate, plays more intelligible without scenes than they afterwards were with them."

such a task? I should be ashamed of myself if I had
even thought this. Germany has not as yet made herself
ridiculous by any Bouhours and I, for my part, have not
the least inclination towards the part. I am convinced
that no people in the world have been specially endowed
with any mental gift superior to that of any other
people. It is true we say the meditative Englishman,
the witty Frenchman. But who made this distinction?
Certainly not nature, who divided all things equally
among all. There are as many witty Englishmen as
Frenchmen and as many meditative Frenchmen as meditative Englishmen, while the bulk of the people is
neither one nor the other. What then do I mean? I
mean to say that the French might very well have
what as yet they have not got, a true tragedy; and why
have they not got it? Voltaire ought to have known
himself very much better if he meant to alight on the
reason.

I mean they have not got it because they deem they
have had it for a long time; in this belief they are
certainly confirmed by something they possess beyond all
other nations, by their vanity, but this is no gift of
nature. Nations are like individuals; in his youth
Gottsched was deemed a poet, because in those days, it
was not known how to distinguish between the poetaster
and the poet. By-and-by philosophy and criticism
explained this difference and if Gottsched had but kept
pace with this century, if his opinion and his taste had
been enlarged and purified together with the opinion and
taste of his age, he might perhaps from a poetaster have
become a poet. But since he had so often heard himself
called the greatest poet, since his vanity persuaded him
that this was so, he remained what he was. It was
impossible for him to attain what he believed he already
possessed and the older he grew the more obstinately and
unblushingly he maintained himself in this fancied
possession.

It seems to me the same thing has happened with the
French. Scarcely had Corneille torn their theatre a
little from the state of barbarism, than they already
believed themselves quite close to perfection. They

deemed that Racine had given it the finishing touch and after this no one questioned (which indeed they never had done) whether the tragic poet could not be yet more pathetic, more touching, than Corneille and Racine. It was taken for granted that this was impossible, and all the emulation of the successive poets was limited to the endeavour to be as like as possible to the one or the other. For a hundred years they have thus deceived themselves and in part their neighbours. Now let some one come and tell them this and see what they will reply.

Of the two it is Corneille who has done the greatest harm and exercised the most pernicious influence on these tragedians. Racine only seduced by his example, Corneille by his examples and doctrines together, the latter especially, which were accepted as oracles by the whole nation (excepting a few pedants, a Hedelin, a Dacier who, however, often did not know themselves what they desired) and followed by all succeeding poets. I would venture to prove bit by bit that these doctrines could produce nothing but the most shallow, vapid and untragical stuff.

The rules of Aristotle are all calculated to produce the greatest tragic effect. What does Corneille do with them ? He brings them forward falsely and inaccurately and because he still finds them too severe, he endeavours with one and the other to introduce *quelques modérations, quelques favorables interprétations* and thus weakens and disfigures, misinterprets and frustrates every rule, and why ? *pour n'être pas obligé de condamner beaucoup de poëmes que nous avons vu réussir sur nos théâtres ;* an excellent reason!

I will rapidly mention the chief points, some of them I have touched on already but for the sake of connexion I must mention them again.

1. Aristotle says tragedy is to excite pity and fear, Corneille says oh, yes, but as it happens, both together are not always necessary, we can be contented with one of them, now pity without fear, another time fear without pity. Else where should I be, I the great Corneille with my Rodrigue and my Chimène? These good children awaken pity, very great pity, but scarcely fear. And again where should I be with my Cleopatra, my Prusias, and my Phocas? Who can have pity on these wretches? but

they create fear. So Corneille believed and the French believed it after him.

· 2. Aristotle says tragedy should excite pity and fear, both, be it understood, by means of one and the same person. Corneille says: if it so happens very good. It is not however absolutely necessary and we may employ two different persons to produce these two sensations as I have done in my ' Rodogune.' This is what Corneille did and the French do after him.

3. Aristotle says by means of the pity and fear excited in us by tragedy our pity and our fear and all that is connected with them are to be purified. Corneille knows nothing of all this and imagines that Aristotle wished to say tragedy excites our pity in order to awaken our fear, in order to purify by this fear the passions which had drawn down misfortunes upon the person we commiserate. I will say nothing of the value of this aim, enough that it is not Aristotle's and that since Corneille gave to his tragedies quite another aim they necessarily became works totally different from those whence Aristotle had deduced his theories, they needs became tragedies which were no true tragedies. And such not only his but all French tragedies became because their authors did not think of the aim of Aristotle, but the aim of Corneille. I have already said that Dacier wished to unite both aims, but even this mere union would have weakened the former and tragedy would have remained beneath its highest effect; added to this Dacier, as I have shown, had only a very imperfect conception of the former and it was no wonder if he therefore imagined that the French tragedies of his age rather attained the former than the latter aim. He says (' Poét. d'Arist.' chap. 6th, rem. 8): "Notre tragédie peut réussir assez dans la première partie, c'est-à-dire qu'elle peut exciter et purger la terreur et la compassion. Mais elle parvient rarement à la dernière, qui est pourtant la plus utile, elle purge peu les autres passions, ou comme elle roule ordinairement sur des intrigues d'amour, si elle en purgeoit quelqu'une, ce seroit celle-là seule, et par là il est aisé de voir qu'elle ne fait que peu de fruit." Now the truth is exactly the contrary. We could sooner find French tragedies which satisfied the latter intention than the former. I know several

French plays which distinctly represent the ill-consequences of some passion from which we may draw many good lessons regarding this passion. But I know none that excite my pity in the degree in which tragedy should excite it, while I certainly know various Greek and English plays which can excite it. Various French plays are very clever, instructive works, which I think worthy of all praise, only they are not tragedies. Their authors could not be otherwise than of good intellect; in part they take no mean rank among poets, only they are not tragic poets, only their Corneille and Racine, their Crébillon and Voltaire have little or nothing of that which makes Sophokles Sophokles, Euripides Euripides, Shakespeare Shakespeare. These latter are rarely in opposition to Aristotle's essential demands, the former are so constantly. For to proceed—

No. 82.

4. Aristotle says we must not let any perfect man suffer in a tragedy without any fault on his part, for this is too terrible. Very true, says Corneille: "Such an event awakens more displeasure and hatred against him who has caused these sufferings than pity for him whom they befall. The former sensation therefore, which is not to be the real aim of tragedy, could stifle the latter if it were not treated skilfully. The spectator would depart discontented because too much anger would be mixed with this pity, while he would have been pleased if his pity alone had been excited." "But," says Corneille; for with a but he must come hobbling after, "if this cause falls away if the poem is so arranged that the virtuous man who suffers excites more pity for himself than displeasure against him who makes him suffer, what then? Oh, then," says Corneille " *J'estime qu'il ne faut point faire de difficulté d'exposer sur la scène des hommes très-vertueux.*" I cannot understand how any one could talk such nonsense against a philosopher, how one can pretend to understand him by letting him say things of which he never thought. Aristotle says the wholly unmerited misfortune of a virtuous man is no matter for a tragedy, because it is terrible. Out of this " because " Corneille twists an " in so far " a mere condition

under which it ceases to be tragic. Aristotle says: It is
entirely terrible and on that account untragical. Corneille
says it is untragical in so far as it is terrible. Aristotle
sees the terrible in the misfortune itself; Corneille sees it
in the displeasure we feel against its author, he does not or
will not see that this terrible is something quite different
from this displeasure, that even if the latter were quite
removed the former might yet exist in full measure. It
is enough for him that by this *quid pro quo* sundry of his
plays seem justified which he pretends to have made so
little contrary to the rules of Aristotle that he is even
arrogant enough to suppose that such pieces had only been
lacking to Aristotle for him to model his doctrines according to them and to abstract from them the manner in
which the misfortune of a wholly virtuous man may
nevertheless become an object of tragedy. He says " En
voici deux ou trois manières, que peut-être Aristote n'a
su prévoir, parce qu'on n'en voyait pas d'exemples sur les
théâtres de son temps." By whom are these examples ? By
whom else but by himself ? and which are these two or
three forms ? We shall soon see. He says " The first
form is when a very virtuous man is persecuted by a
very vicious one, but escapes the danger in which the
vicious one is himself entrapped, as is the case in ' Rodogune ' and ' Heraclius ' where it would be quite intolerable
if in the first play Antiochus and Rodogune and in the
second Heraclius, Pulcheria and Martian had perished,
while Cleopatra and Phokas had triumphed. Misfortunes
of the former awaken pity, which is not stifled by the
abhorrence we feel for their persecutors, because we incessantly hope that some lucky chance will occur that will
save them." Let Corneille persuade whom he can that
Aristotle did not know this form; he knew it so well
that if he did not wholly reject it, he at least emphatically declared it to be more fitted for comedy than tragedy.
How was it possible that Corneille could forget this ? But
it happens thus to all who assume beforehand that their
cause is the cause of truth. Now in fact this form does
not really belong to the case in question. For according
to this the virtuous man does not become unhappy but
only finds himself on the road to misfortune which may

excite compassionate anxiety for him without being terrible. Now as to the second form Corneille says: "It
may also happen that a very virtuous man is persecuted
and killed by command of another who is not sufficiently
vicious to incur our whole displeasure, since he may display more weakness than wickedness in his persecution of
the virtuous man. When Felix lets his son-in-law
Polyeucte perish, it is not from excessive zeal against the
Christians, which would render him worthy of detestation,
but rather from servile fear, which makes him afraid of
saving him in the presence of Severus, of whose hatred
and revenge he stands in awe. We therefore feel some
displeasure against Felix and blame his conduct, but this
displeasure does not outweigh the pity which we feel for
Polyeucte and does not hinder him at the end of the play
from regaining the good graces of the spectators by his
marvellous conversion." I fancy tragic bunglers existed
at all times and even at Athens. Why then should Aristotle have been in want of a play of similar construction
in order to become as enlightened as Corneille? This is
folly! Nervous, weak, undecided characters like Felix
are but another fault in plays of this stamp, and contribute
to render them both cold and repellent without on the
other hand making them less terrible. For as I said
before, the terrible does not consist in the displeasure or
disgust that they awaken, but in the misfortune itself
that befalls the innocent, regardless whether their persecutors are wicked or weak; whether they have treated them
thus cruelly with or without intention. The mere thought
itself is so terrible that there should be human beings
who can be wretched without any guilt of their own. The
heathens endeavoured to keep this terrible thought as far
away from them as possible, and *we* should nourish it? *we*
should take pleasure in spectacles that confirm it; *we*,
whom religion and reason should have convinced that it is
as false as it is blasphemous. The same would have certainly held good of the third form even if Corneille himself had not forgotten to state which this is.

5. Corneille has amendments to make even to that which
Aristotle says regarding the unfitness of an utter villain,
whose misfortunes can excite neither pity nor fear, to be a

hero of tragedy. He admits that he cannot excite pity but he certainly can fear. For although none among the spectators should deem themselves capable of such vices and consequently need not fear a similar fate, yet each one may harbour in himself some imperfection allied to these vices and be on his guard against them by means of the fear of proportionate, if not of the same, unhappy consequences. Now this is founded on the false conception which Corneille had of fear and of the purification of the passions to be awakened in tragedy. It contradicts itself. For I have already shown that the excitation of pity is inseparable from the excitation of fear, and if it were possible that the villain could excite our fear he must necessarily excite our pity. Since Corneille himself admits that he cannot do this, therefore he cannot do the other, and he therefore remains quite unfit to attain the aim of tragedy. Aristotle indeed considers the villain as yet more unfitted for this than the perfect man, for he expressly demands that if a hero of mediocre kind cannot be found he should be chosen rather better than worse. The reason is evident, a man can be very good and yet possess more than one fault, by means of which he throws himself into an immeasurable misfortune, and excites our pity and sorrow without being in the least terrible, because it is the natural consequence of his errors. What Dubos[1] says of them as of villains in tragedy is not what Corneille desires. Dubos would permit them in inferior parts only, would only use them as tools to make the chief personages less guilty, would use them as foils. Corneille demands that the principal interest should centre in them as in his 'Rodogune' and it is this which sins against the intention of tragedy. Dubos observes very justly that the misfortune of an inferior villain makes no impression on us. We hardly notice the death of Narcissus in 'Britannicus.' On this account therefore the poet should avoid employing them as much as possible. For if their misfortunes do not effectually forward the aims of tragedy, if they are merely secondary means by which the poet endeavours to effect his aim the better with other

---

[1] Réflexions crit. T. I. sect. xv.

persons, it is incontestable that his play would be better
still if he could produce the same effect without them.
The more simple a machine, the less springs and wheels
and weights it has, the more perfect it is.

No. 83.

6. Finally, to speak of the misconception of the first
and most important quality demanded by Aristotle with
regard to the morals of the tragic personages. These
should be good. Good? says Corneille. "If good here
means the same as virtuous, then it will fare badly with
the greater part of the ancient and modern tragedies, for
they abound in wicked and villainous persons, or at
least in such as are affected by weakness that cannot
subsist beside virtue." Corneille is especially solicitous for
his Cleopatra in 'Rodogune.' He will by no means allow
the goodness demanded by Aristotle to pass for moral
goodness. It must be another sort of goodness that agrees
with moral badness, as well as with moral goodness.
Nevertheless, Aristotle meant nothing but moral goodness,
only he made a distinction between virtuous persons and
persons who displayed virtuous morals under certain circumstances. In short Corneille connects a false idea with
the word morals and what the proæresis is by means of
which—according to our philosopher—free actions become
good or bad morals, he has not understood. I cannot just
now enter into a detailed proof of my assertion, which can
only be done satisfactorily by means of the connexion and
the syllogistic sequence of all the ideas of the Greek critic.
I therefore postpone it for another opportunity, the rather
as in the present instance it is necessary to show what an
unlucky *détour* Corneille took when he missed the right
road, this *détour*, this expedient resulted in this; that
Aristotle had understood under goodness of morals the
brilliant and elevated character of some virtuous or
criminal habit such as might properly and suitably
belong to the person who was introduced (" le caractère
brillant et élevé d'une habitude vertueuse ou criminelle,
selon qu'elle est propre et convenable à la personne
qu'on introduit "). He says, " Cleopatra in ' Rodogune ' is

extremely wicked, there is no murder from which she
shrinks if only she can maintain herself upon the throne,
which she prefers to all else in the world, so intense is
her love of dominion. But all her crimes are connected
with a certain grandeur of soul which has in it something
so elevated that while we condemn her actions, we must
still admire the source whence they flow. I venture to
say the same of the Liar. Lying is unquestionably a
vicious habit, but Dorante utters his lies with such presence
of mind, such vivacity that the imperfection suits him
extremely well and the spectator is bound to confess that
though the art of lying thus may be a vice yet no block-
head would be capable of it." In very truth Corneille
could not have had a more pernicious idea; if we carry it
out there is an end to all truth, and all delusion, to all
moral benefit of tragedy. For virtue which is always
modest and simple, becomes vain and romantic by assuming
this brilliant character, while vice thus varnished will
dazzle us from whatever point of view we regard it.
What folly to desire to deter by the unhappy consequences of vice if we conceal its inner ugliness! The
consequences are accidental, and experience teaches that
they are as often fortunate as unfortunate. This refers to
the purification of the passions as conceived by Corneille.
As I conceive it, as Aristotle taught it, it can by no
means be connected with this deceptive splendour. The
false foil thus laid beneath vice makes me recognise perfections where there are none, makes me have pity
where I should have none. It is true Dacier had
already contradicted this explanation, but on untenable
reasons, and those which he accepted together with Père
Le Bossu were almost equally detrimental to the plays, at
least to their poetical perfection. He maintains that "the
morals should be good" means nothing more than "well
expressed," "qu'elles soient bien marquées." This is certainly a rule which rightly comprehended deserves in its
proper place the whole attention of the dramatic poet.
If only our French models did not prove too clearly that
" well expressed " has been mistaken for " strongly expressed." The expression has been over-charged, pressure
has been put upon pressure until at last the personages

characterised have become personified characters and vicious or virtuous human beings have been converted into haggard skeletons of vice or virtue.

Herewith I will break off from the matter; whoever is equal to it will be able to make his own application to 'Richard.'   .   .   .   .

No. 84.

On the fifty-first evening Diderot's 'Le Père de Famille' was performed.

As this excellent play—it only pleased the Parisians moderately—is likely to all appearance to hold its place on our stage for some time, I hope to have occasion and space enough to pour out all I have noted down from time to time concerning the piece itself and the whole dramatic system of the author.

I will go back very far. Diderot did not for the first time express his dissatisfaction with the theatre of his nation in the 'Fils naturel' and the dialogues appended. Several years earlier he had already signified that he had not the high conception of it with which his fellow-countrymen deceive themselves, and Europe lets itself be deceived by them. But he expressed this in a book in which one would certainly not search for such like matters; in a book in which a tone of *persiflage* is so predominant, that to most readers, even that which is good common-sense therein, seems nothing but farce and mockery. Beyond doubt Diderot had his reasons for preferring at first to bring out his most secret sentiments in such a book. A wise man often says in joke what he intends afterwards to repeat in earnest.

This book is called 'Les Bijoux indiscrets' and Diderot now disclaims having written it. Diderot does well, but yet he has written it and must have written it if he does not wish to be a plagiarist. It is moreover certain that only such a young man could have written this book as would afterwards be ashamed to have written it.

It is just as well if the smallest possible number of my readers know this book; I will take good care not to make them acquainted with it beyond what serves my purpose.

An emperor—I know not where nor who—had made

various jewels reveal so many ugly things by means of a magic ring, that his favourite would not hear any more about it. She rather preferred to break with her own sex on this account, anyway she resolved that for a fortnight she would limit her intercourse solely to the sultan's majesty and a few wits. These were Selim and Riccaric: Selim a courtier and Riccaric a member of the imperial academy, a man who had studied the ancients, and, without being a pedant, was a great admirer of them. The favourite was once conversing with him when their conversation turned on the miserable nature of academic speeches, concerning which no one was more uneasy than the sultan himself, because it annoyed him to hear himself incessantly praised at the expense of his father and his forefathers, foreseeing that the academy would some day sacrifice his fame in like manner to the fame of his successor. Selim, as a courtier, had agreed to all the sultan had said and thus the conversation was led on to the theatre, which conversation I herewith impart to my readers.

" I think you are in error, sir," replied Riccaric to Selim. " The academy is still the sanctuary of good taste, neither sages nor poets can point to halcyon days to which we could not oppose others taken from our own times. Our theatre was held and is still held the best in all Africa. What a masterpiece is Tuxigraphe's ' Tamerlane ! ' It combines the pathetic of Eurisope with the sublime of Azophe. It is the purely classical."

" I saw the first performance of ' Tamerlane,' said the favourite, " and thought the thread of the play was very rightly conducted, the dialogue very eloquent, *les bienséances* well observed."

" What a difference, madame, between an author like Tuxigraphe who has been nurtured on the ancients and the greater number of our modern writers ! " said Riccaric.

" But these moderns " said Selim " whom you abuse so lustily are yet far removed from being as contemptible as you suppose. Or is it possible that you find no genius, no invention, no fire, no character, no description, no tirades in them? What care I for the rules so long as I am amused. Truly it is not the comments of the wise Almudir, or the learned Abdaldok, nor the poetics of the

acute Facardin, all of which I have not read, that make
me admire the plays of Aboulcazem, Muhardar, and Alba-
boukre, and of so many other Saracens.   Are there then
other rules than the imitation of nature?   And have we
not the same eyes as those with which these studied?"

"Nature," replied Riccaric, "shows itself to us every
moment in various guises.   All are true, but all are not
equally beautiful.   To make a good choice from among
them, this is what we must learn from the works of
which you do not seem to think much.   They are the
collected experiences of the authors and their predecessors.   However intelligent we may be we only acquire
our ideas one after the other, and one individual would
flatter himself vainly if he deemed that he could observe
for himself, in the short space of a lifetime, all that has
been discovered for him in so many centuries.   Were this
not so we could maintain that a science might owe its
origin, its development and its perfection to one single
mind, which as you know is against all experience."

"From this," replied Selim, "nothing further follows
but that the moderns who can make use of all the
treasures which have been collected up to their day, must
be richer than the ancients, or if this comparison does
not please you, that they must necessarily see further
from the shoulders of the giants on which they have
stept, than these can see themselves.   In truth what are
their natural history, their astronomy, their navigation,
their mechanics, their arithmetic in comparison to ours?
Why therefore should we not be equally superior to them
in eloquence and poetry?"

"Selim," said the favourite, "the difference is great
and Riccaric can explain this to you some other time.
He can tell you why our tragedies are worse than those
of the ancients; but that they are so I can easily take
upon myself to prove to you.   I cannot accuse you of
not having read the ancients.   You have acquired too
much elegant knowledge for the theatre of the ancients
to be unknown to you.   Now I ask you to put aside
certain ideas that refer to their customs, their manners
and their religion, and which offend you only because
circumstances have changed, and then tell me whether

their subjects are not always noble, choice and interesting? Does not the action develop quite naturally? does
not the simple dialogue approach very near to nature?
are the complications in the least forced? is the interest
divided? the action overladen with episodes? Transport
yourself in thought to the island of Alindala, examine all
that took place there, listen to all that has been said from
the moment that young Ibrahim and the wily Forfanti
landed, approach the cave of the unhappy Polipsile, lose
no word of his murmurs and then tell me whether the
smallest thing occurs that could disturb your illusion?
Name to me a single modern play which can bear the
same test, which can lay claim to the same degree of
perfection and you shall have conquered."

" By Bramah!" said the Sultan yawning, "madame
has made us an excellent academic address!"

" I do not understand the rules," continued the favourite,
"and still less the learned words in which they have been
clothed. But I know that only the true pleases and
touches. I know also that the perfection of a drama
consists in the accurate imitation of an action, at which
the spectator deems he is present, his illusion not being
destroyed by any interruption. Now is there anything
in the least resembling this in the tragedies you praise
so highly?"

No. 85.

" Do you praise their subjects? These are generally so
involved and various that it would be a miracle if so many
things could really occur in so short a time. The destruction or the preservation of a kingdom, the marriage of a
princess, the fall of a prince, all this occurs as rapidly as
we turn our hands. Is a conspiracy concerned? It is
planned in the first act, in the second it is already
hatched, in the third all the measures have been taken,
all obstructions removed, the conspirators are ready; in
the next there will be a revolution, an encounter, even a
pitched battle. And all this you call well-developed,
interesting, warm, probable? I can forgive such an
opinion to you least of all, who know how much it often
costs to bring about the most miserable intrigue and

how much time is lost in the smallest political affair over preliminaries, conferences and discussions."

"It is true madame" replied Selim, "our plays are a little overladen; but that is a necessary evil; without the help of episodes we should be chilled."

"That is to say: in order to give fire and spirit to the imitation of an action, this action must be represented neither as it is nor as it should be. Can anything more absurd be imagined? Scarcely, unless it were that the violins play a lively air, some merry sonata, while the spectators are to be in anxiety concerning the prince who is on the point of losing his beloved, his throne and his life."

"Madame," said Mongogul, "you are quite right; we ought to play sad airs and I will go and order some." So saying he got up and went out and Selim, Riccaric and the favourite continued the conversation among themselves.

"At least madame" replied Selim "you will not deny that if the episodes destroy our illusion, the dialogue puts us back into that state. I do not know who understands that better than our tragic poets."

"Then no one understands it" she replied. "The wit, the playful and the stilted elements that reign therein are removed a thousand, thousand miles from nature. The author tries in vain to hide himself, he does not escape my eyes and I see him continually behind his personages. Cinna, Sertorius, Maximus, Æmilia are at all moments Corneille's speaking-tubes. Our old Saracens did not converse together thus. If you like, Riccaric can translate some passages to you and you will hear the simple nature that speaks from their mouths. I should so like to say to the moderns: Gentlemen instead of endowing your personages with wit at all moments, why do you not seek to put them into positions that would give them some?"

"To judge by what madame has said as to the course and the dialogue of our dramas, it would not seem as if you would accord much indulgence to their *dénouement*" said Selim.

"No, certainly not," replied the favourite, "there are a hundred bad ones for one that is good. One is not sufficiently led up to, the other occurs as by a miracle. If the author does not know what to do with a person whom he has dragged from scene to scene through five acts, he finishes him off quickly with a dagger thrust, all the world begins to weep and I, I laugh as though I were mad. Again did ever any one speak as we declaim? Do princes and kings walk differently from other men? Do they ever gesticulate like madmen and possessed creatures? And do princesses howl when they speak? It is generally assumed that we have brought tragedy to a high degree of perfection, and I for my part hold it to be almost proved that of all species of literature attempted by the Africans during the last centuries just this has remained the most imperfect."

The favourite had just got to this point in her abuse of our theatrical works, when Mongogul re-entered. "Madame" he said, "you will do me a favour if you proceed. You see I understand how to shorten the art of poetry when I find it too long."

"Let us assume" continued the favourite, "that a man came here fresh from Angote who had never heard of a play in his life, but who was not wanting either in knowledge or good sense, who knew what could happen at a court, who was not unacquainted with the intrigues of courtiers, the jealousies of ministers and the machinations of women. Supposing I said to such a man in confidence: 'My friend, dreadful things are at work in the seraglio. The prince, who is angry with his son because he suspects him of loving Manimonbande, is a man whom I hold capable of the most cruel vengeance. To all appearance this matter must have sad consequences. If you like I will contrive that you shall be a witness of all that passes.' He accepts my proposal and I lead him into a box protected by a grating, out of which he can see the theatre, which he thinks is the sultan's palace. Do you believe that notwithstanding all the gravity I endeavour to maintain, this stranger's illusion will last for a moment? Must you not rather concede that he will laugh in my face in the first scene as he sees the stilted walk of the actors, their strange dresses, their exaggerated gestures, and hears their language spoken with strange emphasis in rhymed and measured speech ? Will he not say straight out either that I am making sport of him or that the prince and all his court are demented ? "

" I admit," said Selim, " that this assumed case makes me hesitate ; but could you not consider that we go to a play with the knowledge that we are about to assist at the imitation of an action, not at the action itself."

" Should this knowledge hinder the action from being represented in the most natural manner possible ?" asked the favourite.

Here the conversation gradually passes on to other matters that do not concern us. Let us turn and consider what we have read. Beyond question Diderot clear and simple ! But at that time all these truths were spoken to the winds. They did not rouse any feeling in the French public until they were repeated with all didactic solemnity and accompanied by examples in which the author endeavoured to depart from some of these criticised faults and to tread the paths of nature and illusion. Then envy awoke criticism. Oh now it was clear why Diderot did not deem the theatre of his nation at the acme of perfection which they believed it to be, why he saw so many faults in their lauded masterpieces ; only and solely to make room for his own plays ! He had to decry the method of his predecessors because he felt that if he pursued this method he would find himself immeasurably below them. He had to be a miserable charlatan despising all strange treacle in order that no one should buy any but his own. Thus the Palissots fell upon his plays.

Beyond question he had given them some excuse in his ' Fils naturel.' This first attempt is by no means equal to the ' Père de famille.' There is too much monotony in the characters, they are too romantic, the dialogue is stilted and archaic, a pedantic mixture of new-fangled philosophical sentences ; all these matters gave to censure an easy field. . . . Neither can it be denied that the form which Diderot gave to the accompanying dialogues and the tone he adopted in them, were somewhat vain and pompous, that he brought forward various comments which were not new and not peculiar to him as though they were

wholly new discourses and that other comments had not the
profundity they seemed to have in his dazzling language.

No. 86.

For example, Diderot maintains[1] that in human nature
there are at most a dozen comic characters of prominent
feature, and that the little varieties in the human character
cannot be so happily treated as the purely unmixed
characters. He therefore proposed that classes instead
of characters should be brought upon the stage and desired
that their treatment should form the especial labour of
serious comedy. He says, " Until now character has been
the chief work of comedy and class distinctions were
something accidental; now however the social standing
must be the chief consideration and the character the
accidental. The whole intrigue used to be drawn from
the character, the circumstances under which it best
evinced itself were carefully chosen and interwoven. In
future the duties, prejudices, and inconveniences of a social
standing must serve for the groundwork of a play. This
source seems to me far more productive, of far greater
extent, of far greater utility, than the source of character.
If the character was a little exaggerated, then the spectator
would say to himself, this is not I. But he cannot deny
that the class represented is his class, he cannot possibly
mistake his duties. He is forced to apply that which he
hears to himself."

Palissot's objections to this are not groundless.[2] He
denies that nature is so poor in original characters that
the comic poets have already exhausted them. Molière saw
enough new characters before him and believed that he
had scarcely treated the smallest part of those that could
be treated. The passage in which he rapidly constructs
various of these is as curious as it is instructive, for it
makes us suspect that the Misanthrope would scarcely
have remained his *non plus ultra* if he had lived longer.[3]

---

[1] The dialogue following ' Le fils naturel.'

[2] ' Petites Lettres sur de grands Philosophes,' Letter II.

[3] ' Impromptu de Versailles,' Sc. II.: " Eh ! mon pauvre Marquis,
nous lui (à Molière) fournirons toujours assez de matière, et nous ne

Palissot himself is not infelicitous in adding some new characters of his own observation; the stupid Mæcenas with his servile clients; the man in the wrong place; the suspicious man whose elaborately conceived attacks are wrecked on the simple honesty of a worthy man, the pseudo-philosopher; the eccentric, the hypocrite with social virtues, since the religious hypocrites are somewhat out of fashion. Truly there are no common vistas thus displayed to eyes that can look well into the distance that here opens out into the endless. Here is harvest enough for the few reapers who may dare to venture upon it!

And if the comic characters are really so few and these few have been exhausted, will social classes help us out of this perplexity, objects Palissot? Let us choose one as an example, the position of judge. Must I not give this judge a character? Must he not be sad or merry, serious or careless, affable or violent? And will it not be merely this character which lifts him out of the range of a metaphysical abstraction and converts him into a real being? And consequently will not the foundations of the intrigue and the moral of the play once more rest upon character?

---

prenons guères le chemin de nous rendre sages par tout ce qu'il fait et tout ce qu'il dit. Crois-tu qu'il ait épuisé dans ses comédies tous les ridicules des hommes, et sans sortir de la cour, n'a-t-il pas encore vingt caractères de gens, où il n'a pas touché? N'a-t-il pas, par exemple, ceux qui se font les plus grandes amitiés du monde, et qui, le dos tourné, font galanterie de se déchirer l'un l'autre? N'a-t-il pas ces adulateurs à outrance, ces flatteurs insipides qui n'assaisonnent d'aucun sel les louanges qu'ils donnent, et dont toutes les flatteries ont une douceur fade qui fait mal au cœur à ceux qui les écoutent? N'a-t-il pas ces lâches courtisans de la faveur, ces perfides adorateurs de la fortune, qui vous encensent dans la prospérité, et vous accablent dans la disgrâce? N'a-t-il pas ceux qui sont toujours mécontents de la cour, ces suivants inutiles, ces incommodes assidus, ces gens, dis-je, qui pour services ne peuvent compter que des importunités et qui veulent qu'on les récompense d'avoir obsédé le prince dix ans durant? N'a-t-il pas ceux qui caressent également tout le monde, qui promènent leurs civilités à droite, à gauche, et courent à tous ceux qu'ils voyent avec les mêmes embrassades, et les mêmes protestations d'amitié?—— Va, va, Marquis, Molière aura toujours plus de sujets qu'il n'en voudra, et tout ce qu'il a touché n'est que bagatelle au prix de ce qui reste."

Consequently will not class distinctions again become the accidental?

It is true that Diderot might reply to this: Certainly the person whom I dignify with a standing must also have his individual character; but I desire that this should be such as does not clash with the duties and circumstances of his class but rather harmonises well with them. Therefore if this person is a judge, it is not open to me to make him serious or careless, affable or violent; he must needs be serious and affable and both in the degree that his occupation demands.

This, I say, Diderot might have replied; but then he would have approached another danger, namely the danger of perfect characters. His class personages would never do anything else but what they must do according to their duty and conscience, they would act exactly according to rote. Do we expect this in comedy? Can such representations be attractive enough? Will the advantage we may hope from them be great enough to compensate the labour of creating a new species, of writing a new poetics?

The danger rock of perfect characters does not seem to me to have been sufficiently observed by Diderot. In his plays he rather steers straight towards it and in his critical sea-charts he finds no warning signals. He rather finds matters in it that advise him to direct his course thither. It is only needful to recall what he says on contrasting the characters of Terence's 'Adelphi.' The two contrasted fathers are depicted with equal force, so that the subtlest critic would be perplexed to name the chief personage, whether Micio or Demea. If he pronounces a verdict before the last act he might easily be amazed on finding that he whom he held throughout five acts to be a sensible man, is nothing but a fool, and that he whom he deemed a fool is actually the more sensible man. We should be almost inclined to say at the commencement of the fifth act of this drama, that the author had been forced by the difficulty of contrast, to abandon his end and to reverse the whole interest of the play. What has become of this? We no longer know for whom to interest ourselves. At the beginning we were with Micio against

Demea, and in the end we are for neither. We almost demand a third father to hold the mean between these two and show wherein they have failed.

Not I. I earnestly beg to be excused this third father, whether in the same play or by himself. What father does not think he knows what a father should be? We all think ourselves to be on the right road; we only ask now and then to be warned against aberrations on either side.

Diderot is right; it is better if the characters are only different, not contrasted. Contrasted characters are less natural, and augment the romantic aspect that in any case is seldom lacking to dramatic events. For one gathering in common life wherein the contrast of character is shown as saliently as the dramatist demands, there are thousands where they are merely different. Very true. But is not a character that always moves in the same grooves marked out by reason and virtue, a still greater phenomenon? Among twenty gatherings in common life, we shall sooner find ten in which fathers take totally opposed paths in the education of their children, than one that can show the ideal father. And this true father is always the same, is singular though the variations from him may be endless. Consequently the plays that bring forward the true father will be individually more unnatural, collectively more monotonous, than those which introduce fathers of various principles. It is also certain that those characters which in society seem merely different, contrast themselves of their own accord as soon as conflicting interests put them in motion. It is moreover quite natural that they should then be eager to seem yet more opposed than they really are. The vivacious man will be fire and flame against him who seems to be acting in a lukewarm manner, and the lukewarm man will be cold as ice in order that the other may commit as many indiscretions as may eventually be useful to him.

Nos. 87 and 88.

In like manner other remarks of Palissot's, if not quite just, are not wholly false. He plainly enough discerns the ring into which he would thrust his lance, only in the eagerness of his attack his lance shifts its place, and he just misses the ring. Thus among other things he says of 'Le fils naturel,' "What a strange title! the natural son! Why is the piece so called? What influence does Dorval's birth exert? What event does it provoke? To what situations does it give rise? What void does it fill? What can have been the intention of the author? To serve up a few observations against the prejudice of illegitimate birth? What sensible being does not know of his own accord how unjust is such a prejudice?"

Diderot might have replied to this: This circumstance was needful to the complication of my fable; without it it would have been far more improbable that Dorval should not know his sister, and his sister not know of a brother. It was open to me to borrow the title thence and I might have borrowed the title from a yet more trifling circumstance. If Diderot had replied thus, would Palissot not have been refuted?

Meanwhile the character of the natural son is open to quite another objection with which Palissot could have attacked the poet far more sharply. Namely this, that the circumstance of illegitimate birth and consequent neglect and seclusion imposed on Dorval for many years, is a circumstance too peculiar and singular, must have had too much influence on the formation of his character, for it to have that universality which according to Diderot's own doctrine is demanded in a comic character. This subject tempts me to a digression on this doctrine, and why need I resist such a temptation in a work of this kind?

Diderot says: "The comic genus has species, and the tragic has individuals. I will explain. The hero of a tragedy is such and such a man; he is Regulus, or Brutus, or Cato, and no other. The prominent persons in a comedy, on the other hand, must represent a large number of mankind. If we accorded to them one peculiar physiognomy so that only one single individual could resemble them, comedy would lapse back into its childhood. Terence seems to me to have once fallen into this error. His Heautontimorumenos is a father who sorrows over the

fearful resolution to which he has driven his son by excessive rigour and who therefore punishes himself by curtail-
ing his food and clothing, avoiding society, dismissing his
servants, and cultivating his fields with his own hands.
It may be said there are no such fathers: The largest
city would scarcely furnish one example of such rare
sorrow in a century."

In the first place concerning the Heautontimorumenos:
if this character is really to be censured, the blame falls
on Menander, not on Terence. Menander was the creator
of this being, to whom, to all appearance he accorded a
far more extended *rôle* than he plays in Terence's imitation, in which his sphere is limited, because of the double
intrigue.[1] But that it comes from Menander, would

---

[1] That is, if the sixth line of the prologue—

"Duplex quæ ex argumento facta est simplici"

—was really so written by the poet and is not meant to be understood
otherwise than Dacier and after her, the new English translator of
Terence, Colman, explain it. "Terence only meant to say that he had
doubled the characters ; instead of one old man, one young gallant, one
mistress, as in Menander, he has two old men, &c. He therefore adds,
very properly, 'novam esse ostendi,' which certainly could not have been
implied had the characters been the same in the Greek poet." Even
Adrian Barkandus, nay even the old glossa interlinealis of Ascensius
did not read the *duplex* otherwise; 'propter senes et juvenes,' says
this one, and the other writes, 'nam in hac latina senes duo, adolescentes
item duo sunt.' And yet this rendering will not satisfy me, because
I cannot see what remains of the play if we take away the persons by
whom Terence doubled the characters of the old man and the lovers.
I cannot conceive how Menander could treat this subject without
Chremes and Clitipho, both are so interwoven that I cannot think of
a complication or solution without them. I will not even name
another explanation by which Julius Scaliger made himself ridiculous.
Also that which was given by Eugraphius and adopted by Faerne is
quite absurd. In this perplexity the critics have sought to change
now the *duplex*, now the *simplici* in the line, which the MSS. in a
measure justify. Some read—

   'Duplex quæ ex argumento facta est duplici,'
others,
   'Simplex quæ ex argumento facta est duplici.'

What remains but that some one should now come and read—

   'Simplex quæ ex argumento facta est simplici'?

alone have checked me from condemning Terence on its
account. The saying ὦ Μένανδρε καὶ βίε, πότερος ἄρ᾽ ὑμῶν

And quite seriously, this is how I should like to read it. Let any one
refer to the passage in the context and ponder my reasons.

> 'Ex integra Græca integram comœdiam
> Hodie sum acturus Heautontimorumenon:
> Simplex quæ ex argumento facta est simplici.'

It is well known what was reproached to Terence by his envious
co-labourers at the theatre—

> 'Multa contaminasse Græcas, dum facit
> Paucas latinas'

—for he was in the habit of welding two Greek plays into one Latin one.
Thus he combined his 'Andria' from the 'Andria' and 'Perinthia' of
Menander; his 'Eunuchus' from the 'Eunuchus' and the 'Colax'
of the same poet; his 'Brothers' from the 'Brothers' of Menander and
a play of Diphilus. On account of this reproach he justifies himself
in the prologue to his 'Heautontimorumenos.' He admits the fact,
but denies that he has acted otherwise than many good poets before
him :—

> 'Id esse factum hic non negat
> Neque se pigere, et deinde factum iri autumat,
> Habet bonorum exemplum: quo exemplo sibi
> Licere id facere, quod ille fecerunt, putat.'

'I have done it,' he says, 'and I think I shall often do it again.'
This refers to former plays but not to the present one, the 'Heautontimorumenos,' for this was not taken from two Greek plays but from
a single one of this name. And this is what he meant to say in the
contested line as I propose reading it—

> 'Simplex quæ ex argumento facta est simplici.'

'As simple as the play of Menander, so simple is my play,' is what
Terence would say; 'I have put in nothing from other plays, but only
taken from a single one of the same name. It is taken as long as it
is from the Greek play, and the Greek play is all in my Latin one, I
therefore give

> 'Ex integra Græca integram comœdiam.'

The meaning that Faerne found given to *integra* in an old gloss that
it was as much as *a nullo tacta* is manifestly false here, because it
would only apply to the first integra, but nowise to the second
integram. And therefore I believe my supposition and reading will
bear attention. Only the following line will evoke opposition :—

> 'Novam esse ostendi, et quæ esset.'

πότερον ἐμιμήσατο is certainly rather frigid than witty, but would it have been said at all of a poet who was capable of describing characters whereof a large town could only show a specimen once in a century? True, in a hundred and more plays one such character might have escaped him. The most productive head can write itself empty, and when imagination can recall no more real subjects for imitation, it composes such, and these generally become caricatures. Diderot thinks he has observed that Horace who had such delicate taste, had already perceived the fault in question, and had censured it lightly in passing.

The passage is said to be in the second satire of the first book, where Horace desires to show that fools are in the habit of falling from one exaggeration into its opposite. He says that Fufidius fears to be held extravagant.

It will be said: 'If Terence admits that he has taken the whole play from a single play of Menander's, how can he pretend to have proved that his play is new, "novam esse"?' I can easily remove this difficulty by an explanation of these words, of which I venture to aver that it is the only true one, although it has only been said by me and no commentator, so far as I know, has even distantly surmised it. I say that the words

'Novam esse ostendi, et quæ esset'

do not refer to that which Terence makes the prologue say in the former plays, but 'apud ædiles' must be understood. 'Novus' does not here mean what has arisen in Terence's own head, but only what was not existent before in Latin. He says, 'that my play is a new play, that it is such a play as has never before appeared in Latin, that I have myself translated it from the Greek, this I have proved to the ædiles who bought it of me.' To agree with me in this it is only needful to recall the dispute he had concerning his 'Eunuchus' with the ædiles. He had sold this to them as a new translation from the Greek, but his adversary, Lavinius, tried to persuade the ædiles that it was not from the Greek, but taken from the plays of Nævius and Plautus. It is true that the 'Eunuchus' had much in common with these plays, yet still Lavinius's accusation was false, for Terence had only drawn from the same Greek source, whereat Nævius and Plautus had drawn before him, without his knowledge. Therefore to guard against similar calumnies with his 'Heautontimorumenos' what was more natural than that he showed the ædiles the Greek original, and instructed them concerning its contents? Nay the ædiles may even have demanded this of him, and this is the reference:—

'Novam esse ostendi, et quæ esset.' "

What does he do? He lends monthly at five per cent.
and gets himself paid in advance. The more another
needs the money, the more interest he demands. He knows
the names of all the youths who are of good family, and
are entering the world, but who have to complain of hard
fathers. Perhaps you expect that this man makes a show
that matches with his revenues? Far from it! He is his
own most cruel enemy and the father in the comedy who
punishes himself for his son's departure cannot torture
himself worse: *non se pejus cruciaverit.* This "worse," this
pejus Diderot insists has a double meaning; in one sense it
applies to Fufidius, and in another to Terence; such incidental hits were, he thinks, quite in the character of Horace.

This may be the case without its being applied to the
passage in question. For here it seems to me, the incidental allusion would damage the main sense. Fufidius
is not so great a fool if there are more such fools. If the
father in Terence tortures himself thus foolishly, if he had
as little cause to torture himself as Fufidius, he shares this
absurdity and Fufidius becomes less absurd and singular.
Only if Fufidius is as hard and cruel against himself
without cause, as the father in Terence is with cause, if
he does from vile avarice what the other does from remorse
and sorrow only, then we shall deem the former quite
contemptible and ridiculous, while we consider the latter
pitiable. And certainly every great sorrow is of the
nature of the sorrow of this father; if it does not forget
itself it tortures itself. It is against all experience that
an example of such sorrow is found only once in a hundred
years. Every sorrow acts somewhat in this manner, only
more or less so and with some difference or other. Cicero had
studied the nature of sorrow more deeply. In the behaviour
of the Heautontimorumenos he saw nothing more than
what all mourners would do, not only when they are
carried away by feeling, but as they think they must
continue in cold blood.[2] "Hæc omnia recta, vera, debita
putantes faciunt in dolore; maximeque declaratur, hoc
quasi officii judicio fieri, quod si qui forte, cum se in
luctu esse vellent, aliquid fecerunt humanius, aut si

---

[2] Tusc. Quæst. lib. iii. c. 27.

hilarius locuti essent, revocant se rursus ad mœstitiam, peccatique se insimulant, quod dolere intermiserint : pueros vero matres et magistri castigare etiam solent, nec verbis solum, sed etiam verberibus, si quid in domestico luctu hilarius ab iis factum est, aut dictum ; plorare cogunt. Quid ille Terentianus ipse se puniens ? " &c.

Menedemus, this is the name of the self-torturer in Terence, is not so hard upon himself from sorrow, but why he denies himself even the smallest luxury is chiefly that he may save the more for his absent son and thus secure in the future a pleasant life to him whom he has forced to embrace such an unpleasant one. What is there in this that a hundred fathers would not do? If Diderot thinks that the peculiar and the singular consists therein, that Menedemus fells, digs, ploughs, he has in his haste thought more of the customs of our times than of those of the ancients. True, a rich modern father would not so easily do this ; very few would know how to set about it, but the rich high-born Romans and Greeks were well acquainted with all agricultural labours and were not ashamed to use their hands.

But granted that all be exactly as Diderot says ; let the character of this self-torturer on account of this singularity, on account of this trait peculiar to him be as unsuited to a comic character as may be :—has not Diderot fallen into the same fault? What can be more eccentric than the character of his Dorval, what character could have more of a peculiar trait than the character of this natural son? Diderot lets him say of himself, " Immediately after my birth I was cast upon a spot that might be called the boundary between society and solitude, and when I opened my eyes and searched for the links that connected me with mankind I could scarcely find any traces of them. For thirty years I wandered about lonely, unknown, unheeded, without feeling the affection of any human being, without meeting any human being who sought mine." That a natural child should search in vain for its parents, that it should look in vain for a person connected with it by the closer ties of blood, is very natural and might happen to nine out of ten. But that he could wander about

for thirty whole years in the world, without having felt
the affection of any human being, that he should not have
met one human being who sought for his affection, this I
am almost inclined to say is absolutely impossible. Or if
it were possible what a number of quite peculiar circumstances must have arisen on both sides, on the side of the
world, and on the side of this so long isolated being, to
make this sad possibility a reality. Century upon century must pass before it could ever become possible again.
At least may Heaven grant that I may never otherwise
conceive of humanity. I would rather else that I had
been born a bear and not a man. It is not possible; no
man can be so lost among men. Cast him whither you
will, if he only falls among men he falls among beings
who before he has had time to look about him are ready
on all sides to attach themselves to him. If not the noble
then it is the lowly; if not the happy, then it is the unhappy; but human beings they always will be. Just so a
drop of water need only touch the surface of water to be
received by and to be absorbed in it, be the water what it
will, pond or well, stream or lake, belt or ocean.

Now this solitude of thirty years among mankind is to
have formed the character of Dorval. What character
could resemble him? Who will recognise himself even in
the smallest particle in him?

I find that Diderot saved himself a loophole. Subsequently to the passage I have quoted; he says "In the
serious genus characters will often be as general as in the
comic, only that they will always be less individual in the
comic than in the tragic." He would therefore reply, the
character of Dorval is no comic character, it is a character
such as serious drama demands and just as this must
fill the place between comedy and tragedy so also the
characters must hold the mean between the comic and
the tragic characters. They need not be as general as the
former if only they are not as entirely individual as the
latter, and of this nature the character of Dorval might be.

Thus we have happily returned to the point from
which we started; we wished to investigate whether it
is true that tragedy has individuals, and comedy species,
that is to say whether it is true that the persons in a

comedy must seize and represent a great number of men
while at the same time the hero of tragedy is only this or
that man, only Regulus or Brutus or Cato. If this is
true, then what Diderot says of the personages of the
middle species, which he calls serious comedy, presents
no difficulties, and the character of Dorval would not be
so blameworthy. But if it is not true then this also
falls of its own accord, and no justification can arise
for the character of the natural son from such an arbitrary
division.

No. 89.

I must first notice that Diderot has left his assertion
without any proof. He must have regarded it as a truth
that no person could or would doubt, which it was only
necessary to know in order to understand its reason. Can
he have found this in the true name of the tragical
hero? because these are called Achilles, Alexander, Cato,
Augustus; and because Achilles, Alexander, Cato, Augustus
were real people can he have assumed therefrom that
all that the poet lets them say and act in tragedy can
only belong to these so-called persons and to no one else
in the world? It would almost seem so.

But Aristotle had refuted this error two thousand
years ago and pointed to the truth of the essential
difference between history and poetry, as well as the
greater benefit conferred by the latter than by the former.
He did this so luminously, that I need only quote his
words to arouse no small wonder how Diderot could have
held an opposite view in so obvious a matter.

Aristotle says[1] after he has established the essential
qualities of the poetic fable. " From this is therefore shown
that it is not the poet's duty to relate what has occurred,
but to relate of what nature these occurrences might
have been, their probability or necessity. For historians
and poets are not distinguished by metrical or unmetrical
speech, for the books of Herodotus might be converted
into metre and they would nevertheless be nothing
more when metrical, than what they are in unmetrical

---

[1] Poetics, 9th chap.

language, a history. They are distinguished herein that the one relates what has occurred, the other relates of what nature the occurrence has been. Therefore poetry is more philosophical and useful than history. Poetry refers to the general and history to the particular. The general is how such and such a man would speak or act according to probability or necessity and this is what poetry regards when giving its names. The particular, on the contrary, is what Alcibiades has done or suffered. All this has been manifestly shown in comedy, for if the fable is constructed according to probability the distinctive names are given afterwards, not as with the iambic poet who remains with the individual. In tragedy we hold by names already existent for the reason that the possible is credible and we do not believe that possible that has not occurred, while that which has occurred must obviously be possible because it would not have occurred if it had not been possible. Yet in some tragedies there are only one or two well-known names and the rest are invented, in some there are none at all, as in Agathon's 'Flower.' In this play actions and names are equally invented, but it does not on this account please the less."

In this passage which I have quoted according to my own translation, trying to be as literal as possible, various matters have been misunderstood or not understood at all by the commentators whom I could consult. What belongs to the matter in hand I must mention.

It is unquestionable that Aristotle makes no distinctions between the personages in tragedy and comedy in regard to their generality. Both, not even excluding the persons in epics,—all persons of poetical imitation without distinction, are to speak and act not only as would become them individually and alone, but as each of them would and must speak or act according to the nature of the same circumstances. In this καθόλου, in this generality, is the sole reason why poetry is more philosophical and more instructive than history; and if it is true that those comic poets who would give especial physiognomies to their personages, so that only a single individual in the world could be like them, would turn back comedy into its childhood and pervert it into satire as

Diderot says; it is equally true that those tragic poets who
would only represent such and such a man, only Cæsar
or Cato according to their individualities without at the
same time showing how these individualities are connected
with the character of Cæsar and Cato that they may
have in common with others, weaken tragedy and debase
it to history.

But Aristotle also says that poetry aims at this generality of the persons by the names accorded them (οὗ
στοχάζεται ἡ ποίησις ὀνόματα ἐπιτιθεμένη) which is specially
marked in comedy. It is this which the commentators
have been satisfied to quote from Aristotle but have not
in the least explained. Many of them have expressed
themselves concerning it in such a manner that we can
clearly see they either had no ideas at all or quite false ones.
The question is : how does poetry regard the generality of
these personages when it accords them names, and how
has this regard to the generality of the person been long
visible especially in comedy ?

The words : ἔστι δὲ καθόλου μὲν, τῷ ποίῳ τά ποι ἄττα συμ-
βαίνει λέγειν, ἢ πράττειν κατὰ τὸ εἰχὸς ἢ τὸ ἀναγκαῖον, οὗ στοχάζεται ἡ ποίησις ὀνόματα ἐπιτιθεμένη, is translated by Dacier
as : " une chose générale, c'est ce que tout homme d'un tel ou
d'un tel caractère, a dû dire, ou faire vraisemblablement
ou nécessairement, ce qui est le but de la poésie lors même
qu'elle impose les noms à ses personnages." Herr Curtius
translates in the same manner " the general is that which
a certain man thinks that a certain character would speak
or do according to probability or necessity. This general
is the goal of poetry even if it imposes names on its
personages." In their annotations also both agree; the
one says entirely what the other says. They both explain what is meant by the general, they both say that
this general is the goal of poetry, but how poetry regards
this general when bestowing its names, of this no one says
a word. The Frenchman with his " lors même," the German with his " even if " show plainly that they knew
nothing or understood nothing of what Aristotle would
say for this " lors même " and " even if " means nothing
more with them than " although " and consequently they
make Aristotle merely say that notwithstanding that

poetry accords to her personages names of individual
persons she does not aim at the peculiarity of these persons but at the general. The words of Dacier[2] which I will
quote in a note show this plainly. Now it is true that
this is not false, but neither does it exhaust the meaning
of Aristotle. Not enough that poetry, regardless of the
names taken by individual persons, aims at generality,
Aristotle says that with these names it aims at generality,
οὗ στοχάζεται. I should imagine that both are not the same
thing, and if they are not the same thing we are
necessarily thrown upon the question at which does it
aim. To this question the commentators do not reply.

No. 90.

How it aims towards it, says Aristotle, this I have
plainly shown long ago in comedy : ἐπὶ μὲν οὖν τῆς κωμῳδίας
ἤδη τοῦτο δῆλον γέγονεν· συστάσαντες γὰρ τὸν μῦθον διὰ τῶν

---

[2] Aristote prévient ici une objection, qu'on pouvait lui faire, sur la
définition, qu'il vient de donner d'une chose générale ; car les ignorants
n'auraient pas manqué de lui dire, qu'Homère, par exemple, n'a point
en vue d'écrire une action générale et universelle, mais une action
particulière, puisqu'il raconte ce qu'on fait de certains hommes, comme
Achille, Agamemnon, Ulysse, etc., et que, par conséquent, il n'y a
aucune différence entre Homère et un historien, qui aurait écrit les
actions d'Achille. Le philosophe va au-devant de cette objection, en
faisant voir que les poëtes, c'est-à-dire, les auteurs d'une tragédie ou
d'un poëme épique, lors même qu'ils imposent les noms à leurs personnages, ne pensent en aucune manière à les faire parler véritablement,
ce qu'ils seraient obligés de faire, s'ils écrivaient les actions particulières et véritables d'un certain homme, nommé Achille ou Édipe, mais
qu'ils se proposent de les faire parler et agir nécessairement ou vraisemblablement : c'est-à-dire, de leur faire dire et faire tout ce que des
hommes de ce même caractère devaient faire et dire en cet état, ou
par nécessité, ou au moins selon les règles de la vraisemblance ; ce
qui prouve incontestablement que ce sont des actions générales et
universelles."
Herr Curtius says nothing else in his annotation, only he endeavours to show the general and particular in examples which
do not fully prove that he has understood the matter to its depth.
For according to them it would only be personified characters whom
the poet makes speak and act, whereas they should be characterised
persons.

εἰκότων, οὕτω τὰ τύχοντα ὀνόματα ἐπιτιθέασι, καὶ οὐχ ὥσπερ οἱ
ἰαμβοποιοὶ περὶ τῶν καθ᾽ ἕκαστον.

For this passage I must also quote the translations of
Dacier and Curtius. Dacier says: "C'est ce qui est déjà
rendu sensible dans la comédie, car les poëtes comiques,
après avoir dressé leur sujet sur la vraisemblance, imposent
après cela à leurs personnages tels noms qu'il leur plaît, et
n'imitent pas les poëtes satyriques, qui ne s'attachent qu'aux
choses particulières," and Curtius says "In comedy this
has long been visible, for after the writers of comedy have
arranged the plan of their fable according to probability,
they give to their personages arbitrary names and do not
set themselves a particular goal like the iambic poets."
What do we find in these translations of that which
Aristotle wished chiefly to say? Neither lets him say anything more than that the comic poets did not act like the
iambic (that is to say the satiric poets) and dwell on the
particular, but went towards the general in their personages, to whom they gave arbitrary names, "tels noms qu'il
leur plaît." Granted that τὰ τύχοντα ὀνόματα means arbitrary
names, what have both translators done with οὕτω? Did
they think this οὕτω meant nothing? and yet here it
means all, for according to this οὕτω the comic poet does
not only give arbitrary names to his personages, but he
gave them these arbitrary names so, οὕτω. And how so?
So that with these names themselves they aimed at the
general: οὗ στοχάζεται ἡ ποίησις ὀνόματα ἐπιτιθεμένη, and
how did this happen? About this I should like to find a
word in the annotations of Dacier and Curtius.

Without further digression it happened as I am about
to tell. Comedy gave names to its personages, names
which by means of the grammatical derivation and composition or by some other meaning expressed the characteristic of these personages, in a word they gave them
speaking names, names it was only needful to hear in
order to know at once of what nature those would be
who bore those names. I will quote a passage from
Donatus on this subject. He says on occasion of the first
line of the first act of 'The Brothers' "Nomina person-
arum in comœdiis duntaxat, habere debent rationem et
etymologiam. Etenim absurdum est, comicum aperte

argumentum confingere: vel nomen personæ incongruum
dare vel officium quod sit a nomine diversum.[1] Hinc
servus fidelis Parmeno: infidelis vel Syrus vel Geta:
miles Thraso vel Polemon; juvenis Pamphilus: matrona
Myrrhina, et puer ab odore Storax: vel a ludo et a
gesticulatione Circus: et item similia. In quibus sum-
mum Poëtae vitium est, si quid et contrario repugnans
contrarium diversumque protulerit, nisi per ἀντιφράσιν
nomen imposuerit joculariter, ut Misargyrides in Plauto
dicitur trapezita." Whoever wishes to be convinced of
this by more examples let him study the names in
Plautus and Terence. Since their plays are all derived
from the Greek, so the names come from the same source,
and in their etymology have always a reference to the
social condition, the mode of thought, and so forth that
these personages had in common with others, even if we
cannot now clearly and certainly trace this etymology.

I will not linger over this well-known matter, but I am
astonished that Aristotle's commentators did not remember
it when Aristotle so unquestionably refers to it. What can
be more true, more clear, than what the philosopher says
of the consideration poetry must evince towards the general in choice of names? What can be more unquestionable
than this, ἐπὶ μὲν τῆς κωμῳδίας ἤδη τοῦτο δῆλον γέγονεν, and that
this consideration has been long openly evinced, especially
in comedy? From its first origin, that is as soon as the
iambic poet rose from the particular to the general, as

---

[1] This sentence might easily be misunderstood. For instance, if we
were to understand it as if Donatus held this as something absurd,
"comicum aperte argumentum confingere." This is not at all
Donatus's meaning. He wished to say it would be absurd if the comic
poet who manifestly invents his theme should give to his personages
awkward names or occupations at variance with their names. For
since the whole subject is wholly the invention of the poet, it was
entirely his own free choice what names he gave to his personages,
and what standing or occupation he meant to connect with these
names. Perhaps Donatus should not have expressed himself so
dubiously, and by the change of a single syllable this difficulty is
avoided. Read either "absurdum est, comicum aperte argumentum
confingentem vel nomen personæ," etc., or else "aperte argumentum
confingere et nomen personæ," etc.

soon as instructive comedy arose out of wounding satire,
sprang the endeavour to indicate this general by means
of the names. The braggart cowardly soldier was not
named like this or that leader of this or that race, he was
called Pyrgopolinices, Captain Wallbreaker. The miserable sycophant who flattered him, was not called like some
poor devil in the city, but was named Artotrogus, Crumb-
cutter. The youth who plunges his father into debt by
his extravagances, especially in the matter of horses, was
not called like this or that noble citizen, he was named
Phidippides, Master Sparehorse.

It might be objected that such suggestive names may
be an invention of the newer Greek comedy to whose
poets the use of real names was gravely forbidden, and
that Aristotle did not know this newer comedy and consequently could take no cognizance of it in his rules. The
latter is maintained by Hurd,[2] but it is as false, as it is false

<hr/>

[2] Hurd, in his dissertation on the various provinces of the drama,
says : " From the account of Comedy, here given, it may appear that
the idea of this drama is much enlarged beyond what it was in Aristotle's time; who defines it to be an imitation of light and trivial
actions, provoking ridicule. His notion was taken from the state and
practice of the Athenian stage; that is from the old or middle comedy
which answers to this description. The great revolution, which the
introduction of the new comedy made in the drama, did not happen
till afterwards." But Hurd merely assumes this, in order that his
explanation of comedy may not be exactly opposed to that of Aristotle. Aristotle certainly lived to see the newer comedy, and he
especially considers it in his ' Nicomachean ethics,' where he treats of
becoming and unbecoming jokes (lib. iv. cap. 14) ἰδοὺ δ᾽ ἄν τις καὶ ἐκ
τῶν κωμῳδιῶν τῶν παλαιῶν καὶ τῶν καινῶν. Τοῖς μὲν γὰρ ἦν γελοῖον ἡ
αἰσχρολογία, τοῖς δὲ μᾶλλον ἡ ὑπόνοια. It might perhaps be said that
under new comedy, middle comedy was here meant, for when there
was no new, the middle was necessarily thus called. It might be
added that Aristotle died in the very Olympiad in which Menander's
first play was performed and the very year before (Eusebius, in
Chronico ad Olymp. cxiv. 4). But it is not correct to reckon the
commencement of the new comedy from Menander. Menander was the
first poet of this epoch according to poetical value, but not according
to time. Philemon, who belongs to it, wrote much earlier, and the
transition from the middle to the new comedy was so imperceptible that
Aristotle cannot possibly have lacked examples thereof. Even Aristophanes had given a sample of this genus, his ' Kokalos ' was so
constructed that Philemon could make it his own with few alterations.
We read in the Life of Aristophanes : Κόκαλον ἐν ᾧ εἰσάγει φθορὰν καὶ

that the older Greek comedy only employed real names.
Even in those plays whose foremost and sole object it
was to make a certain well-known person hated and
ridiculous nearly all the other names except that of
this person were inventions, and invented with reference
to their standing and character.

No. 91.

Indeed the real names themselves we may say not un-
frequently aimed more at the general than the particular.
Under the name of Sokrates, Aristophanes did not seek to
make Sokrates ridiculous and suspicious, but all sophists
who meddled with the education of young people. The
dangerous sophists in general were his theme, and he only
called this one Sokrates because Sokrates was decried as
such an one. Hence a number of traits that did not fit
Sokrates, so that Sokrates himself could calmly stand up
in the theatre and offer himself for comparison. But how
much is the nature of the comedy misapprehended, if
these inexact traits be regarded as nothing but arbitrary
calumnies, and not regarded as that which they are,
enlargement of the individual characters, an elevation
from the personal to the general.

Here much might be said concerning the use generally
of real names in Greek comedy, which has not been
so exactly explained by scholars as it well merits. It
might be noticed that this custom was by no means
universal in older Greek comedy[1] and that only this or

ἀναγνωρισμὸν καὶ τἄλλα πάντα ἃ ἐζηλώσε Μένανδρος. Now as Aristophanes furnishes samples of all varieties of comedy, so Aristotle could
adapt his explanation of comedy from them all. He did this, and
comedy afterwards received no enlargement for which this explanation
became too narrow. If Hurd had rightly understood it, he would not
have needed to have recourse to an assumed ignorance of Aristotle
in order to place his own ideas of comedy, right enough in themselves,
beyond the pale of all disagreement with those of Aristotle.

[1] If, according to Aristotle, the scheme of comedy is borrowed from
the Margites of Homer, οὐ ψόγον, ἀλλὰ τὸ γελοῖον δραματοποιήσαντος,
then, according to all appearance, fictitious names were introduced
from the beginning. For Margites was probably not the real name of
a certain person, since Μαργείτης was more probably made from μάργης,

that poet occasionally ventures upon it,[2] and that consequently it cannot be regarded as a distinctive feature of
this epoch in comedy.[3]   It might be shown that when at

---

than that μάργης should have arisen from Μαργείτης. We find it
especially mentioned by various poets of older comedy that they
refrained from all allusions, which would not have been possible with
real names, for instance, Pherekrates.

[2] Personal satire was so little an essential feature of the older comedy,
that we rather know that poet very well who first ventured upon
it. It was Cratinus who first τῷ χαρίεντι τῆς κωμῳδίας τὸ ὠφέλιμον
προσέθηκε, τοὺς κακῶς πράττοντας διαβάλλων, καὶ ὥσπερ δημοσίᾳ μάστιγι
τῇ κωμῳδίᾳ κολάζων. Even he only ventured at first upon vulgar
disreputable people, from whose resentment he had nothing to fear.
Aristophanes would not be deprived of the honour of being the first to
venture upon the great ones of the state (Ir. v. 750).

> οὐκ ἰδιώτας ἀνθρωπίσκους κωμῳδῶν, οὐδὲ γυναῖκας,
> ἀλλ' Ἡρακλέους ὀργήν τιν' ἔχων, τοῖσι μεγίστοις ἐπιχείρει.

Nay, he would even have wished to have regarded this boldness as his
peculiar privilege. He was very jealous when he saw that so many
other poets, whom he despised, followed him herein.

[3] Which nevertheless nearly always happens. People even go further
and try to maintain that with the real names real events were connected in which the invention of the poet had taken no part. Even
Dacier says : " Aristote n'a pu vouloir dire qu'Épicharmus et Phormis
inventèrent les sujets de leurs pièces, puisque l'un et l'autre ont été
des poëtes de la vieille comédie, où il n'y avait rien de feint, et que ces
aventures feintes ne commencèrent à être mises sur le théâtre, que du
temps d'Alexandre le Grand, c'est-à-dire dans la nouvelle comédie "
(Remarque sur le chap. v. de la Poët. d'Arist.). One might really
fancy that any one who could say this could never even have taken a
peep into Aristophanes. The argument, the fable of old Greek
comedy, was as much invented as the arguments and fables of the
moderns can be. Not one of the remaining dramas of Aristophanes
represents an event that really occurred, and how can we say that the
poet has not invented it because it alludes in part to real events?
When Aristotle assumes as established ὅτι τὸν ποιητὴν μᾶλλον τῶν
μύθων εἶναι δεῖ ποιητήν, ἢ τῶν μέτρων : would he not have been forced
to exclude the authors of old Greek comedy from the class of poets if he
had believed that they had not invented the arguments of their plays ?
But as, according to him, it may be compatible with the poetical
invention of tragedy to borrow names and events from history, it must
also have been the case with comedy. It cannot possibly have been
in keeping with his notions that comedy, by using real names and
alluding to real events, fell back into the iambic love of satire ;
rather he must have believed that καθόλου ποιεῖν λόγους ἢ μύθους was
quite compatible with it. He asserts this of the older comic poets,

last it was strictly forbidden by law, still there always
remained certain persons who were either expressly
excluded from the protection of the law or else were silently
regarded as so excluded. In the plays of Menander people
enough were called by their real names and made ridiculous.[4] But I will not wander from one digression into
another.

I will only make the application to the real names in
tragedy. Just as the Aristophanic Sokrates neither represents nor is intended to represent the individual man of that
name ; just as this personified ideal of a vain and dangerous
school-wisdom only gained the name of Sokrates because
Sokrates was in part known as such a deceiver and
tempter, in part was to become better known as such a one ;
just as the poet was decided in his choice of the name by
the circumstance that the name of Sokrates combined and
should combine yet more the mere conception of character
and position ; so also the conception of character we are
accustomed to combine with the names Regulus, Cato,
Brutus decided the tragic poet in giving these names to his
personages. He introduces a Regulus, a Brutus, not to
make us acquainted with the real adventures of these men,
not to revive their memories, but to entertain us with such
adventures as might and must occur to men of their
character. Now it is true that we have deduced this
character from the real events of their lives, but it does
not therefore follow that their character must lead us back
to these events. Not rarely it will lead us far more
briefly and naturally to quite others with which those

Epicharmus, Phormis and Krates, and would certainly not have denied
it to Aristophanes, even though he knew how much he had taken off
not only Kleon and Hyperbolus, but also Perikles and Sokrates.

[4] The severity with which Plato in his ' Republic' interdicted that
any one should be made ridiculous in comedy was never exercised in
the real Republic. (μήτε λόγῳ, μήτε εἰκόνι, μήτε θυμῷ, μήτε ἄνευ θυμοῦ,
μηδαμὸς μηδένα τῶν πολίτων κωμῳδεῖν.) I will not prove by citation that
in Menander's plays many à cynic philosopher, many a courtesan is
mentioned by name ; it might be replied that this scum of humanity
did not belong to the citizens. But Ktesippus, the son of Chabrias,
was certainly an Athenian citizen, as good as any, and see what
Menander says of him (Menandri, Fr. p. 137, edit. Cl.).

real ones have nothing in common save that they have
flowed from one source, but by paths that cannot be followed, and over tracts of land that have fouled their purity.
In this case the poet will certainly prefer the fictitious to
the real, and yet leave to his personages their real names.
And this for a double reason; in the first place because we
are accustomed to think of a character as it is shown in
its generality in connexion with this name; secondly,
because real names seem to be attached to real occurrences,
and all that has once occurred is more credible than what
has not occurred.   The first of these reasons springs from
the connexion in general of the Aristotelian conceptions;
it is fundamental, and it was not needful for Aristotle
to dwell upon it more circumstantially.   The second on
the contrary required it, as springing from extraneous
causes.   But this lies beside my way just now, and the
commentators in general have misunderstood it less than
the former.

And now to return to Diderot's assertion. If I may
think that I have rightly explained Aristotle's teaching,
then I may also believe that my explanation has proved
that the matter itself cannot possibly be otherwise than
as Aristotle teaches. The characters in tragedy must be
as general as the characters in comedy. The difference
maintained by Diderot is imaginary, or else Diderot must
comprehend under the generality of a character something
quite different from what Aristotle meant thereby.

No. 92.

And why should not the latter be the case? Do I not
find that another and no less excellent critic expresses himself in the same way as Diderot, and seems to contradict
Aristotle almost as flatly, and yet fundamentally contradicts him as little, so that I must acknowledge him among
all critics as the one who has spread most light concerning
this matter.

This is the English commentator on Horace's Poetics,
Hurd . . . Hurd has appended an essay on the various provinces of drama to his commentary. For he thought that
he had observed that up to his time only the general laws

of this mode of poetry had been considered, without establishing the limits of the various species. Yet this must also take place in order to pronounce a fair judgment on the special merits of each species. After therefore defining the intention of drama in general and of the three species—tragedy, comedy, and farce, he deduces from their general and their special objects those qualities which they have in common as well as those which distinguish them.

Among the latter he counts in regard to comedy and tragedy these; that a true occurrence is more suitable to tragedy, a fictitious one to comedy. He thus proceeds: "The same genius in the two dramas is observable in their draught of characters. Comedy makes all characters general; tragedy, particular. The 'Avare' of Molière is not so properly the picture of a covetous man, as of covetousness itself. Racine's 'Nero' on the other hand is not a picture of cruelty, but of a cruel man."

Hurd seems to conclude thus. If tragedy demands a real occurrence, then the characters must be true, that is, must be constructed as they really exist in the individuals. If on the other hand comedy can be satisfied with fictitious occurrences, if probable occurrences in which characters can display themselves in all their range are more acceptable to it than real ones that do not permit of such wide scope; then its characters may and must of themselves be more general than they exist in nature, seeing that such generality assumes in our imagination a kind of entity, which has exactly the same relation to the real existence of the individual as the probable has to the actual.

I will not now examine whether this mode of conclusion is not a mere circle. I will merely accept the conclusion as it lies and as it directly contradicts the teaching of Aristotle. But as I have said, it only seems so to do, as is demonstrated from Hurd's extended explanation.

He says: "Yet here it will be proper to guard against two mistakes, which the principles now delivered may be thought to countenance.

"The *first* is with regard to *tragic* characters, which I say are *particular*. My meaning is, that they are *more* particular than those of comedy. That is, the *end* of tragedy does not require or permit the poet to draw together so many of those characteristic circumstances which show the manners, as comedy. For in the former of these dramas, no more of *character* is shown, than what the course of the action necessarily calls forth. Whereas, all or most of the features, by which it is usually distinguished are sought out and industriously displayed in the latter.

" The case is much the same as in *portrait-painting*, where if a great master be required to draw a *particular face*, he gives the very lineaments he finds in it; yet so far resembling to what he observes of the same turn in other faces, as not to affect any minute circumstances of peculiarity. But if the same artist were to design a *head* in general, he would assemble together all the customary traits and features, anywhere observable through the species, which should best express the idea, whatever it was, he had conceived in his own mind and wanted to exhibit in the picture.

" There is much the same difference between the two sorts of *dramatic* portraits. Whence it appears that in calling the tragic character *particular*, I suppose it only *less representative* of the kind than the comic, not that the draught of so much character as it is concerned to represent shall not be *general*, the contrary of which I have asserted and explained at large elsewhere.[1]

" Next I have said, the characters of just comedy are *general*. And this I explain by the instance of the ' Avare ' of Molière which conforms more to the idea of *avarice*, than to that of the real *avaricious man*. But here again, the reader will not understand me, as saying this in the strict sense of the words. I even think Molière faulty in the instance given; though, with some necessary explanation, it may well enough serve to express my meaning.

[1] At the words in Horace's ' Poetics ' : " Respicere exemplar vitæ morumque jubebo Doctum imitatorem, et veras hinc ducere voces," where Hurd shows that the truth here demanded by Horace means such an expression as conforms to the general nature of things, while falsehood means that which, however suitable to the particular instance in view, does yet not correspond to such general nature.

" The view of the comic scene being to delineate characters, this end, I suppose, will be attained most perfectly, by making these characters as *universal* as possible. For thus the person shown in the drama being the representative of all characters of the same kind, furnishes in the highest degree the entertainment of *humour*. But then this universality must be such as agrees not to our idea of the *possible* effects of the character as conceived in the abstract, but to the *actual* exertion of its powers, which experience justifies and common life allows. Molière, and before him Plautus, had offended in this; that for a picture of the *avaricious man*, they presented us with a fantastic, unpleasing draught of the *passion of avarice*. I call this a *phantastic* draught because it hath no archetype in nature. And it is, farther, an *unpleasing* one for, being the delineation of a *simple passion unmixed* it wanted all those

   " ' Lights and shades, whose well accorded strife
     Gives all the strength and colour of our life.'

All these *lights* and *shades* (as the poet finely calls the intermixture of many passions, which, with the *leading* or principal ones form the human character) must be blended together in every picture of dramatic manners, because the avowed business of the drama is to image real life. Yet the draught of the *leading* passion must be as general as this strife in nature permits, in order to express the intended character more perfectly."

No. 93.

" All which again is easily illustrated in the instance of painting. In *portraits of character*, as we may call those that give a picture of the *manners*, the artist, if he be of real ability, will not go to work on the possibility of an abstract idea. All he intends, is to show that some one quality *predominates;* and this he images strongly, and by such signatures as are most conspicuous in the operation of the *leading passion*. And when he hath done this, we may, in common speech or in compliment, if we please, to his art, say of such a portrait that it images to us not the *man* but the *passion;* just as the ancients observed of the famous statue of Apollodorus by Silarion, that it expressed not the angry *Apollodorus*, but his passion of anger.[1] But by this must be understood only that he has well expressed the leading parts of the designed character. For the rest he treats his *subject* as he would any other ; that is, he represents the *concomitant affections*, or considers merely that general symmetry and proportion which are expected in a human figure. And this is to copy nature, which affords no specimen of a man turned all into a single passion. No metamorphosis could be more strange or incredible. Yet portraits of this vicious taste are the admiration of common starers, who, if they find a picture of a *miser* for instance (as there is no commoner subject of moral portraits) in a collection, where every muscle is strained, and feature hardened into the expression of this idea, never fail to profess their wonder and approbation of it. On this idea of excellence, Le Brun's book of the Passions must be said to contain a set of the unjustest *moral portraits*. And the characters of Theophrastus might be recommended, in a dramatic view, as preferable to those of Terence.

" The *virtuosi* in the fine arts would certainly laugh at the former of these judgments. But the latter, I suspect, will not be thought so extraordinary. At least if one may guess from the practice of some of our best comic writers and the success which such plays have commonly met with. It were easy to instance in almost all plays of character. But if the reader would see the extravagance of building dramatic manners on abstract ideas, in its full light, he needs only turn to Ben Jonson's ' Every Man out of his Humour ' ;[2] which under the name of the *play of character*

---

[1] " Non hominem ex ære fecit, sed iracundiam."—Plin. xxxiv. 8.

[2] Ben Jonson has named two comedies after " humour," the one 'Every Man in his Humour,' the other 'Every Man out of his Humour.' The word " humour " had come up in his time, and was misused in the most absurd manner. This abuse, as well as its real meaning, he expresses in the following lines :—

> " As when some one peculiar quality
> Doth so possess a man, that it doth draw
> All his affects, his spirits, and his powers,
> In their constructions, all to run one way,
> This may be truly said to be a humour.   [But

is in fact, an unnatural, and, as the painters call it, *hard* delineation of a group of *simply existing passions*, wholly chimerical, and unlike to anything we observe in the commerce of real life. Yet this comedy has always had its admirers. And *Randolph* in particular, was so taken with the design, that he seems to have formed his *Muse's looking-glass* in express imitation of it.

"Shakespeare, we may observe, is in this as in all the other more essential beauties of the drama, a perfect model. If the discerning reader peruse attentively his comedies with this view, he will find his *best-marked* characters discoursing through a great deal of their *parts* just like any other, and only expressing their essential and leading qualities occasionally, and as circumstances concur to give an easy exposition to them. This singular excellence of his comedy was the effect of his copying faithfully after nature, and of the force and vivacity of his genius, which

---

> But that a rook by wearing a pied feather,
> The sable hatband, or the three-piled ruff,
> A yard of shoe-tye, or the Switzer's knot
> On his French garters should affect a humour!
> Oh! it is more than most ridiculous."

In the history of Humour, therefore, these two plays of Jonson are important documents, and the second even more than the first. The humour we now especially ascribe to the English was then chiefly affectation, and it was notably to make this affectation ludicrous that Jonson depicted humour. To take the matter accurately, only such affected humour, never the real thing, should form the theme of a comedy. For only the desire to be distinguished from others, to be remarkable through some peculiarity, is a general human weakness, which, according to the nature of the means chosen, can be very absurd or very culpable. But that whereby Nature herself, or a long-continued habit that has become second nature, marks out an individual man from all others, is far too special to accord with the general philosophical intentions of the drama. The overladen humour in many English plays might consequently form their distinctive, but not their best feature. It is certain that not a trace of humour is found in the drama of the ancients. The old dramatic poets, indeed the old poets in general, possessed the artistic secret of individualising their characters without the aid of humour. The old historians and orators certainly evince humour now and then, when for instance historical truth or the exposition of certain facts demands an accurate description καθ' ἕκαστον. . . .

made him attentive to what the progress of the scene suc-
cessively presented to him; whilst *imitation* and *inferior
talents* occasion little writers to wind themselves up into
the habit of attending perpetually to their main view and
a solicitude to keep their favourite characters in constant
play and agitation.   Though in this illiberal exercise of
their wit, they may be said to use *the persons of their drama*
as a certain facetious sort do their *acquaintance,* whom they
urge and tease with their civilities, not to give them a
reasonable share in the conversation, but to force them to
play *tricks* for the diversion of the company."

No. 94.

So much for the generality of the comic character and
the limits of this generality, according to Hurd's idea!
But it will still be necessary to quote the second passage,
where he tells us he has explained in how far the tragic
characters, though they are only particular, yet partake
of a generality, before we can draw any conclusion whether,
and how far, Hurd agrees with Diderot and both agree
with Aristotle.

" *Truth* in poetry, means such an expression, as conforms
to the general nature of things; *falsehood,* that, which
however suitable to the particular instance in view, doth
yet not correspond to such *general nature.*   To attain to
this *truth* of expression in dramatic poetry, two things are
prescribed : first, a diligent study of the Socratic philosophy, and secondly, a masterly knowledge and comprehension of human life.   The first, because it is the peculiar
distinction of that school : *ad veritatem vitæ propius accedere*
(Cic. de Orat. lib. 1, c. 51) and the latter, as rendering the
imitation more universally striking.   This will be understood in reflecting *that truth may be followed too closely in
works of imitation ;* as is evident in two respects.   For first,
the artist, when he would give a copy of nature, may
confine himself too scrupulously to the exhibition of
particulars, and so fail of representing the general idea of
the *kind.*   Or, second, in applying himself to give the
general idea, he may collect it from an enlarged view of
real life, whereas it were still better taken from the nobler

conception of it as subsisting only in the *mind*. This last is the kind of censure we pass upon the Flemish school of painting, which takes its model from real nature, and not, as the Italian, from the contemplative idea of beauty. The former corresponds to that other fault objected also to the Flemish masters, which consists in their copying from particular, odd and grotesque nature in contradistinction to general and graceful nature.

" We see then that in deviating from particular and partial, the poet more faithfully imitates *universal* truth. And thus an answer occurs to that refined argument which Plato invented and urged, with such seeming complacency, against *poetry*. It is that *poetical imitation is at a great distance from truth*. " Poetical expression," says the philosopher, " is the copy of the poet's own conceptions; the poet's conception of things, and things, of the standing archetype, as existing in the divine mind. Thus the poet's expression, is a copy at third hand, from the primary, original truth " (Plato, de Rep. lib. x.). Now the diligent study of this rule of the poet obviates this reasoning at once. For, by abstracting from existences all that peculiarly respects and discriminates the *individual*, the poet's conception, as it were neglecting the intermediate particular objects, catches, as far as may be, and reflects the divine archetypal idea and so becomes itself the copy or image of truth. Hence too we are taught the force of that unusual encomium on poetry by the great critic, *that it is something more severe and philosophical than history*, φιλοσο-φώτερον καὶ σπουδαιότερον ποίησις ἱστορίας ἐστίν. The reason follows, which is now very intelligible ; ἡ μὲν γὰρ ποίησις μᾶλλον τὰ καθόλου ἡ δ' ἱστορία τὰ καθ' ἕκαστον λέγει (Poetics cap. 9). And this will further explain an essential difference, as we are told, between the two great rivals of the Greek stage. Sophokles, in return to such as objected a want· of truth in his characters, used to plead, *that he drew men such as they ought to be, Euripides such as they were—* Σοφόκλης ἔφη αὐτὸς μὲν οἵους δεῖ ποιεῖν, Εὐριπίδης δὲ οἷοι εἰσί (Poetics, cap. 25). The meaning of which is, Sophokles from his more extended commerce with mankind, had enlarged and widened the narrow, partial conception,. arising from the contemplation of *particular* characters, into a complete comprehension of the *kind*. Whereas the philosophic Euripides, having been mostly conversant in the academy, when he came to look into life, keeping his eye too intent on single, really existing personages, sunk the *kind* in the *individual;* and so painted his characters naturally indeed, and *truly*, with regard to the objects in view, but sometimes without that general and universally striking likeness, which is demanded to the full exhibition of poetical truth.[1]

"But here an objection meets us, which must not be overlooked. It will be said, "that philosophic speculations are more likely to render men's views *abstract* and *general* than to confine them to *individuals*. This latter is a fault arising from the *small number* of objects men happen to contemplate : and may be removed not only by taking a view of many *particulars*, which is knowledge of the world ; but also by reflecting on the *general nature* of men, as it appears in good books of morality. For the writers of such books form their *general* notion of human nature from an extensive experience (either their own or that of others) without which their writings are of no value." The answer, I think, is this. *By reflecting on the general nature of man* the philosopher learns what is the tenor of action arising from the predominancy of certain qualities or properties : *i.e.* in general, what that conduct is, which

---

[1] This explanation is greatly to be preferred to that which Dacier gives of this passage in Aristotle. It is true that according to the wording of the translation, Dacier seems to say exactly what Hurd says ; "que Sophocle faisait ses héros, comme ils devaient être et qu'Euripide les faisait comme ils étaient." But in reality he combines an entirely different idea with it. Hurd understands in the expression ' as they should be,' the general abstract idea of kind, according to which the poet must depict his personages, rather than according to their individual peculiarities. But Dacier understands by this a higher moral perfection, such as man is able to attain, although he seldom attains it, and it is this, he says, with which Sophokles generally endowed his personages. "Sophocle tâchait de rendre ses imitations parfaites, en suivant toujours bien plus ce qu'une belle nature était capable de faire, que ce qu'elle faisait." But it is just this higher moral perfection that does not belong to the general idea, it pertains to the individual, but not to the kind, and therefore the poet who endows his personages with it, is really representing them rather in the manner of Euripides than in that of Sophokles. The further treatment of this matter deserves more than a note.

the imputed character requires. But to perceive clearly
and certainly, how far, and with what degree of strength
this or that character will, on particular occasions, most
probably show itself, this is the fruit only of a knowledge
of the world. Instances of a want of this knowledge cannot be supposed frequent in such a writer as Euripides;
nor, when they occur, so glaring as to strike a common
reader. They are niceties, which can only be discerned
by the true critic; and even to *him*, at this distance of
time, from an ignorance of the Greek manners, that may
possibly appear a fault, which is a real beauty. It would
therefore be dangerous to think of pointing out the places,
which Aristotle might believe liable to this censure in
Euripides. I will however presume to mention one, which,
if not justly criticised, will, at least, serve to illustrate
my meaning.

No. 95.

"The story of his 'Electra' is well known. The poet
had to paint in the character of this princess, a virtuous,
but fierce resentful woman; stung by a sense of personal
ill-treatment, and instigated to the revenge of a father's
death, by still stronger motives. A disposition of this
warm temperament, it might be concluded by the philosopher in his closet, would be prompt to show itself.
Electra would, on any proper occasion, be ready to vow
her resentment, as well as to forward the execution of her
purpose. But to what lengths would this *resentment* go?
i.e. what degree of fierceness might Electra express,
without affording occasion to a person widely skilled in
mankind and the operation of the passions, to say, "This
is improbable"? Here abstract theories will be of little
service. Even a moderate acquaintance with real life will
be unable to direct us. Many individuals may have
fallen under observation, that will justify the poet in
carrying the expression of such a *resentment* to any
extreme. History would perhaps furnish examples, in
which a virtuous resentment hath been carried even
further than is here represented by the poet. What way
then of determining the precise bounds and limits of it?

Only by observing in numerous instances, *i.e.* from a large extensive knowledge of practical life, how far it usually, in such characters, and under such circumstances, prevails. Hence a difference of representation will arise in proportion to the extent of that *knowledge.* Let us now see how the character before us, hath in fact, been managed by Euripides.

In that fine scene, which passes between Electra and Orestes, whom as yet she suspects not to be her brother, the conversation very naturally turns upon Electra's distresses, and the author of them, Clytemnestra, as well as on her hopes of deliverance from them by the means of Orestes. The dialogue upon this proceeds :—

OR. What then of Orestes, were he to return to this Argos?

EL. Ah! wherefore that question, when there is no prospect of his return at all?

OR. But supposing he should return, how would he go about to revenge the death of his father?

EL. In the same way, in which that father suffered from the daring attempts of his enemies.

OR. And would you then dare to undertake with him the murder of your mother?

EL. Yes, with that very steel, with which she murdered my father.

OR. And am I at liberty to relate this to your brother, as your fixed resolution?

EL. I desire only to live, till I have murdered my mother.

The Greek is still stronger.

θάνοιμι, μητρὸς αἷμ᾽ ἐπισφάζασ᾽ ἐμῆς.

May I die, as soon as I have murdered my mother!

Now that this last sentence is absolutely unnatural, will not be pretended. There have been doubtless many examples, under the like circumstances, of an expression of revenge carried thus far. Yet, I think, we can hardly help being a little shocked at the fierceness of *this* expression. At least Sophokles has not thought fit to carry it to that extreme. In him, Electra contents herself with saying to Orestes, on a similar occasion :—

" The conduct of this affair now rests upon you. Only
let me observe this to you, that, had I been left alone, I
would not have failed in one of these two purposes, either
to deliver myself gloriously, or to perish gloriously."

" Whether this representation of Sophokles be not more
agreeable to *truth* as collected from wide observation: *i.e.*
from human nature at large, than that of Euripides, the
capable reader will judge. If it be the reason I suppose
to have been, that Sophokles painted his characters such
as, attending to numerous instances of the same kind, he
would conclude they ought to be; Euripides, such, as a
narrower sphere of observation had persuaded him they
were."

Most excellent! Even regardless of my intention in
quoting these long passages from Hurd they unquestionably contain so many subtle observations, that my readers
will probably relieve me from making any excuses on the
score of this interpolation. I am only afraid lest over it
he should have lost sight of my intention. It was this:
to show that Hurd also, like Diderot, accorded particular
characters to tragedy and general ones to comedy, and
yet nevertheless did not wish to contradict Aristotle, who
demands the generality of all poetic characters and
consequently also of the tragic ones. Hurd thus explains
himself: the tragic character must be particular, or
rather less general than the comic, *i.e.* it must be less
representative of its kind, while at the same time the
little that it is deemed well to show of it, must be conceived according to the generality demanded by Aristotle.[1]

Now comes the question whether Diderot also wishes to
be thus understood? And why not, if he desires to be
found nowhere in contradiction to Aristotle? It may be
permitted to me who am concerned that two thinking
heads should not say Yes and No about the same matter,
to foist this exposition upon Diderot, to lend him this
subterfuge.

But rather let me say another word about this subterfuge. It seems to me an evasion and yet no evasion. For

[1] In calling the tragic character *particular*, I suppose it only less
representative of the kind than the comic, not that the draught of so
much character as it is concerned to represent should not be *general.*

obviously the word *general* is taken in a double and quite different sense. The one in which Hurd and Diderot deny it to tragic characters, is not the same in which Hurd assents to it for them. Certainly the subterfuge just rests on this; but how if the one exactly excludes the other?

In the first sense a *general* character means a character in which what has been observed in one or more individuals, is welded together; in a word, an *overladen* character. It is more the personified idea of a character than a characterized person. In the other sense a *general* character means a character in which a certain average, a certain mean proportion has been taken from many or all individuals; in a word a *common* character, not in so far as concerns the character itself but in as far as the degree and measure of the same is common.

Hurd is quite right in explaining Aristotle's καθόλου as generality in the second sense. But if Aristotle demands this generality as well from the comic as the tragic characters, how is it possible that the same character can also possess the other generality? How is it possible that it should at the same time be *overladen* and *common*? And even granted it were not nearly as overladen as the characters in the censured play of Jonson's, granted it might still represent an individual, and that examples really existed that it showed itself as strongly and consistently in some human beings; would it not therefore be yet more *uncommon* than is permitted by the Aristotelian generality?

This is the difficulty! I here remind my readers that these sheets are to contain anything rather than a dramatic system. I am therefore not bound to resolve all the difficulties I raise. My thoughts may seem less and less connected, may even seem to contradict themselves, what matter if only they are thoughts amid which may be found matter for individual thinking! I only want here to scatter *Fermenta cognitionis*.

No. 96.

On the fifty-second evening Herr Romanus's ' Brothers'
was repeated.

Or rather I should say the ' Brothers' of Herr Romanus.
Donatus remarks on the occasion of the ' Brothers' by
Terence: " Hanc dicunt fabulam secundo loco actam,
etiam tum rudi nomine poëtæ; itaque sic pronunciatam,
Adelphoi Terenti, non Terenti Adelphoi, quod adhuc
magis de fabulæ nomine poëta, quam de poëtæ nomine
fabula commendabatur." Herr Romanus has issued his
comedies without his name, but his name has got known
by their means. Those plays of his that have kept their
place on our boards are a recommendation to his name,
which is named in provinces in Germany where without
them it would never have been heard. What ill-fate
kept this man from continuing his labours for the stage
until the plays had ceased to commend his name and his
name commended the plays instead!

The most of what we Germans possess in the domain of
belles-lettres are attempts by young people. Indeed, the
prejudice is almost universal among us that it only befits
young people to labour in this field. Men, it is said,
have more serious studies, more important business to
which Church or State invites them. Verses and
comedies are named playthings; it is possible that they
are not useless exercises with which we may occupy
ourselves up to at most our twenty-fifth year. As soon
as we approach manhood we ought carefully to dedicate
all our strength to a useful profession. If this profession
leaves us a little time wherein to write something, still
we ought to write nothing but what can coexist with
its gravity and its civic dignity; a neat compendium of
the higher faculties, a good chronicle of our dear native
town, an edifying sermon and such like.

Thence it arises that our *belles-lettres* have such a
youthful, ay a childish appearance compared with, I will
not say, the literature of the ancients, but even compared with that of all modern educated nations, and that
they will long, long retain it. It is not actually wanting
in blood and life, in colour and fire, but power and nerves,

marrow and bones are greatly lacking. It has as yet so few works which a man, practised in thinking, cares to take up, when he wishes for once to think for his recreation and invigoration, outside the uniform tedious circle of his daily occupations. What nourishment can such a man find, for instance, in our most puerile comedies? Puns, proverbs, jokes that can be heard daily in the streets, such stuff may cause laughter in the pit that enjoys itself as best it can, but whoever desires to be amused beyond mere titillation, whoever wishes to laugh with his reason, he goes to the theatre once and never goes again.

Who has nothing, can give nothing. A young man just entering upon the world himself, cannot possibly know and depict the world. The greatest comic genius shows itself empty and hollow in its youthful works; Plutarch[1] even says of the first plays of Menander that they are not to be compared with his later and better plays. And he adds that we may thence conclude what he would still have produced had he lived longer. And how young is it supposed that Menander died? How many comedies is it supposed that he had already written? Not less than a hundred and five and not younger than fifty-two.

None of all our deceased comic poets, who are worth naming lived to that age; none of those now living are as yet so old; none of either have written a fourth part as many plays. And should not criticism have the same to say concerning them which it has just said of Menander? Let her only venture and speak out.

But it is not only the authors who listen with displeasure. We have now, Heaven be praised, a generation of critics whose highest criticism consists in making all criticism suspicious. They vociferate: "Genius! Genius! Genius overcomes all rules! What genius produces is rules!" Thus they flatter genius; I fancy in order that they too may be held geniuses. But they too evidently betray that they do not feel a spark of it in themselves,

---

[1] 'Επιτ. τῆς συγκρίσεως 'Αριστ. καὶ Μενάν. p. 1588. Ed. Henr. Stephani.

when they add in one and the same breath: "Rules oppress genius." As if genius could be oppressed by anything in the world! And yet more by something that, as they themselves admit, is deduced from it. Not every critic is a genius; but every genius is a born critic. He has the proof of all rules within himself. He comprehends, remembers and follows only those that express his feelings in words. And these his feelings expressed in words should be able to limit his activity? Reason with him about this as much as you will, he only understands you in so far as he recognises your general axioms in a momentarily objective case, and he only remembers this particular case, and during work this affects his powers neither more nor less than the remembrance of a felicitous example or of an individual experience would do. To maintain therefore that rules and criticism can oppress genius, means to maintain in other words, that example and practice can do this; means not only limiting genius to itself but even to its first attempts.

These wise gentlemen know as little what they want when they lament so amusingly over the unfavourable impression which criticism makes on the public. They would like to persuade us that no one any longer thinks a butterfly bright and beautiful since the large magnifying glass has shown us that these colours are but dust.

"Our theatre," they say, "is yet of too tender an age to bear the monarchical sceptre of criticism. It is almost more needful to show the means how the ideal can be attained than to demonstrate how far we are still removed from that ideal. The stage must reform by examples, not by rules. It is easier to reason than to invent."

Now does that mean clothing ideas in words, or does it not rather mean seeking thoughts to put to words and finding none? And who are they after all, who talk so much of examples and invention? What examples have they furnished? What have they invented? The cunning fellows! When examples come before them for judgment they wish for rules; and if they are to judge rules, then they would rather have examples. Instead of proving that a criticism is false, they demonstrate that it is too severe and then think they have neutralized it. Instead of confuting a line of argument, they note that invention is harder than reasoning and think they have confuted it!

Whoever reasons rightly, invents, and whoever desires to invent must be able to reason. Only those who are not fitted for either believe that they can separate the one from the other.

But why do I detain myself over these chatterers? I will go my way and remain regardless of what the grass-hoppers chirp by the roadside. Even a step aside to crush them is too much honour. The end of their summer is not long to await.

Therefore, without further introduction, to the comments I promised to make on the occasion of the first representation of Herr Romanus's 'Brothers.' The principal of these will relate to the changes he deemed it needful to make in Terence's fable, in order to bring it nearer to our manners.

What indeed can be said in general as to the necessity of such changes? If we find so little objection to see Roman or Greek customs depicted in tragedy, why not also in comedy? Whence the rule, if it is a rule, to place the scene of the one in a distant land, among a strange people, and to place the other in our homes? Whence the necessity, which we impose on the poet, of depicting in the former as accurately as may be the manners of the people among whom his action takes place, when we only demand in the latter that our own manners be depicted by him? Pope says of this, that on first sight, this appears mere obstinacy, mere whim, but that it has its reason in nature. What we chiefly seek in comedy is a faithful picture of common life, of whose fidelity, however, we cannot be so easily assured if we see it disguised in strange fashions and customs. In tragedy on the other hand, it is the action that chiefly attracts our attention, and in order to use a native event for the stage we should have to take greater liberties with the action, than a well-known history permits.

No. 97.

This solution, strictly speaking, might not prove satis-factory in all plays.   For admitting that foreign manners do not meet the requirements of comedy as well as native ones, the question remains whether native manners do not bear a better relation to the intention of tragedy than foreign ones?   This question is not answered by the difficulty of making a native event serviceable for the stage without too marked and offensive changes.   True, native manners demand native events, but if with these tragedy attained its aim more easily and certainly, then it ought to be better to surmount all the difficulties that stand in the way of this treatment than to fall short of the essential intention which is unquestionably its aim. Neither will all native events demand such marked and offensive changes, and we are not obliged to treat of those that require them.   Aristotle has already remarked that there can and may be events that have occurred exactly in the manner the poet requires.   Since such however are rare, he has decided that the poet should trouble himself less about the minority among his spectators who are perhaps instructed concerning the exact circumstances, than about discharging his duty.

The advantage possessed by native customs in comedy rests on the intimate acquaintance we have with them. The poet does not first need to acquaint us with them; he is therefore relieved from all requisite descriptions and hints, he can at once let his personages act in accord-ance with their customs without first having tediously to describe these customs.   Native customs therefore facilitate his labour and enhance the illusion of the spectator.

Now wherefore should the tragic poet resign this important double advantage?   He too has reason to facilitate his labour as much as may be, and not to squander his strength on side issues but to husband it for the main object.   For him too all depends on the illusion of the spectator.   It may be replied that tragedy does not greatly need customs, that it can completely dispense with them.   But in that case it does not need foreign

customs, and of the little it desires to have and to show
of customs, it will still be better if these are taken from
native customs rather than from foreign ones.

The Greeks at least never based either their comedies
or their tragedies on any customs but their own.   They
rather preferred to lend foreign peoples their Greek
customs when they drew the material of their tragedies
from abroad, than to endanger stage effect by incomprehensible barbaric customs.   They laid little or no weight
on costume—which is so anxiously regarded by our tragic
poets.   The proof of this can manifestly be shown in the
' Persian Women' of Æschylus, and the reason why they
held themselves so little bound by costume is easily to be
deduced from the intention of tragedy.

But I am plunging too far into that portion of the
problem which just now concerns me the least.   Now
when I insist that native customs would be more conformable with tragedy than foreign ones, I assume that
they unquestionably are so in comedy.   And if they are
so, or if I at least believe that they are so, then I cannot
do otherwise than approve the changes which Herr
Romanus made with this intention in the play of Terence.

He was right to transform a fable in which such speci-
fically Greek and Roman customs are so intimately interwoven.   The example only retains its power by means of
its inherent probability, which every one judges by what
is most familiar to him.   All application falls away if we
have first to place ourselves in strange surroundings with
an effort.   But such a transformation is no easy matter.
The more perfect the fable, the less can the smallest part
of it be changed without destroying the whole.   And
woe if we then content ourselves with patches instead of
transforming in the real sense of the word !

* * * * * *

Nos. 101, 102, 103, and 104.

Numbers a hundred and first to fourth ?   I had intended
that the yearly issue of these papers should consist of a
hundred numbers.   Fifty-two weeks—two numbers a week
makes certainly a hundred and four.   But why, among
all workmen, should the weekly journalist be the only

one to have no holidays? And only four in a whole year, that is not too much!

But Dodsley and Company[1] have expressly promised a hundred and four numbers to the public in my name. I must therefore not make these good people liars.

The only question is how am I best to set about it? My material is already cut out, I shall have to patch or to enlarge. But that sounds so bungling. There occurs to me,—what should have occurred to me at once,—that habit of the actors to let a little play succeed their chief representation. The play may deal with what it likes and need not stand in the least connexion with the preceding. Such an after-play then may fill these pages which I had intended to have spared to myself.

First a word concerning myself. For why should not an after-play have a prologue, beginning with a " Poeta cum primum animum ad scribendum appulit"? When a year and a day ago some good folk in this place conceived the idea of trying whether something more could not be done for the German theatre, than could be done under the management of a so-called director, I do not know how it was that they thought of me and dreamed that I could be useful to such an undertaking. I was just standing idly in the market-place, no one wanted to hire me, beyond doubt because no one knew how to use me until these friends came. Until now all occupations of my life have been very indifferent to me; I have never pushed myself into any or offered myself, but neither have I ever refused even the most insignificant to which I felt myself drawn by any kind of predilection.

Whether I would concur in the foundation of the local theatre? to this I could reply easily. My only reasons for hesitation were these, whether I could, and how I could best do so?

I am neither actor nor poet.

It is true that I have sometimes had the honour of being taken for the latter, but only because I have been misunderstood. It is not right to draw such liberal

---

[1] [The assumed name of the piratical reprinters of Lessing's journal. —Tr.]

inferences from the few dramatic attempts I have ventured. Not every one who takes up a brush and lays on colours is a painter. The earliest of my attempts were made at that time of life when we are but too apt to regard inclination and facility as genius. What is tolerable in my later attempts is due, as I am well aware, simply and solely to criticism. I do not feel within myself the living spring that works itself out of its native strength and breaks forth out of its own strength into such rich, fresh, clear streams. I must force everything out of myself by pressure and pipes. I should be poor, cold, shortsighted if I had not learnt in a measure to borrow foreign treasures to warm myself at foreign fires and to strengthen my eyes by the glasses of art. I am therefore always ashamed or annoyed when I hear or read anything in disparagement of criticism. It is said to suppress genius, and I flattered myself that I had gained from it something very nearly approaching to genius. I am a lame man who cannot possibly be edified by abuse of his crutch.

But certainly like the crutch which helps the lame man to move from one place to another and yet cannot make him a runner, so it is with criticism. If by its aid I can produce something which is better than another who has my talents would make without it, yet it costs me much time, I must be free from all other occupations, must not be interrupted by arbitrary distractions, I must have all my learning at hand, I must be able calmly to recollect at every point all the observations I have ever made regarding customs and passions. Hence for a workman who is to furnish a theatre with novelties, no one could be worse suited than I.

Consequently I shall take care to refrain from doing for the German theatre what Goldoni did for the Italian, to enrich it in one year with thirteen new plays. Yes, I should leave that alone even if I could do it. I am more suspicious of first thoughts than even John de la Casa or old Shandy[2] could be. For even if I do not hold them to

---

[2] "An opinion John de la Casa, Archbishop of Benevento, was afflicted with, which opinion was, that whenever a Christian was writing a book (not for his private amusement, but) where his intent and purpose was *bonâ fide* to print and publish it to the world, his first thoughts were always the temptations of the evil one. My father

be temptations of the evil one, either of the real or the allegorical devil, I still think that first thoughts are the first and that the best does not even in all soups swim on the top. My first thoughts are certainly not better by a hair's-breadth than anybody's first thoughts and anybody's first thoughts had best be kept in the background.

At last they hit upon the plan to use that in me which makes me such a slow, or as my more energetic friends deem, such a lazy workman; criticism. And thus arose the idea of these papers.

It pleased me, this idea. It reminded me of the Didaskalia of the Greeks, *i.e.* of the short notices of the kind which even Aristotle thought it worth while to write on the plays of the Greek stage. It reminded me how, a long time ago, I had laughed over the highly learned Casaubon who, from sheer reverence for the solid in scholarship, conceived that Aristotle's chief aim in these Didaskalia had been the rectification of chronology.[3] For in very truth it would have been an everlasting disgrace to Aristotle if he had concerned himself more with the poetical value of plays, with the influence of customs, with the education of taste, than with the Olympiads, than with the years of the Olympiads and with the names of the archons under which they were first performed.

I had had the intention of calling my journal the 'Hamburg Didaskalia.' But the title sounded too foreign and now I am very glad I preferred the present one. What I chose to bring or not to bring into a Dramaturgy, rested with me; at least Lione Allacci could not prescribe to me.

---

was hugely pleased with this theory of John de la Casa, and (had it not cramped him a little in his creed) I believe would have given ten of the best acres in the Shandy estate to have been the broacher of it; but as he could not have the honour of it in the literal sense of the doctrine, he took up with the allegory of it. 'Prejudice of education,' he would say, 'is the devil,' &c." ('Life and Opinions of Tristram Shandy,' vol. v. p. 74).

[3] Animadv. in Athenæum, lib. vi. cap. 7: Διδασκαλία accipitur pro eo scripto, quo explicatur ubi, quando, quomodo et quo eventu fabula aliqua fuerit acta.—Quantum critici hac diligentia veteres chronologos adjuverint, soli æstimabunt illi, qui norunt quam infirma et tenuia præsidia habuerint, qui ad ineundam fugacis temporis rationem primi animum appulerunt. Ego non dubito, eo potissimum spectasse Aristotelem, cum διδασκαλίας suas componeret.

But the learned think they know what a Didaskalia should be like, if only from the extant Didaskalia of Terence which this same Casaubon calls *breviter et eleganter scriptas*. I had no inclination to write my Didaskalia either so briefly or so elegantly, and our contemporaneous Casaubons would have excellently shaken their heads when they found how rarely I touched upon any chronological circumstance that could at some future period throw light on an historical fact when millions of other books should be lost. They would have searched and to their astonishment not found, in my pages, what year of Louis XIV. or XV. first saw such or such a French masterpiece performed, whether at Paris or Versailles, in presence of princes of the blood or not in the presence of princes of the blood.

What else these papers were to have been, concerning this I explained myself in my preface; what they have really become, this my readers know. Not wholly that which I promised to make them, something different and yet I think nothing worse.

They were to accompany every step which the art of the poet as well as the actor should take here.

Of the second half I was very soon weary. We have actors but no mimetic art. If in past times there was such an art, we have it no longer; it is lost, it must be discovered anew. There is enough superficial chatter on the subject in various languages, but special rules, known to every one, pronounced with distinctness and precision, according to which the blame or the praise of an actor can be defined in a particular case, of such I scarcely know two or three. Thence it arises that all our reasoning about this subject always seems so vacillating and dubious, and that it is small wonder if the actor who possesses nothing but a happy routine, feels himself offended by it in all ways. He will never think himself praised enough and will always believe himself blamed too much; ay, he will often not even know whether he has been praised or blamed. Indeed the observation was made long ago that the sensitiveness of artists, with regard to criticism, rises just in that ratio in which the certainty, precision, and number of their principles regarding their art decline. This much in my own defence and in defence of those without whom I should not need to excuse myself.

But how about the first half of my promise? With this the *here* has certainly up to now been very little taken into consideration; and how could it be? The barriers are scarcely opened yet, and it was desired to see the competitors already at the goal; at a goal that every moment was placed further and further away from them. If the public asks, " What has been done?" and answers itself with a sarcastic, "Nothing," then I ask on my part, " What has the public done in order that something might be achieved?" Nothing also, ay, and something worse than nothing. Not enough that it did not help on the work, it did not even permit to it its natural life-course. Out on the good-natured idea to procure for the Germans a national theatre, when we Germans are not yet a nation! I do not speak of our political constitution, but only of our social character. It might almost be said that this consists in not desiring to have an individual one. We are still the sworn copyists of all that is foreign, especially are we still the obedient admirers of the never sufficiently admired French. All that comes to us from beyond the Rhine is beautiful, charming, exquisite, divine. We would rather belie our sight and hearing than find it otherwise. We would rather let ourselves be persuaded that clumsiness is unconstraint; impudence, grace; grimace, expression; a jingle of rhymes, poetry; howling, music; than in the least doubting the superiority in all that is good, beautiful, elevated and correct which this amiable people, this first people in the world, as they are in the habit of modestly calling themselves, have received from just fate as their portion.

But this *locus communis* is so stale, and its nearer application might easily grow so bitter, that I will rather break off from it.

Instead of following the steps which the art of the dramatic poet might have taken here, I was consequently obliged to linger over those that it would have previously had to take, in order afterwards to run its course with larger and more rapid strides. They were the steps that one who has lost his way must retrace in order to get back to the right path and keep his goal straight before him.

Every one may boast of his industry. I believe I have studied the art of dramatic writing, and studied it more than twenty who practise it. I have also practised it so far as it is needful in order to be able to speak my say; for I know well that as the painter does not like to be blamed by one who does not know how to hold a brush, so it is with the poet. I have at least attempted what he must achieve, and can judge whether that can be done though I cannot effect it myself. . . . . .

But it is possible to study until one has studied oneself deep into error. What therefore assures me that this has not happened to me, that I do not mistake the essence of dramatic art is this, that I acknowledge it exactly as Aristotle deduced it from the countless masterpieces of the Greek stage. I have my own thoughts about the origin and foundation of this philosopher's poetics which I could not bring forward here without prolixity. I do not however hesitate to acknowledge (even if I should therefore be laughed to scorn in these enlightened times) that I consider the work as infallible as the Elements of Euclid. Its foundations are as clear and definite, only certainly not as comprehensible and therefore more exposed to misconstruction. Especially in respect to tragedy, as that concerning which time would pretty well permit everything to us, I would venture to prove incontrovertibly, that it cannot depart a step from the plumbline of Aristotle, without departing so far from its own perfection.

In this conviction I set myself the task of judging in detail some of the most celebrated models of the French stage. For this stage is said to be formed quite in accordance with the rules of Aristotle, and it has been particularly attempted to persuade us Germans that only by these rules have the French attained to the degree of perfection from which they can look down on all the stages of modern peoples. We have long so firmly believed this, that with our poets, to imitate the French was regarded as much as to work according to the rules of the ancients.

Nevertheless this prejudice could not eternally stand against our feelings. These were fortunately roused from their slumbers by some English plays, and we at last experienced that tragedy was capable of another quite different effect from that accorded by Corneille and Racine. But, dazzled by this sudden ray of truth, we rebounded to the edge of another prejudice. Certain rules with which the French had made us acquainted, were too obviously lacking to the English plays. What did we conclude thence? This, that without these rules the aim of tragedy could be attained, ay, that these rules were even at fault if this aim were less attained.

Now even this deduction might have passed. But with these rules we began to confound all rules, and to pronounce it generally as pedantry to prescribe to genius what it must do or leave alone. In short we were on the point of wantonly throwing away the experience of all past times and rather demanding from the poet that each one should discover the art anew.

I should be vain enough to deem I had done something meritorious for our theatre, if I might believe that I have discovered the only means of checking this fermentation of taste. I may at least flatter myself that I have worked hard against it, since I have had nothing more at heart than to combat the delusion concerning the regularity of the French stage. No nation has more misapprehended the rules of ancient drama than the French. They have adopted as the essential some incidental remarks made by Aristotle about the most fitting external division of drama, and have so enfeebled the essential by all manner of limitations and interpretations, that nothing else could necessarily arise therefrom but works that remained far below the highest effect on which the philosopher had reckoned in his rules.

. . . .

It is the absolute truth, that the systematic reprint by which it has been sought to make these papers more popular, is the only cause why their publication has been so deferred and why they must be wholly abandoned. Before I say a word more about this, I may be permitted to clear myself of any suspicion of selfishness. The theatre

itself has paid the expenses in the hopes of receiving back
a considerable portion from the sale of the paper. I lose
nothing by the failure of this hope.   Neither am I
annoyed that I cannot bring forward the materials I had
collected for the continuation.   I draw back my hand as
willingly from this plough as I placed it there. . . .

I cannot and will not deny that these last sheets have
been written almost a year later than their date suggests.
The sweet dream of founding a national theatre here in
Hamburg has already faded, and as far as I have now
learnt to know this place, it might be the very last where
such a dream could ever find realization.

But that too can be all the same to me. I should not
like to appear as if I held the failure of efforts in which
I have taken part a signal misfortune.   They are of
no particular value just because I have taken part in
them.   But how, if endeavours of greater import should
fail owing to the same ill-services through which mine
have failed ?   The world loses nothing because I only
bring out two volumes of dramaturgy instead of five or
six.   But it might lose if a more useful work by a better
author were thus hindered, and if there were actually
people who laid express plans that the most useful work,
begun under similar circumstances, should and must come
to an untimely end.

A CATALOGUE OF SELECTED DOVER BOOKS
IN ALL FIELDS OF INTEREST

A CATALOGUE OF SELECTED DOVER BOOKS
IN ALL FIELDS OF INTEREST

WHAT IS SCIENCE?, *N. Campbell*
The role of experiment and measurement, the function of mathematics, the nature of scientific laws, the difference between laws and theories, the limitations of science, and many similarly provocative topics are treated clearly and without technicalities by an eminent scientist. "Still an excellent introduction to scientific philosophy," H. Margenau in *Physics Today.* "A first-rate primer . . . deserves a wide audience," *Scientific American.* 192pp. 5⅜ x 8.
S43   Paperbound $1.25

THE NATURE OF LIGHT AND COLOUR IN THE OPEN AIR, *M. Minnaert*
Why are shadows sometimes blue, sometimes green, or other colors depending on the light and surroundings? What causes mirages? Why do multiple suns and moons appear in the sky? Professor Minnaert explains these unusual phenomena and hundreds of others in simple, easy-to-understand terms based on optical laws and the properties of light and color. No mathematics is required but artists, scientists, students, and everyone fascinated by these "tricks" of nature will find thousands of useful and amazing pieces of information. Hundreds of observational experiments are suggested which require no special equipment. 200 illustrations; 42 photos. xvi + 362pp. 5⅜ x 8.
T196   Paperbound $2.00

THE STRANGE STORY OF THE QUANTUM, AN ACCOUNT FOR THE GENERAL READER OF THE GROWTH OF IDEAS UNDERLYING OUR PRESENT ATOMIC KNOWLEDGE, *B. Hoffmann*
Presents lucidly and expertly, with barest amount of mathematics, the problems and theories which led to modern quantum physics. Dr. Hoffmann begins with the closing years of the 19th century, when certain trifling discrepancies were noticed, and with illuminating analogies and examples takes you through the brilliant concepts of Planck, Einstein, Pauli, Broglie, Bohr, Schroedinger, Heisenberg, Dirac, Sommerfeld, Feynman, etc. This edition includes a new, long postscript carrying the story through 1958. "Of the books attempting an account of the history and contents of our modern atomic physics which have come to my attention, this is the best," H. Margenau, Yale University, in *American Journal of Physics.* 32 tables and line illustrations. Index. 275pp. 5⅜ x 8.
T518   Paperbound $2.00

GREAT IDEAS OF MODERN MATHEMATICS: THEIR NATURE AND USE, *Jagjit Singh*
Reader with only high school math will understand main mathematical ideas of modern physics, astronomy, genetics, psychology, evolution, etc. better than many who use them as tools, but comprehend little of their basic structure. Author uses his wide knowledge of non-mathematical fields in brilliant exposition of differential equations, matrices, group theory, logic, statistics, problems of mathematical foundations, imaginary numbers, vectors, etc. Original publication. 2 appendixes. 2 indexes. 65 ills. 322pp. 5⅜ x 8.
T587   Paperbound $2.00

THE MUSIC OF THE SPHERES: THE MATERIAL UNIVERSE — FROM ATOM TO QUASAR, SIMPLY EXPLAINED, *Guy Murchie*
Vast compendium of fact, modern concept and theory, observed and calculated data, historical background guides intelligent layman through the material universe. Brilliant exposition of earth's construction, explanations for moon's craters, atmospheric components of Venus and Mars (with data from recent fly-by's), sun spots, sequences of star birth and death, neighboring galaxies, contributions of Galileo, Tycho Brahe, Kepler, etc.; and (Vol. 2) construction of the atom (describing newly discovered sigma and xi subatomic particles), theories of sound, color and light, space and time, including relativity theory, quantum theory, wave theory, probability theory, work of Newton, Maxwell, Faraday, Einstein, de Broglie, etc. "Best presentation yet offered to the intelligent general reader," *Saturday Review*. Revised (1967). Index. 319 illustrations by the author. Total of xx + 644pp. 5⅜ x 8½.
T1809, T1810 Two volume set, paperbound $4.00

FOUR LECTURES ON RELATIVITY AND SPACE, *Charles Proteus Steinmetz*
Lecture series, given by great mathematician and electrical engineer, generally considered one of the best popular-level expositions of special and general relativity theories and related questions. Steinmetz translates complex mathematical reasoning into language accessible to laymen through analogy, example and comparison. Among topics covered are relativity of motion, location, time; of mass; acceleration; 4-dimensional time-space; geometry of the gravitational field; curvature and bending of space; non-Euclidean geometry. Index. 40 illustrations. x + 142pp. 5⅜ x 8½.   S1771 Paperbound $1.35

HOW TO KNOW THE WILD FLOWERS, *Mrs. William Starr Dana*
Classic nature book that has introduced thousands to wonders of American wild flowers. Color-season principle of organization is easy to use, even by those with no botanical training, and the genial, refreshing discussions of history, folklore, uses of over 1,000 native and escape flowers, foliage plants are informative as well as fun to read. Over 170 full-page plates, collected from several editions, may be colored in to make permanent records of finds. Revised to conform with 1950 edition of Gray's Manual of Botany. xlii + 438pp. 5⅜ x 8½.   T332 Paperbound $2.25

MANUAL OF THE TREES OF NORTH AMERICA, *Charles Sprague Sargent*
Still unsurpassed as most comprehensive, reliable study of North American tree characteristics, precise locations and distribution. By dean of American dendrologists. Every tree native to U.S., Canada, Alaska; 185 genera, 717 species, described in detail—leaves, flowers, fruit, winterbuds, bark, wood, growth habits, etc. plus discussion of varieties and local variants, immaturity variations. Over 100 keys, including unusual 11-page analytical key to genera, aid in identification. 783 clear illustrations of flowers, fruit, leaves. An unmatched permanent reference work for all nature lovers. Second enlarged (1926) edition. Synopsis of families. Analytical key to genera. Glossary of technical terms. Index. 783 illustrations, 1 map. Total of 982pp. 5⅜ x 8.
T277, T278 Two volume set, paperbound $5.00

IT'S FUN TO MAKE THINGS FROM SCRAP MATERIALS,
Evelyn Glantz Hershoff
What use are empty spools, tin cans, bottle tops? What can be made from
rubber bands, clothes pins, paper clips, and buttons? This book provides
simply worded instructions and large diagrams showing you how to make
cookie cutters, toy trucks, paper turkeys, Halloween masks, telephone sets,
aprons, linoleum block- and spatter prints — in all 399 projects! Many are easy
enough for young children to figure out for themselves; some challenging
enough to entertain adults; all are remarkably ingenious ways to make things
from materials that cost pennies or less! Formerly "Scrap Fun for Everyone."
Index. 214 illustrations. 373pp. 5⅜ x 8½.　　　　T1251　Paperbound $1.50

SYMBOLIC LOGIC and THE GAME OF LOGIC, *Lewis Carroll*
"Symbolic Logic" is not concerned with modern symbolic logic, but is instead
a collection of over 380 problems posed with charm and imagination, using
the syllogism and a fascinating diagrammatic method of drawing conclusions.
In "The Game of Logic" Carroll's whimsical imagination devises a logical game
played with 2 diagrams and counters (included) to manipulate hundreds of
tricky syllogisms. The final section, "Hit or Miss" is a lagniappe of 101 additional puzzles in the delightful Carroll manner. Until this reprint edition,
both of these books were rarities costing up to $15 each. Symbolic Logic:
Index. xxxi + 199pp. The Game of Logic: 96pp. 2 vols. bound as one. 5⅜ x 8.
　　　　　　　　　　　　　　　　　　　　　　　T492　Paperbound $2.00

MATHEMATICAL PUZZLES OF SAM LOYD, PART I
selected and edited by M. Gardner
Choice puzzles by the greatest American puzzle creator and innovator. Selected
from his famous collection, "Cyclopedia of Puzzles," they retain the unique
style and historical flavor of the originals. There are posers based on arithmetic,
algebra, probability, game theory, route tracing, topology, counter and sliding
block, operations research, geometrical dissection. Includes the famous "14-15"
puzzle which was a national craze, and his "Horse of a Different Color" which
sold millions of copies. 117 of his most ingenious puzzles in all. 120 line
drawings and diagrams. Solutions. Selected references. xx + 167pp. 5⅜ x 8.
　　　　　　　　　　　　　　　　　　　　　　　T498　Paperbound $1.25

STRING FIGURES AND HOW TO MAKE THEM, *Caroline Furness Jayne*
107 string figures plus variations selected from the best primitive and modern
examples developed by Navajo, Apache, pygmies of Africa, Eskimo, in Europe,
Australia, China, etc. The most readily understandable, easy-to-follow book in
English on perennially popular recreation. Crystal-clear exposition; step-by-
step diagrams. Everyone from kindergarten children to adults looking for
unusual diversion will be endlessly amused. Index. Bibliography. Introduction
by A. C. Haddon. 17 full-page plates, 960 illustrations. xxiii + 401pp. 5⅜ x 8½.
　　　　　　　　　　　　　　　　　　　　　　　T152　Paperbound $2.25

PAPER FOLDING FOR BEGINNERS, *W. D. Murray and F. J. Rigney*
A delightful introduction to the varied and entertaining Japanese art of
origami (paper folding), with a full, crystal-clear text that anticipates every
difficulty; over 275 clearly labeled diagrams of all important stages in creation.
You get results at each stage, since complex figures are logically developed
from simpler ones. 43 different pieces are explained: sailboats, frogs, roosters,
etc. 6 photographic plates. 279 diagrams. 95pp. 5⅜ x 8⅜.
　　　　　　　　　　　　　　　　　　　　　　　T713　Paperbound $1.00

PRINCIPLES OF ART HISTORY,
H. Wölfflin
Analyzing such terms as "baroque," "classic," "neoclassic," "primitive," "picturesque," and 164 different works by artists like Botticelli, van Cleve, Dürer, Hobbema, Holbein, Hals, Rembrandt, Titian, Brueghel, Vermeer, and many others, the author establishes the classifications of art history and style on a firm, concrete basis. This classic of art criticism shows what really occurred between the 14th-century primitives and the sophistication of the 18th century in terms of basic attitudes and philosophies. "A remarkable lesson in the art of seeing," *Sat. Rev. of Literature*. Translated from the 7th German edition. 150 illustrations. 254pp. 6⅛ x 9¼. T276 Paperbound $2.00

PRIMITIVE ART,
Franz Boas
This authoritative and exhaustive work by a great American anthropologist covers the entire gamut of primitive art. Pottery, leatherwork, metal work, stone work, wood, basketry, are treated in detail. Theories of primitive art, historical depth in art history, technical virtuosity, unconscious levels of patterning, symbolism, styles, literature, music, dance, etc. A must book for the interested layman, the anthropologist, artist, handicrafter (hundreds of unusual motifs), and the historian. Over 900 illustrations (50 ceramic vessels, 12 totem poles, etc.). 376pp. 5⅜ x 8. T25 Paperbound $2.50

THE GENTLEMAN AND CABINET MAKER'S DIRECTOR,
Thomas Chippendale
A reprint of the 1762 catalogue of furniture designs that went on to influence generations of English and Colonial and Early Republic American furniture makers. The 200 plates, most of them full-page sized, show Chippendale's designs for French (Louis XV), Gothic, and Chinese-manner chairs, sofas, canopy and dome beds, cornices, chamber organs, cabinets, shaving tables, commodes, picture frames, frets, candle stands, chimney pieces, decorations, etc. The drawings are all elegant and highly detailed; many include construction diagrams and elevations. A supplement of 24 photographs shows surviving pieces of original and Chippendale-style pieces of furniture. Brief biography of Chippendale by N. I. Bienenstock, editor of *Furniture World*. Reproduced from the 1762 edition. 200 plates, plus 19 photographic plates. vi + 249pp. 9⅛ x 12¼. T1601 Paperbound $3.50

AMERICAN ANTIQUE FURNITURE: A BOOK FOR AMATEURS,
Edgar G. Miller, Jr.
Standard introduction and practical guide to identification of valuable American antique furniture. 2115 illustrations, mostly photographs taken by the author in 148 private homes, are arranged in chronological order in extensive chapters on chairs, sofas, chests, desks, bedsteads, mirrors, tables, clocks, and other articles. Focus is on furniture accessible to the collector, including simpler pieces and a larger than usual coverage of Empire style. Introductory chapters identify structural elements, characteristics of various styles, how to avoid fakes, etc. "We are frequently asked to name some book on American furniture that will meet the requirements of the novice collector, the beginning dealer, and . . . the general public. . . . We believe Mr. Miller's two volumes more completely satisfy this specification than any other work," *Antiques*. Appendix. Index. Total of vi + 1106pp. 7⅞ x 10¾. T1599, T1600 Two volume set, paperbound $7.50

THE BAD CHILD'S BOOK OF BEASTS, MORE BEASTS FOR WORSE CHILDREN, and A MORAL ALPHABET, *H. Belloc*
Hardly and anthology of humorous verse has appeared in the last 50 years without at least a couple of these famous nonsense verses. But one must see the entire volumes — with all the delightful original illustrations by Sir Basil Blackwood — to appreciate fully Belloc's charming and witty verses that play so subacidly on the platitudes of life and morals that beset his day — and ours. A great humor classic. Three books in one. Total of 157pp. 5⅜ x 8.
T749   Paperbound $1.00

THE DEVIL'S DICTIONARY, *Ambrose Bierce*
Sardonic and irreverent barbs puncturing the pomposities and absurdities of American politics, business, religion, literature, and arts, by the country's greatest satirist in the classic tradition. Epigrammatic as Shaw, piercing as Swift, American as Mark Twain, Will Rogers, and Fred Allen, Bierce will always remain the favorite of a small coterie of enthusiasts, and of writers and speakers whom he supplies with "some of the most gorgeous witticisms of the English language" (H. L. Mencken). Over 1000 entries in alphabetical order. 144pp. 5⅜ x 8.   T487   Paperbound $1.00

THE COMPLETE NONSENSE OF EDWARD LEAR.
This is the only complete edition of this master of gentle madness available at a popular price. *A Book of Nonsense, Nonsense Songs, More Nonsense Songs and Stories* in their entirety with all the old favorites that have delighted children and adults for years. The Dong With A Luminous Nose, The Jumblies, The Owl and the Pussycat, and hundreds of other bits of wonderful nonsense. 214 limericks, 3 sets of Nonsense Botany, 5 Nonsense Alphabets, 546 drawings by Lear himself, and much more. 320pp. 5⅜ x 8.   T167   Paperbound $1.50

THE WIT AND HUMOR OF OSCAR WILDE, *ed. by Alvin Redman*
Wilde at his most brilliant, in 1000 epigrams exposing weaknesses and hypocrisies of "civilized" society. Divided into 49 categories—sin, wealth, women, America, etc.—to aid writers, speakers. Includes excerpts from his trials, books, plays, criticism. Formerly "The Epigrams of Oscar Wilde." Introduction by Vyvyan Holland, Wilde's only living son. Introductory essay by editor. 260pp. 5⅜ x 8.   T602   Paperbound $1.50

A CHILD'S PRIMER OF NATURAL HISTORY, *Oliver Herford*
Scarcely an anthology of whimsy and humor has appeared in the last 50 years without a contribution from Oliver Herford. Yet the works from which these examples are drawn have been almost impossible to obtain! Here at last are Herford's improbable definitions of a menagerie of familiar and weird animals, each verse illustrated by the author's own drawings. 24 drawings in 2 colors; 24 additional drawings. vii + 95pp. 6½ x 6.   T1647   Paperbound $1.00

THE BROWNIES: THEIR BOOK, *Palmer Cox*
The book that made the Brownies a household word. Generations of readers have enjoyed the antics, predicaments and adventures of these jovial sprites, who emerge from the forest at night to play or to come to the aid of a deserving human. Delightful illustrations by the author decorate nearly every page. 24 short verse tales with 266 illustrations. 155pp. 6⅝ x 9¼.
T1265   Paperbound $1.50

THE PRINCIPLES OF PSYCHOLOGY,
William James
The full long-course, unabridged, of one of the great classics of Western literature and science. Wonderfully lucid descriptions of human mental activity, the stream of thought, consciousness, time perception, memory, imagination, emotions, reason, abnormal phenomena, and similar topics. Original contributions are integrated with the work of such men as Berkeley, Binet, Mills, Darwin, Hume, Kant, Royce, Schopenhauer, Spinoza, Locke, Descartes, Galton, Wundt, Lotze, Herbart, Fechner, and scores of others. All contrasting interpretations of mental phenomena are examined in detail—introspective analysis, philosophical interpretation, and experimental research. "A classic," *Journal of Consulting Psychology*. "The main lines are as valid as ever," *Psychoanalytical Quarterly*. "Standard reading ... a classic of interpretation," *Psychiatric Quarterly*. 94 illustrations. 1408pp. 5⅜ x 8.

T381, T382　Two volume set, paperbound $5.25

VISUAL ILLUSIONS: THEIR CAUSES, CHARACTERISTICS AND APPLICATIONS,
M. Luckiesh
"Seeing is deceiving," asserts the author of this introduction to virtually every type of optical illusion known. The text both describes and explains the principles involved in color illusions, figure-ground, distance illusions, etc. 100 photographs, drawings and diagrams prove how easy it is to fool the sense: circles that aren't round, parallel lines that seem to bend, stationary figures that seem to move as you stare at them — illustration after illustration strains our credulity at what we see. Fascinating book from many points of view, from applications for artists, in camouflage, etc. to the psychology of vision. New introduction by William Ittleson, Dept. of Psychology, Queens College. Index. Bibliography. xxi + 252pp. 5⅜ x 8½.　　　T1530　Paperbound $1.50

FADS AND FALLACIES IN THE NAME OF SCIENCE,
Martin Gardner
This is the standard account of various cults, quack systems, and delusions which have masqueraded as science: hollow earth fanatics, Reich and orgone sex energy, dianetics, Atlantis, multiple moons, Forteanism, flying saucers, medical fallacies like iridiagnosis, zone therapy, etc. A new chapter has been added on Bridey Murphy, psionics, and other recent manifestations in this field. This is a fair, reasoned appraisal of eccentric theory which provides excellent inoculation against cleverly masked nonsense. "Should be read by everyone, scientist and non-scientist alike," R. T. Birge, Prof. Emeritus of Physics, Univ. of California; Former President, American Physical Society. Index. x + 365pp. 5⅜ x 8.　　　T394　Paperbound $2.00

ILLUSIONS AND DELUSIONS OF THE SUPERNATURAL AND THE OCCULT,
D. H. Rawcliffe
Holds up to rational examination hundreds of persistent delusions including crystal gazing, automatic writing, table turning, mediumistic trances, mental healing, stigmata, lycanthropy, live burial, the Indian Rope Trick, spiritualism, dowsing, telepathy, clairvoyance, ghosts, ESP, etc. The author explains and exposes the mental and physical deceptions involved, making this not only an exposé of supernatural phenomena, but a valuable exposition of characteristic types of abnormal psychology. Originally titled "The Psychology of the Occult." 14 illustrations. Index. 551pp. 5⅜ x 8. T503 Paperbound $2.75

FAIRY TALE COLLECTIONS, *edited by Andrew Lang*
Andrew Lang's fairy tale collections make up the richest shelf-full of traditional children's stories anywhere available. Lang supervised the translation of stories from all over the world—familiar European tales collected by Grimm, animal stories from Negro Africa, myths of primitive Australia, stories from Russia, Hungary, Iceland, Japan, and many other countries. Lang's selection of translations are unusually high; many authorities consider that the most familiar tales find their best versions in these volumes. All collections are richly decorated and illustrated by H. J. Ford and other artists.

THE BLUE FAIRY BOOK. 37 stories. 138 illustrations. ix + 390pp. 5⅜ x 8½.
T1437   Paperbound $1.75

THE GREEN FAIRY BOOK. 42 stories. 100 illustrations. xiii + 366pp. 5⅜ x 8½.
T1439   Paperbound $1.75

THE BROWN FAIRY BOOK. 32 stories. 50 illustrations, 8 in color. xii + 350pp. 5⅜ x 8½.
T1438   Paperbound $1.95

THE BEST TALES OF HOFFMANN, *edited by E. F. Bleiler*
10 stories by E. T. A. Hoffmann, one of the greatest of all writers of fantasy. The tales include "The Golden Flower Pot," "Automata," "A New Year's Eve Adventure," "Nutcracker and the King of Mice," "Sand-Man," and others. Vigorous characterizations of highly eccentric personalities, remarkably imaginative situations, and intensely fast pacing has made these tales popular all over the world for 150 years. Editor's introduction. 7 drawings by Hoffmann. xxxiii + 419pp. 5⅜ x 8½.
T1793   Paperbound $2.25

GHOST AND HORROR STORIES OF AMBROSE BIERCE,
edited by E. F. Bleiler
Morbid, eerie, horrifying tales of possessed poets, shabby aristocrats, revived corpses, and haunted malefactors. Widely acknowledged as the best of their kind between Poe and the moderns, reflecting their author's inner torment and bitter view of life. Includes "Damned Thing," "The Middle Toe of the Right Foot," "The Eyes of the Panther," "Visions of the Night," "Moxon's Master," and over a dozen others. Editor's introduction. xxii + 199pp. 5⅜ x 8½.
T767   Paperbound $1.50

THREE GOTHIC NOVELS, *edited by E. F. Bleiler*
Originators of the still popular Gothic novel form, influential in ushering in early 19th-century Romanticism. Horace Walpole's *Castle of Otranto*, William Beckford's *Vathek*, John Polidori's *The Vampyre*, and a *Fragment* by Lord Byron are enjoyable as exciting reading or as documents in the history of English literature. Editor's introduction. xi + 291pp. 5⅜ x 8½.
T1232   Paperbound $2.00

BEST GHOST STORIES OF LEFANU, *edited by E. F. Bleiler*
Though admired by such critics as V. S. Pritchett, Charles Dickens and Henry James, ghost stories by the Irish novelist Joseph Sheridan LeFanu have never become as widely known as his detective fiction. About half of the 16 stories in this collection have never before been available in America. Collection includes "Carmilla" (perhaps the best vampire story ever written), "The Haunted Baronet," "The Fortunes of Sir Robert Ardagh," and the classic "Green Tea." Editor's introduction. 7 contemporary illustrations. Portrait of LeFanu. xii + 467pp. 5⅜ x 8.
T415   Paperbound $2.00

EASY-TO-DO ENTERTAINMENTS AND DIVERSIONS WITH COINS, CARDS, STRING, PAPER AND MATCHES, *R. M. Abraham*
Over 300 tricks, games and puzzles will provide young readers with absorbing fun. Sections on card games; paper-folding; tricks with coins, matches and pieces of string; games for the agile; toy-making from common household objects; mathematical recreations; and 50 miscellaneous pastimes. Anyone in charge of groups of youngsters, including hard-pressed parents, and in need of suggestions on how to keep children sensibly amused and quietly content will find this book indispensable. Clear, simple text, copious number of delightful line drawings and illustrative diagrams. Originally titled "Winter Nights' Entertainments." Introduction by Lord Baden Powell. 329 illustrations. v + 186pp. 5⅜ x 8½.   T921 Paperbound $1.00

AN INTRODUCTION TO CHESS MOVES AND TACTICS SIMPLY EXPLAINED, *Leonard Barden*
Beginner's introduction to the royal game. Names, possible moves of the pieces, definitions of essential terms, how games are won, etc. explained in 30-odd pages. With this background you'll be able to sit right down and play. Balance of book teaches strategy — openings, middle game, typical endgame play, and suggestions for improving your game. A sample game is fully analyzed. True middle-level introduction, teaching you all the essentials without oversimplifying or losing you in a maze of detail. 58 figures. 102pp. 5⅜ x 8½.   T1210 Paperbound $1.25

LASKER'S MANUAL OF CHESS, *Dr. Emanuel Lasker*
Probably the greatest chess player of modern times, Dr. Emanuel Lasker held the world championship 28 years, independent of passing schools or fashions. This unmatched study of the game, chiefly for intermediate to skilled players, analyzes basic methods, combinations, position play, the aesthetics of chess, dozens of different openings, etc., with constant reference to great modern games. Contains a brilliant exposition of Steinitz's important theories. Introduction by Fred Reinfeld. Tables of Lasker's tournament record. 3 indices. 308 diagrams. 1 photograph. xxx + 349pp. 5⅜ x 8. T640 Paperbound $2.25

COMBINATIONS: THE HEART OF CHESS, *Irving Chernev*
Step-by-step from simple combinations to complex, this book, by a well-known chess writer, shows you the intricacies of pins, counter-pins, knight forks, and smothered mates. Other chapters show alternate lines of play to those taken in actual championship games; boomerang combinations; classic examples of brilliant combination play by Nimzovich, Rubinstein, Tarrasch, Botvinnik, Alekhine and Capablanca. Index. 356 diagrams. ix + 245pp. 5⅜ x 8½.   T1744 Paperbound $2.00

HOW TO SOLVE CHESS PROBLEMS, *K. S. Howard*
Full of practical suggestions for the fan or the beginner — who knows only the moves of the chessmen. Contains preliminary section and 58 two-move, 46 three-move, and 8 four-move problems composed by 27 outstanding American problem creators in the last 30 years. Explanation of all terms and exhaustive index. "Just what is wanted for the student," Brian Harley. 112 problems, solutions. vi + 171pp. 5⅜ x 8.   T748 Paperbound $1.35

SOCIAL THOUGHT FROM LORE TO SCIENCE,
H. E. Barnes and H. Becker
An immense survey of sociological thought and ways of viewing, studying, planning, and reforming society from earliest times to the present. Includes thought on society of preliterate peoples, ancient non-Western cultures, and every great movement in Europe, America, and modern Japan. Analyzes hundreds of great thinkers: Plato, Augustine, Bodin, Vico, Montesquieu, Herder, Comte, Marx, etc. Weighs the contributions of utopians, sophists, fascists and communists; economists, jurists, philosophers, ecclesiastics, and every 19th and 20th century school of scientific sociology, anthropology, and social psychology throughout the world. Combines topical, chronological, and regional approaches, treating the evolution of social thought as a process rather than as a series of mere topics. "Impressive accuracy, competence, and discrimination . . . easily the best single survey," *Nation*. Thoroughly revised, with new material up to 1960. 2 indexes. Over 2200 bibliographical notes. Three volume set. Total of 1586pp. 5⅜ x 8.
T901, T902, T903   Three volume set, paperbound $8.50

A HISTORY OF HISTORICAL WRITING, *Harry Elmer Barnes*
Virtually the only adequate survey of the whole course of historical writing in a single volume. Surveys developments from the beginnings of historiography in the ancient Near East and the Classical World, up through the Cold War. Covers major historians in detail, shows interrelationship with cultural background, makes clear individual contributions, evaluates and estimates importance; also enormously rich upon minor authors and thinkers who are usually passed over. Packed with scholarship and learning, clear, easily written. Indispensable to every student of history. Revised and enlarged up to 1961. Index and bibliography. xv + 442pp. 5⅜ x 8½.
T104   Paperbound $2.50

JOHANN SEBASTIAN BACH, *Philipp Spitta*
The complete and unabridged text of the definitive study of Bach. Written some 70 years ago, it is still unsurpassed for its coverage of nearly all aspects of Bach's life and work. There could hardly be a finer non-technical introduction to Bach's music than the detailed, lucid analyses which Spitta provides for hundreds of individual pieces. 26 solid pages are devoted to the B minor mass, for example, and 30 pages to the glorious St. Matthew Passion. This monumental set also includes a major analysis of the music of the 18th century: Buxtehude, Pachelbel, etc. "Unchallenged as the last word on one of the supreme geniuses of music," John Barkham, *Saturday Review Syndicate*. Total of 1819pp. Heavy cloth binding. 5⅜ x 8.
T252   Two volume set, clothbound $15.00

BEETHOVEN AND HIS NINE SYMPHONIES, *George Grove*
In this modern middle-level classic of musicology Grove not only analyzes all nine of Beethoven's symphonies very thoroughly in terms of their musical structure, but also discusses the circumstances under which they were written, Beethoven's stylistic development, and much other background material. This is an extremely rich book, yet very easily followed; it is highly recommended to anyone seriously interested in music. Over 250 musical passages. Index. viii + 407pp. 5⅜ x 8.
T334   Paperbound $2.25

THREE SCIENCE FICTION NOVELS,
John Taine
Acknowledged by many as the best SF writer of the 1920's, Taine (under the name Eric Temple Bell) was also a Professor of Mathematics of considerable renown. Reprinted here are *The Time Stream*, generally considered Taine's best, *The Greatest Game*, a biological-fiction novel, and *The Purple Sapphire*, involving a supercivilization of the past. Taine's stories tie fantastic narratives to frameworks of original and logical scientific concepts. Speculation is often profound on such questions as the nature of time, concept of entropy, cyclical universes, etc. 4 contemporary illustrations. v + 532pp. 5⅜ x 8⅜.

T1180   Paperbound $2.00

SEVEN SCIENCE FICTION NOVELS,
H. G. Wells
Full unabridged texts of 7 science-fiction novels of the master. Ranging from biology, physics, chemistry, astronomy, to sociology and other studies, Mr. Wells extrapolates whole worlds of strange and intriguing character. "One will have to go far to match this for entertainment, excitement, and sheer pleasure . . ."*New York Times*. Contents: The Time Machine, The Island of Dr. Moreau, The First Men in the Moon, The Invisible Man, The War of the Worlds, The Food of the Gods, In The Days of the Comet. 1015pp. 5⅜ x 8.

T264   Clothbound $5.00

28 SCIENCE FICTION STORIES OF H. G. WELLS.
Two full, unabridged novels, *Men Like Gods* and *Star Begotten*, plus 26 short stories by the master science-fiction writer of all time! Stories of space, time, invention, exploration, futuristic adventure. Partial contents: *The Country of the Blind, In the Abyss, The Crystal Egg, The Man Who Could Work Miracles, A Story of Days to Come, The Empire of the Ants, The Magic Shop, The Valley of the Spiders, A Story of the Stone Age, Under the Knife, Sea Raiders,* etc. An indispensable collection for the library of anyone interested in science fiction adventure. 928pp. 5⅜ x 8.   T265   Clothbound $5.00

THREE MARTIAN NOVELS,
Edgar Rice Burroughs
Complete, unabridged reprinting, in one volume, of Thuvia, Maid of Mars; Chessmen of Mars; The Master Mind of Mars. Hours of science-fiction adventure by a modern master storyteller. Reset in large clear type for easy reading. 16 illustrations by J. Allen St. John. vi + 490pp. 5⅜ x 8½.

T39   Paperbound $2.50

AN INTELLECTUAL AND CULTURAL HISTORY OF THE WESTERN WORLD,
Harry Elmer Barnes
Monumental 3-volume survey of intellectual development of Europe from primitive cultures to the present day. Every significant product of human intellect traced through history: art, literature, mathematics, physical sciences, medicine, music, technology, social sciences, religions, jurisprudence, education, etc. Presentation is lucid and specific, analyzing in detail specific discoveries, theories, literary works, and so on. Revised (1965) by recognized scholars in specialized fields under the direction of Prof. Barnes. Revised bibliography. Indexes. 24 illustrations. Total of xxix + 1318pp.

T1275, T1276, T1277   Three volume set, paperbound $7.50

HEAR ME TALKIN' TO YA, *edited by Nat Shapiro and Nat Hentoff*
In their own words, Louis Armstrong, King Oliver, Fletcher Henderson, Bunk Johnson, Bix Beiderbecke, Billy Holiday, Fats Waller, Jelly Roll Morton, Duke Ellington, and many others comment on the origins of jazz in New Orleans and its growth in Chicago's South Side, Kansas City's jam sessions, Depression Harlem, and the modernism of the West Coast schools. Taken from taped conversations, letters, magazine articles, other first-hand sources. Editors' introduction. xvi + 429pp. 5⅜ x 8½.   T1726   Paperbound $2.00

THE JOURNAL OF HENRY D. THOREAU
A 25-year record by the great American observer and critic, as complete a record of a great man's inner life as is anywhere available. Thoreau's Journals served him as raw material for his formal pieces, as a place where he could develop his ideas, as an outlet for his interests in wild life and plants, in writing as an art, in classics of literature, Walt Whitman and other contemporaries, in politics, slavery, individual's relation to the State, etc. The Journals present a portrait of a remarkable man, and are an observant social history. Unabridged republication of 1906 edition, Bradford Torrey and Francis H. Allen, editors. Illustrations. Total of 1888pp. 8⅜ x 12¼.
T312, T313   Two volume set, clothbound $25.00

A SHAKESPEARIAN GRAMMAR, *E. A. Abbott*
Basic reference to Shakespeare and his contemporaries, explaining through thousands of quotations from Shakespeare, Jonson, Beaumont and Fletcher, North's *Plutarch* and other sources the grammatical usage differing from the modern. First published in 1870 and written by a scholar who spent much of his life isolating principles of Elizabethan language, the book is unlikely ever to be superseded. Indexes. xxiv + 511pp. 5⅜ x 8½. T1582 Paperbound $2.75

FOLK-LORE OF SHAKESPEARE, *T. F. Thistelton Dyer*
Classic study, drawing from Shakespeare a large body of references to supernatural beliefs, terminology of falconry and hunting, games and sports, good luck charms, marriage customs, folk medicines, superstitions about plants, animals, birds, argot of the underworld, sexual slang of London, proverbs, drinking customs, weather lore, and much else. From full compilation comes a mirror of the 17th-century popular mind. Index. ix + 526pp. 5⅜ x 8½.
T1614   Paperbound $2.75

THE NEW VARIORUM SHAKESPEARE, *edited by H. H. Furness*
By far the richest editions of the plays ever produced in any country or language. Each volume contains complete text (usually First Folio) of the play, all variants in Quarto and other Folio texts, editorial changes by every major editor to Furness's own time (1900), footnotes to obscure references or language, extensive quotes from literature of Shakespearian criticism, essays on plot sources (often reprinting sources in full), and much more.

HAMLET, *edited by H. H. Furness*
Total of xxvi + 905pp. 5⅜ x 8½.
T1004, T1005   Two volume set, paperbound $5.25

TWELFTH NIGHT, *edited by H. H. Furness*
Index. xxii + 434pp. 5⅜ x 8½.   T1189   Paperbound $2.75

La Boheme by Giacomo Puccini,
translated and introduced by Ellen H. Bleiler
Complete handbook for the operagoer, with everything needed for full enjoyment except the musical score itself. Complete Italian libretto, with new, modern English line-by-line translation—the only libretto printing all repeats; biography of Puccini; the librettists; background to the opera, Murger's La Boheme, etc.; circumstances of composition and performances; plot summary; and pictorial section of 73 illustrations showing Puccini, famous singers and performances, etc. Large clear type for easy reading. 124pp. 5⅜ x 8½.
T404 Paperbound $1.00

Antonio Stradivari: His Life and Work (1644-1737),
W. Henry Hill, Arthur F. Hill, and Alfred E. Hill
Still the only book that really delves into life and art of the incomparable Italian craftsman, maker of the finest musical instruments in the world today. The authors, expert violin-makers themselves, discuss Stradivari's ancestry, his construction and finishing techniques, distinguished characteristics of many of his instruments and their locations. Included, too, is story of introduction of his instruments into France, England, first revelation of their supreme merit, and information on his labels, number of instruments made, prices, mystery of ingredients of his varnish, tone of pre-1684 Stradivari violin and changes between 1684 and 1690. An extremely interesting, informative account for all music lovers, from craftsman to concert-goer. Republication of original (1902) edition. New introduction by Sydney Beck, Head of Rare Book and Manuscript Collections, Music Division, New York Public Library. Analytical index by Rembert Wurlitzer. Appendixes. 68 illustrations. 30 full-page plates. 4 in color. xxvi + 315pp. 5⅜ x 8½.
T425 Paperbound $2.25

Musical Autographs from Monteverdi to Hindemith,
Emanuel Winternitz
For beauty, for intrinsic interest, for perspective on the composer's personality, for subtleties of phrasing, shading, emphasis indicated in the autograph but suppressed in the printed score, the mss. of musical composition are fascinating documents which repay close study in many different ways. This 2-volume work reprints facsimiles of mss. by virtually every major composer, and many minor figures—196 examples in all. A full text points out what can be learned from mss., analyzes each sample. Index. Bibliography. 18 figures. 196 plates. Total of 170pp. of text. 7⅞ x 10¾.
T1312, T1313 Two volume set, paperbound $4.00

J. S. Bach,
Albert Schweitzer
One of the few great full-length studies of Bach's life and work, and the study upon which Schweitzer's renown as a musicologist rests. On first appearance (1911), revolutionized Bach performance. The only writer on Bach to be musicologist, performing musician, and student of history, theology and philosophy, Schweitzer contributes particularly full sections on history of German Protestant church music, theories on motivic pictorial representations in vocal music, and practical suggestions for performance. Translated by Ernest Newman. Indexes. 5 illustrations. 650 musical examples. Total of xix + 928pp. 5⅜ x 8½.
T1631, T1632 Two volume set, paperbound $4.50

THE METHODS OF ETHICS, *Henry Sidgwick*
Propounding no organized system of its own, study subjects every major methodological approach to ethics to rigorous, objective analysis. Study discusses and relates ethical thought of Plato, Aristotle, Bentham, Clarke, Butler, Hobbes, Hume, Mill, Spencer, Kant, and dozens of others. Sidgwick retains conclusions from each system which follow from ethical premises, rejecting the faulty. Considered by many in the field to be among the most important treatises on ethical philosophy. Appendix. Index. xlvii + 528pp. 5⅜ x 8½.
T1608 Paperbound $2.50

TEUTONIC MYTHOLOGY, *Jakob Grimm*
A milestone in Western culture; the work which established on a modern basis the study of history of religions and comparative religions. 4-volume work assembles and interprets everything available on religious and folkloristic beliefs of Germanic people (including Scandinavians, Anglo-Saxons, etc.). Assembling material from such sources as Tacitus, surviving Old Norse and Icelandic texts, archeological remains, folktales, surviving superstitions, comparative traditions, linguistic analysis, etc. Grimm explores pagan deities, heroes, folklore of nature, religious practices, and every other area of pagan German belief. To this day, the unrivaled, definitive, exhaustive study. Translated by J. S. Stallybrass from 4th (1883) German edition. Indexes. Total of lxxvii + 1887pp. 5⅜ x 8½.
T1602, T1603, T1604, T1605 Four volume set, paperbound $10.00

THE I CHING, *translated by James Legge*
Called "The Book of Changes" in English, this is one of the Five Classics edited by Confucius, basic and central to Chinese thought. Explains perhaps the most complex system of divination known, founded on the theory that all things happening at any one time have characteristic features which can be isolated and related. Significant in Oriental studies, in history of religions and philosophy, and also to Jungian psychoanalysis and other areas of modern European thought. Index. Appendixes. 6 plates. xxi + 448pp. 5⅜ x 8½.
T1062 Paperbound $2.75

HISTORY OF ANCIENT PHILOSOPHY, *W. Windelband*
One of the clearest, most accurate comprehensive surveys of Greek and Roman philosophy. Discusses ancient philosophy in general, intellectual life in Greece in the 7th and 6th centuries B.C., Thales, Anaximander, Anaximenes, Heraclitus, the Eleatics, Empedocles, Anaxagoras, Leucippus, the Pythagoreans, the Sophists, Socrates, Democritus (20 pages), Plato (50 pages), Aristotle (70 pages), the Peripatetics, Stoics, Epicureans, Sceptics, Neo-platonists, Christian Apologists, etc. 2nd German edition translated by H. E. Cushman. xv + 393pp. 5⅜ x 8.
T357 Paperbound $2.25

THE PALACE OF PLEASURE, *William Painter*
Elizabethan versions of Italian and French novels from *The Decameron*, Cinthio, Straparola, Queen Margaret of Navarre, and other continental sources — the very work that provided Shakespeare and dozens of his contemporaries with many of their plots and sub-plots and, therefore, justly considered one of the most influential books in all English literature. It is also a book that any reader will still enjoy. Total of cviii + 1,224pp.
T1691, T1692, T1693 Three volume set, paperbound $6.75

THE WONDERFUL WIZARD OF OZ, *L. F. Baum*
All the original W. W. Denslow illustrations in full color—as much a part of
"The Wizard" as Tenniel's drawings are of "Alice in Wonderland." "The
Wizard" is still America's best-loved fairy tale, in which, as the author expresses
it, "The wonderment and joy are retained and the heartaches and nightmares
left out." Now today's young readers can enjoy every word and wonderful picture of the original book. New introduction by Martin Gardner. A Baum
bibliography. 23 full-page color plates. viii + 268pp. 5⅜ x 8.
                                                    T691   Paperbound $1.75

THE MARVELOUS LAND OF OZ, *L. F. Baum*
This is the equally enchanting sequel to the "Wizard," continuing the adventures of the Scarecrow and the Tin Woodman. The hero this time is a little
boy named Tip, and all the delightful Oz magic is still present. This is the
Oz book with the Animated Saw-Horse, the Woggle-Bug, and Jack Pumpkin-
head. All the original John R. Neill illustrations, 10 in full color. 287pp.
5⅜ x 8.   T692   Paperbound $1.50

ALICE'S ADVENTURES UNDER GROUND, *Lewis Carroll*
The original *Alice in Wonderland*, hand-lettered and illustrated by Carroll
himself, and originally presented as a Christmas gift to a child-friend. Adults
as well as children will enjoy this charming volume, reproduced faithfully
in this Dover edition. While the story is essentially the same, there are slight
changes, and Carroll's spritely drawings present an intriguing alternative to
the famous Tenniel illustrations. One of the most popular books in Dover's
catalogue. Introduction by Martin Gardner. 38 illustrations. 128pp. 5⅜ x 8½.
                                                    T1482   Paperbound $1.00

THE NURSERY "ALICE," *Lewis Carroll*
While most of us consider *Alice in Wonderland* a story for children of all
ages, Carroll himself felt it was beyond younger children. He therefore provided this simplified version, illustrated with the famous Tenniel drawings
enlarged and colored in delicate tints, for children aged "from Nought to
Five." Dover's edition of this now rare classic is a faithful copy of the 1889
printing, including 20 illustrations by Tenniel, and front and back covers
reproduced in full color. Introduction by Martin Gardner. xxiii + 67pp.
6⅛ x 9¼.   T1610   Paperbound $1.75

THE STORY OF KING ARTHUR AND HIS KNIGHTS, *Howard Pyle*
A fast-paced, exciting retelling of the best known Arthurian legends for young
readers by one of America's best story tellers and illustrators. The sword
Excalibur, wooing of Guinevere, Merlin and his downfall, adventures of Sir
Pellias and Gawaine, and others. The pen and ink illustrations are vividly
imagined and wonderfully drawn. 41 illustrations. xviii + 313pp. 6⅛ x 9¼.
                                                    T1445   Paperbound $1.75

Prices subject to change without notice.

Available at your book dealer or write for free catalogue to Dept. Adsci,
Dover Publications, Inc., 180 Varick St., N.Y., N.Y. 10014. Dover publishes more
than 150 books each year on science, elementary and advanced mathematics,
biology, music, art, literary history, social sciences and other areas.